D1623935

The DRI Model
of the U.S. Economy

by Otto Eckstein

McGRAW-HILL BOOK COMPANY

New York St. Louis San Francisco Auckland Bogotá
Hamburg Johannesburg London Madrid Mexico
Montreal New Delhi Panama Paris São Paulo
Singapore Sydney Tokyo Toronto

Eckstein, Otto.
    The DRI model of the U.S. economy.

    Includes index.
    1. United States — Economic conditions — 1971-1981 —
Mathematical models.   2. United States — Economic
conditions — 1981-   — Mathematical models.   3. Data
Resource, inc.   I. Title.   II. Title: D.R.I. model of the
U.S. economy.
U.S. economy.
HC106.8.E26   1983   330.973'00724   83-13528
ISBN 0-07-018972-2

1234567890   DOC/DOC   89876543

ISBN 0-07-018972-2

TABLE OF CONTENTS

LIST OF TABLES

LIST OF FIGURES

PREFACE

This volume provides an account of the 800-equation Data Resources Model of the U.S. Economy. The model has been used for the last 13 years to forecast the U.S. economy and to analyze various policy proposals. It has also been available as a simulation tool to government agencies and private organizations to develop their own forecasts and policy analyses.

The initial DRI model was developed between 1968 and 1972, but it was rebuilt and substantially elaborated after the OPEC oil shock of 1974. The behavior of the economy changed considerably in the mid-1970s and various aspects of supply and finance needed to be represented more explicitly. The present volume describes the model as it has existed over the last half-dozen years.

The model is reestimated each year, after the national income account revisions become available in July. These reestimates reflect the forecasting and simulation experience of that year, as well as any structural changes that can be identified. The annual revision process has greatly complicated the production of this book because the model is continuously evolving. In general, the book describes the model used in 1981, although some of the simulation exercises were run earlier with model versions of the late 1970s.

This volume contains only a sketchy overview of the 200-equation financial sector of the model. This feature of the model, which is certainly among its most important innovations, will be presented fully in an accompanying volume by Allen Sinai.

The three opening chapters of the book have been published elsewhere in preliminary form. Chapter 1 appeared as an appendix in my book, *The Great Recession*; Chapter 2 was published in the volume, *Large-Scale Macro-Econometric Models*, J. Kmenta and J.B. Ramsey, editors. Chapter 3 appeared in my book, *Core Inflation*.

The DRI model was developed before the rise of the rational expectations school and is a structural model. While Chapter 2 contains some material which deals with the rational expectations issues, a fuller treatment will have to await future publications. The basic rationale for continuing to use structural models in the face of the rational expectations criticism is this: changes in policy regime seem to have been among the minor sources of structural change of the economy and of forecasting error in the actual historical record. The principal obstacles to structural constancy and forecast accuracy seem to lie in the exogenous shocks of wars and OPEC, and in the unpredictability of the exogenous monetary policy variables. The central assumption of the rational expectations school, that the forecasts on which businesses and households make their decisions are free of bias and that markets clear instantaneously, so far do not seem to be confirmed by the historical record. Also, the basic theory underlying spending decisions in the DRI model emphasizes not only expected values, but also their variance, assuming decision-makers to be risk-averse; this is inconsistent with the stronger versions of the rational expectations viewpoint. But there are important lessons to be learned from the exciting recent works of this school. DRI is conducting various experiments based on the new approach, including forecasts using the monetarist, reduced-form versions of rational expectations models as well as adaptations of the large-scale structural model which substitute observable market expectations for some of the most important structural equations. It remains to be seen whether these experiments will lead to improved forecasts.

The presentation of empirical equations presents an expositional problem. Should the nearly incomprehensible mnemonics of the model be presented or should simpler expressions be substituted? Because this book is to be read in conjunction with the actual use of the model, the elaborate mnemonics are shown. Also, the full printout of test statistics is shown. To make this material more readable, each exhibit is self-contained even at the expense of repetition, with all variables defined verbally in each table.

The book does not contain all 800 equations of the model. To present them all would make the book enormous and indigestible, and in any event, the equations are reestimated every year. But the important equations are shown and, in the case of the more detailed sectors of the economy, each type of equation is illustrated by example.

*   *   *

An 800-equation model, reestimated each year, clearly requires a sizable team effort, and many members of DRI's National Forecasting Group have contributed ideas and equations over the years. But a few individuals can be singled out for the importance of their contributions to the effort.

Allen Sinai developed the financial sector, including the elaborate modeling of the flows-of-funds for household and corporations. He also contributed ideas on various final demand equations, particularly in the use of financial variables to integrate the real and financial systems. This work was particularly significant in the case of the equations for investment, where interest costs in relation to cash flow and a comprehensive, multiple-source measure of the cost of capital were introduced. Comprehensive measures of net worth play a role in some of the consumer equations, and the housing equations contain a detailed treatment of the impact of mortgage supplies. These variables heighten the sensitivity of the real sector to financial fluctuations.

Over these 14 years, I have worked with an exceptionally capable series of young economists concentrating on the annual respecifications of the model. Christopher Probyn, who held this post over the last two years, developed model Version 1981C, which is most heavily represented in this volume. Among his predecessors who made major contributions to the model are Edward L. Green, the first to hold this position, Andrea Kusko, Richard Hokenson and Frank Cooper.

Douglas Rice and Robin Siegel developed much of the energy sector, and Rice also made a particularly significant contribution in developing the algorithm which brings the income and expenditure sides into consistency. The equations for exports and imports were initially developed by Christopher Gutry and developed further by Brigitte Sellekaerts. The equations for production, applying time series analysis to input/output estimates, were developed by V. Sundararajan, and developed in later versions by Peter Jones, Edward Green, David Gigante and Michael Cebry. Lester Thurow and Samuel Rea produced the equations for the age-sex-race breakdowns of unemployment, and James Connor developed the industry employment equations.

Important contributions to the consumer sector were made by Edward Green and Gina Rogers. The housing sector has benefitted from the work of Robert Gough and from the earlier versions developed by Eric Herr and Donna Petlock Rubin. Sara Johnson improved the state and local government sector, the wage-price block and the equations for exports and imports. The model simulation program was developed by Robert Lacey, and the initial version of the model was programmed by Rosann Cahn. Terry Glomski and Roberta Gerson contributed to the development of the financial sector. Martin Feldstein developed an initial set of financial equations.

This book has benefitted from a close editorial reading by Allen Sinai. Responsibility for any errors and omissions remains mine, however. The manuscript was produced by Lyn Hadden and she saw the book through the entire publication process.

Otto Eckstein
November 1982
Lexington, Massachusetts

CHAPTER 1

THE DRI MODEL:
HISTORICAL PERSPECTIVE AND AN OVERVIEW

1. Introduction

The Data Resources Quarterly Model of the U.S. Economy (the DRI model) is an 800-equation structure. The model depicts the decision processes of businesses, households, financial institutions and governments, and shows how they interact to produce the economy's broad movements. It is a vehicle for formalizing the existing state of knowledge about the economy's functioning and for processing the information contained in historical and current data. The model is used for forecasting the U.S. economy both short and long term, for policy analysis of a variety of government actions, and for driving the microeconomic models of specific industries, companies, products, costs and other variables of particular importance to private and public agencies.

This volume is an account of the DRI model structure and the characteristics it portrays for the behavior of the actual U.S. economy. It describes the structure in the versions used in the period 1978-81. While many of its essentials have been retained over much of its thirteen-year history of use, changing ideas and data have produced a continuing evolution of its structure.

2. Historical Perspective: The First Generation

Econometric models for advanced industrial economies have gone through three generations. The first generation began with Tinbergen's pre-war models of the Dutch and U.S. economies.[1] After the hiatus of World War II,

---

[1]Jan Tinbergen, *Selected Papers* (Amsterdam: North-Holland Publishing Co., 1959), pp. 36-84, and *Business Cycles in the United States of America: 1919-1932* (Geneva: League of Nations, 1939).

when even the U.S. economy was controlled and planned, Lawrence Klein began the American tradition of model building.[2] The early Klein models of the late 1940s and 1950s were very much in the Keynesian tradition, modeling the circular flow of income and expenditure. The principal equations explained the major components of final demand including consumption, fixed investment, inventories and housing. Government demands and exports were exogenous. The income side accounted for the gross national product in terms of the total wage bill, taxes, profits, and the other components of national income. The models were typically expressed in real terms, with the price-wage mechanisms superimposed in nearly recursive fashion and in highly aggregated terms.

Other investigators built models with some significant variations. Colin Clark[3] developed a quarterly business-cycle model in the late 1940s which emphasized the inventories mechanism as the principal source of short-run variation, basing it on sales expectations and cash balances. Duesenberry, Eckstein and Fromm[4] built a simulation model designed to analyze anti-recession policies in more detail, including the use of decision rules for particular instruments and stochastic simulation experiments. The OBE (later BEA)[5] and Michigan models[6] were based on the earlier work of Klein.

By today's standards, the first-generation models were small, beginning with Klein's original twelve-equation model and expanding to thirty-two equations in the Michigan model. Dynamic structures were much simpler, and the equations were limited to the larger aggregates of the national income accounts because of computational constraints.

3. The Second Generation

The second generation of macroeconometric models began in the early 1960s with the development of the large-scale Brookings model,[7] and continued

[2]Lawrence R. Klein, *Economic Fluctuations in the United States: 1921-1944,* Cowles Commission Monograph No. 11 (New York: Wiley, 1950); and Lawrence R. Klein and Arthur S. Goldberger, *An Econometric Model of the United States, 1929-1952* (Amsterdam: North-Holland Publishing Co., 1955).

[3]Colin Clark, "A System of Equations Explaining the United States Trade Cycle, 1921-1944," *Econometrica* (June 1949), pp. 93-124.

[4]James S. Duesenberry, Otto Eckstein and Gary Fromm, "A Simulation of the U.S. Economy in Recession," *Econometrica* (October 1960), pp. 749-809.

[5]Maurice Liebenberg, Albert A. Hirsch and Joel Popkin, "A Quarterly Econometric Model of the United States: A Progress Report," *Survey of Current Business* (May 1966), pp. 13-39.

[6]Daniel B. Suits, "Forecasting and Analysis with an Econometric Model," *American Economic Review* (March 1962), pp. 104-132.

[7]James S. Duesenberry, Gary Fromm, Lawrence R. Klein and Edwin Kuh, eds., *The Brookings Quarterly Econometric Model of the United States* (Chicago: Rand McNally, 1965).

with the early versions of the Wharton[8] and the Federal Reserve-MIT[9] (now MPS) models. The Data Resources models up to 1974 also fall in this general category. Each represented a sizable team effort spanning several years, and consequently contained considerably more disaggregated and elaborate equations for the final demands, incomes, labor markets, and wages and prices. The Brookings and Fed-MIT models were primarily testing grounds for new theories and the technology of larger-scale model building. The Wharton model went beyond the earlier pioneer forecasting of the Michigan model and earlier Klein models, to provide the first intensive quarterly forecasting effort aimed at replacing previous informal methods. The DRI model was part of the development of the first national economic information system and was primarily designed for forecasting and policy analysis.[10]

These models were larger than their antecedents. The initial version of the Brookings model contained 150 equations, the 1976 Wharton model about 200 equations. The original Fed-MIT model had sixty-six equations, but the later version (MPS) grew to 175 equations. Early versions of the DRI model (e.g., 1971) had about 300 equations. The increased size was due to the desire to model the economic processes more fully as inputs to institutional decision making. Faster computers and better programs allowed the more efficient development of equations and made solutions of larger models practical.

The principal advances sprang out of the general econometric work of the field as a whole. The Brookings model project energized many scholars to make their results usable in the large-model context. The Almon and Koyck methods for estimating distributed lags made more precise dynamic structures possible. Jorgenson's neoclassical theory of investment had become available. The lifetime consumption theories of Modigliani, Ando and Brumberg opened up new possibilities for the consumer sector. The wage and price equations developed by Phillips, Lipsey, Eckstein, Wilson, Fromm, Perry, Schultze and others allowed better—if still inadequate—wage-price sectors. And, particularly in the MPS model, the Jorgenson technique of defining synthetic time series variables derived from profit-maximization

[8]Michael K. Evans and Lawrence R. Klein, *The Wharton Econometric Forecasting Model* (Philadelphia: Economic Research Unit, University of Pennsylvania, 1967).

[9]Frank De Leeuw and Edward M. Gramlich, "The Federal Reserve-MIT Model," *Federal Reserve Bulletin* (June 1969), pp. 11-40; and Albert Ando, Franco Modigliani and Robert Rasche, "Equations and Definitions of Variables for the FRB-MIT-PENN Econometric Model, November 1969," in *Econometric Models of Cyclical Behavior*, Bert Hickman, ed. (Cambridge, Mass.: National Bureau of Economic Research, 1972), pp. 543-598.

[10]Otto Eckstein, *The Data Resources Econometric Forecasting System, A Preliminary Account* (Lexington, Mass.: Data Resources, Inc., April 1970); also "The Organization and Retrieval of Economic Knowledge," Kiel Symposium of the International Economic Association, July 1975, and "Information Processing and Econometric Model Forecasting," Paper presented to the Ottawa Meeting of the Econometric Society, June 1977.

assumptions was carried over into other demand equations: rental price concepts were defined for housing and the consumption of durable goods as a means of introducing neoclassical relative price effects and overcoming the attendant difficulty of multicollinearity.

Besides this general progress in macro-econometrics, the second generation of models was characterized by five major innovations: (1) the use of input-output analysis to calculate production in a time-series framework; (2) the development of financial sectors; (3) the introduction of endogenous behavioral equations for state and local government taxes and expenditures; (4) the use of explicit demographic elements, thereby blurring the previous distinctions between short- and long-run models; and (5) social indicator equations.

3.1 Input-Output Analysis

Input-output analysis was introduced into time series-oriented econometrics by Arrow and Hoffenberg,[11] who developed a technique for combining the fixed-coefficient, Leontief-matrix estimates of industry production with technologically based time trends that shift the relationships, and with systematic cyclical variables. The initial attempts to apply the technique empirically were not successful. The Brookings model[12] used a simpler approach to incorporate input-output into a full-scale econometric model, a technique which combined the fixed-coefficient estimate with an autocorrelative adjustment that automatically corrected the observed errors by extrapolation. The DRI model[13] developed the Arrow-Hoffenberg technique by modeling the trend and cycle influences on production coefficients more elaborately and by correcting for other limitations of the available input-output tables. The current DRI model uses an eighty-four-industry, input-output matrix to calculate the Leontief estimates of production, which are then aggregated and applied in fifty-six quarterly industry production equations.

[11]Kenneth J. Arrow and Marvin Hoffenberg, *A Time Series Analysis of Interindustry Demands* (Amsterdam: North-Holland Publishing Co., 1959).

[12]Franklin M. Fisher, Lawrence R. Klein and Y. Shinkai, "Price and Output Aggregation in the Brookings Econometric Model," in *The Brookings Quarterly Econometric Model of the United States*, eds. J. S. Duesenberry et al. (Chicago: Rand McNally, 1965), pp. 653-679; and Gary Fromm and Lawrence R. Klein, "Solutions of the Complete System," in *The Brookings Model: Some Further Results*, eds. J. S. Duesenberry et al. (Chicago: Rand McNally, 1969), pp. 362-422.

[13]V. Sundararajan, "A Flexible Coefficient Bridge Model: Trend-Cycle Adjustments in Input-Output Analysis," (unpublished, 1971).

3.2 Financial Sectors

The introduction of financial sectors into large-scale models must be credited to Frank De Leeuw, who did the initial work for the Brookings model.[14] This financial sector consisted of nineteen equations for the demand and supply of money, time deposits of commercial banks, U.S. Government securities, household and business debt, savings accounts, and several interest rates. The short-term, 90-day Treasury bill rate was estimated from the relationships among loan demands, commercial bank deposits and the bank reserves provided by monetary policy. The resultant short-term rate then became the principal device for estimating the long-term interest rate through the long-established term-structure theory, modified by the supply of government securities. Interest rates were determinants for several kinds of spending including investment through the cost of capital, housing principally through the relationship between short- and long-term interest rates, and public construction for schools through the long-term rate.

The Federal Reserve-MIT (MPS) model substantially expanded the financial sector, integrating it increasingly with the real sectors. In particular, it added a model of the mortgage market which showed how major financial intermediaries allocated savings inflows to mortgages. The model also strengthened the importance of other financial effects in some spending equations. The mortgage market conditions became prime determinants of housing activity.[15] The stock market became a prime mover of household wealth which, in turn, was a determinant of consumer spending.

The early DRI models modified this approach by assuming a two-sector capital market. The long-term interest rate was determined independently of the short rates, principally from inflation expectations and the supply of liquidity provided by monetary policy in relation to the level of aggregate economic activity.[16] Later editions of the model contained expanded financial sectors of this type, adding twenty-four interest rates, with particularly elaborate modeling of the mortgage market and the behavior of the various financial intermediaries.[17]

---

[14]Frank De Leeuw, "A Model of Financial Behavior," in *The Brookings Quarterly Econometric Model*, eds. J.S. Duesenberry et al., pp. 465-530.

[15]Edward M. Gramlich and Dwight M. Jaffee, eds., *Savings Deposits, Mortgages and Housing* (Lexington, Mass.: D.C. Heath & Co., 1972).

[16]Martin S. Feldstein and Otto Eckstein, "The Fundamental Determinants of the Interest Rate," *Review of Economics and Statistics* (November 1970), pp. 363-375.

[17]Otto Eckstein, Edward W. Green, and Allen Sinai, "The Data Resources Model: Uses, Structure and Analysis of the U.S. Economy," *International Economic Review* (October 1974), pp. 595-615.

3.3 Endogenous State and Local Government Sector

The treatment of the state and local sector as an endogenous behavioral component of the economy was pioneered by Henderson[18] and Gramlich,[19] and first introduced into large-scale models in the Federal Reserve-MIT model. In these studies, local fiscal behavior was endogenously determined from the sector's revenue needs. Eckstein and Halvorsen,[20] in work for the initial DRI model, extended this approach, making outlays dependent upon the financial position of state and local governments and their normal growth of revenues, along with demographic factors, and introduced preferences for balance among tax sources into the revenue equations.

3.4 Demographic Influences

Demographic factors received a major emphasis in the initial DRI models. The shift in age structure created by postwar population changes began to be a significant determinant of macroeconomic behavior in the mid-1960s. Further, improvements in computer technology made it possible to use quarterly models for medium-term analysis and to shift the short-run forecasting horizon beyond the traditional single year. Therefore, short-run models needed to incorporate major features previously limited to long-term analyses, many of which depended on changing demographics. These included the endogenous determination of aggregate supply (potential GNP). Equations for housing demand incorporated the growth in the age groups that represent new demand for housing. Automobile demand was related to the growth of the driving-age population. The health-related consumer services were linked to the growing older population. The demand for state and local government spending was related to the changes in the school-age population.

3.5 Social Indicator Equations

By the early 1970s, it was recognized that successful macroeconomic performance would not automatically alleviate all dimensions of the poverty

---

[18]James M. Henderson, "Local Government Expenditures: A Social Welfare Analysis," *Review of Economics and Statistics* (May 1968), pp. 156-163.

[19]Edward M. Gramlich, "State and Local Governments and Their Budget Constraints," *International Economic Review* (June 1969), pp. 163-182.

[20]Otto Eckstein and Robert F. Halvorsen, "A Behavioral Model of the Public Finances of the State and Local Sector," in *Public Finance and Stabilization Policy, Essays in Honor of Richard A. Musgrave,* Warren Smith and John Culbertson, eds. (Amsterdam: North-Holland Publishing Co., 1974), pp. 309-332.

problem. While the successful employment performance of the 1960s had been of enormous benefit to all groups in the labor force, the benefit had not been uniform, and for some groups unemployment remained high even when the national rate was below 3%. These differences were due to various legacies of the past, such as low human investment, poor work attitudes and job discrimination, as well as the demographic shifts of the mid-1960s when the number of young workers rose sharply. Because economic policy increasingly focussed on attempts to reduce unemployment for specific groups and began to be evaluated in terms of its impact on them, the initial DRI models embodied equations which calculated the detailed structure of unemployment by age, sex and race. These equations also permitted the analysis of labor market policies in a large model context.

3.6 Result: Shrinking Multipliers and Greater Sensitivity to Inflation

Many of the innovations in the second generation of models made them less "Keynesian" compared to their predecessors. The introduction of financial sectors, interest rates, and wealth effects in spending equations gave a greater recognition to the importance of money. Fiscal policy simulations run without accommodating monetary policies showed reduced multiplier effects. In addition, the renewed emphasis on demographic factors reduced the income elasticities in various spending equations, partially shifting the burden of explanation from income growth to population growth. This also served to reduce multipliers.

The introduction of wage equations embodying a near-accelerationist point of view began to build a greater sensitivity to inflation into the models. When combined with long-term interest-rate equations embodying inflation expectations, new links were established which automatically caused extra inflation to reduce real activity. Thus, the second generation of models, which held the stage from 1963 to 1974, had moved a long distance toward a centrist position in the controversy between fiscalists and monetarists.

4. The Third Generation

The third generation of models began after the economic crisis of 1973-75 demonstrated several major shortcomings in the existing framework. None of the second-generation models was able to portray the full violence of the events of those years. The relatively smooth growth of the historical period 1953-73, the sample on which these models were fitted, did not reveal the full cyclical vulnerability of the economy. Nor did their design offer sufficient points of contact with external matters such as raw material prices, oil prices, worldwide booms and recessions, shortages and the financial instability which only became more evident during that period.

The third generation of models was designed to remedy these identifiable shortcomings. The DRI models after 1975 have probably gone furthest in providing a framework for analyzing such events, growing to a size and complexity made possible by the increased scale and speed of third-generation computers. The later machines made it unnecessary to design the model with a recursive block structure, and most of the equations in the model were made simultaneous.

4.1 Major Innovations

The current-vintage DRI model contains eight major innovations compared to its 1963-74 predecessors.

(1) Modeling Sectoral Flows-of-Funds, Balance Sheets, and Financial-Real Interactions:[21] Since 1974, the DRI model has contained explicit simultaneous equations for nonfinancial corporate uses and sources of funds and the balance sheet. Outlays for physical or financial assets are the principal uses of funds, derived from the model's spending equations, expected own and alternate rates of return, and the initial balance sheet configuration. Sources of financing include cash flow, proceeds from the sale of financial assets, accumulation of short- and long-term debt, and new equity issues. The need for external financing is estimated from the gap between internal sources and projected uses of funds. The profile of financing that closes this gap depends upon the expected real, aftertax costs of the various financial instruments and the existing balance sheet position. Given the determination of the various sources and uses of funds for each period, the resulting balance sheet is calculated. Hence, the flows-of-funds behavior determines the nature and composition of the corporate balance sheet.

The balance sheet conditions produced by the corporate flow-of-funds model become significant inputs into the business spending equations. Some

---

[21]The framework underlying the flow-of-funds equations builds on the portfolio theoretic approach in James S. Tobin. "A General Equilibrium Approach to Monetary Theory," *Journal of Money, Credit and Banking* (May 1969), pp. 15-29; and William Brainard and J.S. Tobin, "Pitfalls in Financial Model Building," *American Economic Review, Proceedings* (May 1968), pp. 98-122. See W.H.L. Anderson, *Corporate Finance and Fixed Investment* (Cambridge: Harvard University Press, 1964), for an early model of the corporate flow of funds. For an earlier version of the DRI model treatment, see Allen Sinai, "The Integration of Financial Instability in Large-Scale Macroeconomic Models," Paper presented to the Midwest Economic Association, Chicago, Illinois, April 1975. The development of the financial sector in the DRI model was directed by Allen Sinai.

of the traditional balance-sheet liquidity ratios and the composite interest burden relative to cash flow are variables which help to explain business outlays on fixed investment, inventories and employment. These variables provide an important new set of links from financial conditions to real business spending, and raise the power of monetary policy beyond what had previously been identified through interest rate and cost-of-capital measures.

The innovation of the endogenously determined corporate flow of funds increases the cyclicality of the model's representation of the economy. Near the upper turning point of the cycle, the business balance sheet typically deteriorates sharply: internal cash flow grows slowly while spending commitments are still rising strongly. Debt is accumulated rapidly, and too little of this increase is long-term debt, making the firm more vulnerable to deteriorating financial conditions. Belated turns in monetary policy typically raise the cost of capital sharply, dramatically worsening the balance sheet ratios, thereby reducing business spending on fixed investment, inventories and employment. Conversely, not long after the lower business cycle turning point, business completes the reduction of its commitments, monetary policy eases the cost of capital, and business balance sheets are reliquefied. This helps to set the stage for the upswing in business spending.

Flow-of-funds modeling was applied to the household sector of the DRI model in 1973. A set of equations allocates personal financial savings among the various assets that are available to households including the thrift accounts of various institutions, short-term securities, bonds and stocks. These allocation decisions are determined by relative real, aftertax yields on the various investment media, by the inherited portfolio position at the beginning of the period, by wealth and disposable income. Consumer borrowing, particularly of installment credit, is also estimated, principally from spending behavior. Mortgage indebtedness depends primarily on housing outlays and construction activity and on the costs of other sources of finance.

The asset and debt position of households is an important element in the consumer spending equations. Real net worth, along with income, serves to determine long-term spending growth. Variations in the consumer debt position have a strong influence on short-term changes in automobile sales and other spending categories. These financial elements in the household sector accentuate the cyclicality of the model by making consumer spending vulnerable to past household portfolio imbalances and to short-run variations in the cost and availability of credit.

Finally, the DRI model contains a highly disaggregated representation of mortgage market activity to depict the process which links monetary policy to the housing cycle through the financial system. The savings flows and debt repayments of households supply funds to major financial intermediaries including commercial banks, savings and loan associations, mutual savings banks, and life insurance companies. Depending on relative yields and inherited portfolio positions, these institutions make available varying amounts of funds to the mortgage market. The quantity and price of available mortgages are important determinants of residential construction activity. Housing policy is represented by various instruments including the mortgage purchases of the Federal National Mortgage Association and Government National Mortgage Association, the outstanding advances of the Federal Home Loan Bank Board, the new mortgage commitments from the Federal Home Loan Mortgage Corporation, the required liquidity reserve ratio for savings and loan associations, and direct housing subsidies.

(2) Stage-of-Processing Approach to Prices: Popkin and Earl[22] developed econometric models which trace inflationary impulses from the raw materials stage through semi-finished, finished wholesale and retail prices. At each stage of processing, the prices from the previous stage provide an estimate of material costs. Labor costs and demand measures are added to the equations for the price indexes of the successive stages.

This approach was built into the DRI model in 1974, and permits the model to reflect the impact of alternative OPEC pricing strategies or varying agricultural prices. Among the raw material prices in the sector are the price of world oil, lumber, and the composite wholesale price index for agricultural commodities. The prices of semi-finished goods include such processed materials as metals, paper, and the composite price of energy, as well as fabricated metals. Finished goods prices at wholesale include machinery, transportation equipment and processed foods. At the retail stage, the model includes the consumer price indexes for food, nonfood commodities, and services. GNP deflators are calculated principally from the particular wholesale prices for goods, following the technique employed by the Bureau of Economic Analysis. Deflators for services are based on energy costs, equations for rent, and labor costs.

(3) More Elaborate Modeling of Supply: Impacts on Prices, Inventory Behavior and Aggregate Output: Econometric models represent market behavior rather than government controls of physical quantities or price ceilings. Thus, modeling of supply conditions has to be carried out in the context of market behavior of prices and quantities. The DRI model represents such behavior in several quite elaborate ways. First, the model

---

[22] Joel Popkin, "Consumer and Wholesale Prices in a Model of Price Behavior by Stage of Processing," *Review of Economics and Statistics* (November 1974), pp. 486-501; and Paul H. Earl, *Inflation and the Structure of Industrial Prices* (Lexington, Mass.: D.C. Heath & Co., 1973).

calculates the utilization rates of manufacturing as a whole, the materials industries, and primary processing industries; capacities are estimated from investment outlays for two-digit industries and technological trends. Production is estimated from the flexible-coefficient, input-output block in the model. The utilization rates are important inputs into the stage-of-processing equations for wholesale prices and also play a role in profit and productivity equations.

Utilization rates have long been criticized as imperfect measures, and it must be acknowledged that there is no theoretically airtight way to estimate capacity or utilization. Nonetheless, two decades of econometric modeling of prices, productivity, and profits have shown that even imperfect measures of utilization are essential variables to achieve adequate econometric results. Utilization affects both resource efficiency and strength of demand.

A second important measure was introduced in the DRI model of 1976 which increases the sensitivity of industrial prices to demand, particularly to excess demand. This is the measure of delivery delays, "vendor performance," a widely reported response in a monthly survey of purchasing executives, and one of the well-established leading indicators. It greatly increases the explanatory power of wholesale price equations and makes the model's wage-price block more sensitive to demand.

Third, the model calculates aggregate supply (potential output), which affects the unemployment rate, wages, productivity and prices. Potential real GNP is estimated within a Cobb-Douglas production-function framework, with explicit labor, capital, energy and R&D inputs. The capital stocks of plant and equipment are corrected for pollution abatement requirements to obtain potential capital service flows. The labor input is corrected for demographic variations, the capital stock for the age of capital. Time trends are included to reflect disembodied technological change. This specification permits a fully endogenous growth of potential output that depends on business capital formation, labor productivity, real energy costs, and the effort on R&D that helps create the stock of technology.

When a particular commodity is in an extraordinary supply situation not created by market forces and therefore not reflected in price behavior—e.g., strike disruptions or OPEC embargoes—special model solutions are developed with satisfied demands held back by the particular supply constraint. Either the solution as a whole must be held to feasible values through policies of restraint, or the effects of shortages or allocation schemes must be modelled through the use of add-factors in affected sectors.

(4) "Supply-Side Economics": The last few years have seen a revival of interest and scientific work in the relationship between the tax system and the growth of aggregate supply. There are numerous points of contact between

the tax system and the supply and efficiency of the factors of production. The relationship between the tax system and supply is ultimately summarized by model solutions which link tax changes to changes in potential GNP.

The effects of taxes on the supply of capital and the effect of capital on potential output have been integral parts of the DRI model since an aggregate production function was introduced in the early 1970s. In more recent editions, the supply of labor and the efficiency of resource use as measured by factor productivity respond to the personal tax burden. The effects, which are derived both from time-series analysis and from review of the scientific literature, are not of a magnitude to produce the extreme results necessary to have tax cuts pay for themselves or to lead to dramatic upward revisions of potential growth. But the effects are significant, large enough to make a significant difference to the economy's performance in raising per capita living standards and in creating inflation-reducing productivity advances.

(5) Inventory Behavior and the Inventory-Production-Price Loop: The models have long used the standard econometric theory of inventory behavior, relying on the relationship between expected sales and the stock of inventories as the principal explanation.[23] The adjustment of the actual inventory stock toward the optimal stock occurs gradually, of course. The DRI model contains three significant innovations: the utilization rate of industry affects the desired inventory stock; the corporate debt-service burden affects the speed of adjustment; and a lengthening of delivery periods causes precautionary buying. When manufacturing utilization is high, delivery periods lengthen, and the optimal inventory stock is therefore larger for a given level of expected sales. A heavy debt-service burden, on the other hand, creates shorter adjustment processes, including distress selling in recession.

Since utilization rates are sluggish and imprecise measures for inventory policy, it has proved necessary to develop an approach which corresponds more closely to the highly unstable behavior actually observed. This new approach is based on the use of the vendor performance measure that was found so powerful in price equations. When vendor performance deteriorates, the response of purchasing executives is to become more aggressive, to seek to hold larger inventories, and to place multiple orders.

The equations for vendor performance, production, utilization, inventory investment, and industrial wholesale prices constitute an interdependent loop which easily generates inventory and price cycles. Vendor performance is itself determined by such factors as preceding inventory-sales ratios and

---

[23]Lloyd A. Metzler, "The Nature and Stability of Inventory Cycles," *Review of Economics and Statistics* (August 1941), pp. 113-129; and Michael C. Lovell, "Manufacturers' Inventories, Sales Expectations, and the Accelerator Principle," *Econometrica* (July 1961), pp. 293-314.

utilization rates. Consequently, if utilization exceeds a critical level, vendor performance deteriorates, triggering inventory hoarding. The attempt to build up inventory boosts production. Companies are typically unable to distinguish an increase of sales caused by customer inventory hoarding from an increase validated by final demand. Consequently, they respond to better sales by expanding their own activities, reinforcing the inventory cycle. As inventory investment boosts production, utilization rates are driven higher still, worsening vendor performance and triggering further inventory hoarding. Industrial prices advance to reinforce these destabilizing tendencies. Sooner or later, usually within a quarter or two, the inevitable correction occurs.

(6) Modeling Errors-in-Expectations: The experience of recent years has shown that businesses do make mistakes on occasion by acting on false expectations about the future paths of their markets, prices, and costs. The econometric models of the 1960s and early 1970s emphasized adaptive expectations and sluggishly acting distributed-lag formulations which typically understated the important role of error in the business cycle.

The 1977 version of the DRI model marked the beginning of a major research effort to develop spending equations with sufficiently elaborate expectations mechanisms to make it possible to calculate the deviations between business expectations and actual results. In the initial round of research, it has been found that much progress can be made using simple expectations mechanisms. Thus, several of the model's equations, including inventory investment and employment, contain expectations variables in which the current quarter's sales or production are calculated to exceed the four-quarter-earlier results by the same percentage as experienced in the preceding quarter. This mechanism reflects the reality that business makes virtually all of its decisions on seasonally unadjusted data, on the basis of four-quarter or twelve-month comparisons. When these estimates are contrasted with actual results, the expectational elements allow the model to track previous episodes of errors-in-expectations more precisely, including particularly business spending in 1973 and 1974, as well as the minor inventory cycle of 1976. In the case of producers' durable equipment, where decisions are based on longer-term considerations, the errors-in-expectations are modeled as the deviation between current and expected output, where expectations are formed by a geometric lag on past actual values.

(7) Modeling Consumer Confidence and Uncertainty: It has long been recognized that inflation and unemployment raise the personal saving rate, presumably because consumers become more uncertain about their future incomes. In the DRI model, the consumer sector represents this process more elaborately than before. The consumer sentiment index (University of

Michigan) plays a role in some of the more volatile consumer-spending categories, and the index itself is modeled from observed inflation, unemployment and financial conditions. In addition, the uncertainty of consumer income enters into spending equations: following a period of high variance, consumers will save more because they will project a greater down-risk for their future income expectation. The use of credit further magnifies income risk into a larger consumption risk because of the leverage introduced by outstanding interest and repayment obligations. Thus, both income and financial risk are raised by income variance, with the size of the total effect dependent on the household's debt situation. Expected income variance is modelled from current experience of inflation and unemployment.

The variance variables reduce the multipliers on temporary tax reductions, at least to a small degree. Surcharges and rebates accentuate the variance of consumer income, thereby raising the consumer's expectation of future income variance and increasing saving rates.

(8) A Disaggregated Foreign Trade Sector: The worldwide boom of 1971-73, the subsequent crisis and the changed world energy situation have shown that domestic progress is affected by developments abroad. Therefore, the DRI model now includes a detailed structure of U.S. foreign trade. The equations follow economic theory quite closely, relying on relative prices, relative activity levels, and a few commodity-specific variables. The activity levels of the foreign trading partners are modeled through their production indexes which are typically available more quickly and with less interpretation than their GNP accounts.

In actual forecasting, the DRI U.S. model uses the forecasts developed by the DRI International Group. Simultaneous solution of national macro models in the DRI family is limited to the European economies. The iteration of solutions among Europe, Canada, Japan and the United States is still conducted informally for each forecasting cycle.

However, to make the simulation properties of the U.S. model more realistic, reflection ratios are used for our trading partners. Thus, the DRI U.S. model does not assume that foreign economies and policies are left unaffected by our actions. The U.S. economy is so large that one must calculate its impact on its partners and the reflection of their changed situation on U.S. exports and imports.

(9) Other Innovations in the Third-Generation DRI Models: The annual reworkings of the model, with the benefit of new data, fresh ideas and forecasting and simulation experience, have brought various other innovations into the model.

(a) The industry production equations embody elements of the input-output structure within production. Previously, econometric models used "bridge" equations that were driven entirely by the final demands, reflecting interindustry relations only through the matrix of input-output "bridge" coefficients that derive production from final demands. The DRI model's structure explicitly shows how finished goods production determines materials output, thereby allowing inventory and other changes in a "downstream" industry to impart a greater sensitivity to materials industry activity.

(b) The investment equations, while still using the Jorgenson neoclassical approach as their point of departure, have reintroduced utilization rates as proxies of future business output expectations: current utilization is given some weight in assessing future capacity needs. The debt service burden has been added to reflect the loss of liquidity and balance sheet position caused by the heavy use of debt and high interest rates. Also, a more precise measure for the cost of capital is now employed, reflecting the actual mix of financing and the aftertax cost of both debt and equity capital. These modifications strengthen the balance sheet effects and provide a new channel for monetary policy to act on industry behavior and inflation.

(c) The investment equations applied to the twenty-two industries which comprise the BEA plant and equipment statistics use a uniform neoclassical approach. Of course the dynamic structure of the equations differs among industries because of the great variations found in the structure of their physical capital, and the roles of short-run conditions and errors-in-expectations vary accordingly.

(d) The housing sector explicitly models the demand and supply of three types of housing, relying heavily on financial and profitability factors. Housing demand is modeled from demography, permanent income, wealth, confidence and relative cost vis-a-vis consumption. Market disequilibrium, including vacancy rates and the number of houses for sale, introduces important information into the model and heightens the sector's sensitivity to demand changes. The supply of housing is heavily conditioned by financial factors, including mortgage commitments, mortgage rates and the opportunity costs of other investments, deposit flows, and government financial support of this sector.

(e) The relation between the macroeconomy and the energy sector is made more explicit by disaggregation. Consumer energy demands for electricity, home heating fuels and gasoline are separate equations with appropriate price elasticities and stocks to which they pertain. Industrial energy demand is calculated from industrial production levels and the pertinent price elasticities. By adding estimates of government demands for energy, total energy use is estimated. This model structure is designed to allow simultaneous solution of the DRI macro and energy models.

Table 1.1
The DRI Model

	Stochastic Equations	Nonstochastic Equations	Total Equations	Exogenous Variables
—Final GNP Demands	64	148	212	83
Consumption	19	30	49	5
Housing	8	12	20	2
Business Fixed Investment	7	22	29	11
Inventories	6	6	12	4
Government	10	38	48	34
Foreign	14	40	54	27
—Incomes	15	37	52	6
Wages, Salaries and Supplements	0	6	6	3
Corporate Profits	3	6	9	--
Interest	3	1	4	1
Other	9	24	33	2
—Financial	112	81	193	46
Monetary and Reserve Aggregates	8	14	22	8
Interest Rates and Stock Prices	26	1	27	18
Commercial Bank Loans and Investments	6	1	7	2
Flow of Funds—Households	20	12	32	--
Flow of Funds—Nonfinancial Corporations	25	33	58	10
Flow of Funds—Mortgage Activity	10	12	22	8
Flow of Funds—Government	3	1	4	--
Flow of Funds—Commercial Banks, Savings and Loan Associations, Mutual Savings Banks, Life Insurance Companies and Others	6	1	7	--
Equity Market, Inflation Expectations, and Others	6	3	9	--
Consumer Installment Credit	2	3	5	--
—Supply, Capacity, Operating Rates	6	6	12	5
—Prices, Wages and Productivity	57	37	94	14
—Population Employment, Unemployment, and the Labor Force	9	1	10	14
—Industry	112	96	208	6
Production	59	17	76	4
Investment	24	43	67	--
Capital Stock	0	32	32	--
Employment	29	4	33	2
—TOTAL	375	406	781	174

—Block Structure
First Recursive Block: 57 equations
Simultaneous Block: 455 equations
Later Blocks and Recursive Equations: 269 equations

The model is summarized in Table 1.1, where the categories of behavioral equations, identities, exogenous variables and block structure for solutions are shown.

5. Implications

The third-generation DRI model simulates the properties of the American economy differently than its predecessors. The principal changes can be summarized as follows.

5.1 *The model has become more cyclical.*

As shown above, numerous elements have been developed to simulate actual business-cycle behavior with suitable sensitivity. The impact of balance sheet behavior on spending and of monetary conditions on balance sheets plays a large role. The inventory-production-price loop makes the economy more vulnerable to "pauses" and subcycles, and can compound a major cycle as occurred in 1973-74. The inclusion of new demand measures in the wage-price sectors and the stage-of-processing modeling of such price shocks as world oil prices not only make the model more inflation-prone, but also affect subsequent financial conditions, spending behavior, and help intensify the business cycle as a whole.

Fig. 1.1 shows that the model can generally reproduce the violence of the recent business cycle experience. It contrasts a full, dynamic, 15-year simulation of the model over the years 1966-80 with the actual experience. The simulation is not perfect: the model captures the downturn of 1969-70 too early, but does reflect well the severe recession of 1973-75 as would be expected from the third-generation model improvements. The recession of 1980 is modelled accurately, but only with the aid of a credit control dummy in the credit-dependent categories of consumer expenditures.

5.2 *The fiscal multipliers are modest, temporary and cyclical.*

Fig. 1.2 shows the path for a basic fiscal multiplier, the result of a $5 billion increase in the real volume of federal nonmilitary spending, with monetary policy leaving nonborrowed bank reserves unaffected. The multiplier peaks at 1.6 after two years but then fades away to 0.5 by the fifth year. The downturn is due to higher inflation, higher interest rates, some partial

Figure 1.1
Real Gross National Product,
Dynamic Simulation Versus
Actual Data, 1966-1980

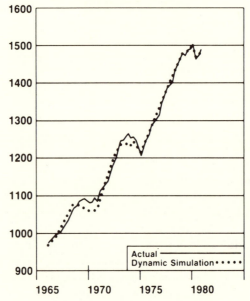

*Simulation based on the DRI model released
in May 1981, with data of that vintage.*

"crowding out" of private credit due to the government deficit, and reduced spending created by deteriorated balance sheets. There are also some accelerator-type, stock-flow adjustment processes in consumer durables, housing and business fixed investment which reinforce the cyclical character of the multiplier.

The secondary drop in the sixth year is due to the crowding out of housing. Aggregate supply is also reduced through crowding out of investment. The specific multiplier values also depend on the base situation on which the exercise is run. In this example, the dynamic historical simulation, beginning in 1966, was used. The multipliers of other fiscal instruments will differ, of course, and assumptions about monetary policy make a big difference. These results are discussed in several later chapters.

Figure 1.2
Impact of a $10 Billion Increase in
Real Nonmilitary Federal Government Spending
on Real GNP
(Starting point: 1966:1)

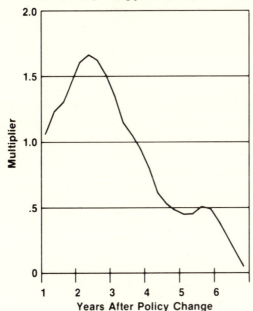

5.3 The monetary multipliers are especially large, though temporary, reflecting the strong influence of money and finance.

Fig. 1.3 shows the path for real GNP that arises from a sustained $1 billion rise in nonborrowed reserves, the key monetary policy instrument in the DRI model. The response of the economy to changes in reserves is relatively quick, with the sharpest advance occurring between the third and seventh quarters of the stimulus. By year four, the effect is near zero, as higher inflation reduces real activity. Ultimately, the cumulative effect of the extra reserves approximates zero as well, as the inflation effect on real activity takes its toll. Nevertheless, it is clear that money and credit have a strong impact on the economy, reflected in the elaborate financial-real linkage mechanisms in the DRI model.

Figure 1.3
Impact of a $1 Billion Rise in
Nonborrowed Reserves:
Ratio of the Change in Real GNP
Relative to the Increment in Nonborrowed Reserves
(Starting point: 1966:1)

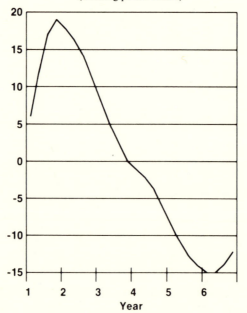

Year

5.4 The Phillips curve has become increasingly nonlinear.

In earlier DRI models, the Phillips curve was already heavily conditioned by the previous history of inflation. But the recent improvements in the model have greatly heightened the sensitivity of prices to demand conditions, and have gradually allowed the DRI model to escape what had been the biggest bugaboo of large-scale models: a short-run Phillips curve which was so insensitive that policy analysis always showed large near-term benefits of stimulus at no near-term cost. Figs. 1.4 and 1.5 show Phillips curves for different time spans. The curves are based on two sets of simulations, one using a period of price stability as the initial condition, the other the actual initial conditions found in the third quarter of 1978, with a previous three-year average inflation rate of 6.2%. In the stable-price-history case, the short-run Phillips curve—the curve after one year—shows a tradeoff of 0.7 in moving from unemployment of 7% to 6%. The tradeoff becomes 1.4 in going from 5% to 4% and rises to 3.2 in going from 4% to 3%. These figures reflect the economic conditions of the 1960s.

When the initial conditions are inflationary, the feasible combinations are less favorable and the tradeoffs become worse. The dominant effect is the persistent element of inflation: the effect of unemployment on inflation is not strong enough to quickly overcome the history, and consequently the Phillips curve stays in worse territory even after four years.

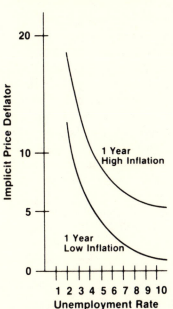
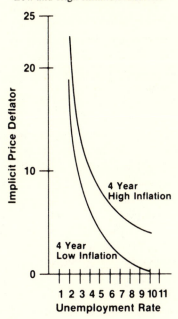
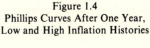

Figure 1.4
Phillips Curves After One Year,
Low and High Inflation Histories

Figure 1.5
Phillips Curves After Four Years,
Low and High Inflation Histories

5.5 Inflation affects spending.

From its beginning in 1969, the DRI model has had the property that higher inflation reduces real activity. This effect was caused mainly by the impact of inflation on interest rates and housing, and by the definition of some spending categories in nominal terms in the early versions.

The third-generation DRI model contains additional relationships between inflation and spending including the impact of inflation on consumer attitudes. When exogenous elements in inflation are increased, all categories of spending are hurt. Business spending is hurt by the higher real capital costs and increased uncertainty. Worsening balance sheets restrain both business and consumer spending. State and local governments cut real purchases because of their worsened budget position.

Counteracting these tendencies is the inducement to accelerate spending in anticipation of inflation. Real interest rates after taxes affect the outlays for some of the bigger consumer durables. Higher expected inflation cuts real interest rates and boosts spending. The net effect of accelerating inflation, including the impact on consumer confidence, is to reduce spending, however.

6. The Output-Inflation Transform

Among the most critical performance characteristics of a modern economy are its output and inflation responses to fiscal or monetary stimulus. If the principal result is increased output rather than inflation at conditions short of full employment, the traditional Keynesian prescription of operating the economy near its full potential is very attractive. On the other hand, if stimulating action leads to very little increased output and mainly to extra inflation, whether through the routine working of markets or through anticipatory expectations of businesses and households, the policy of stimulus will fail.

Econometric models have been very much in the center of the controversy between the Keynesian and the rational expectations schools associated with the above two viewpoints. The models are designed to have each individual component represented as realistically as possible, using historical data as the statistical evidence.

Inevitably, a model built on the historical data will not support either viewpoint, since, as is usually the case in such matters, the evidence falls somewhere in between. The strong assertion of the Keynesian school, that demand inflation only becomes important near full employment, has been recognized to run contrary to the facts for a generation. In the stronger versions of the rational expectations school, there is nearly instant discounting of government policies in people's expectations and therefore virtually no output effects. It does not correspond with the facts, as discussed in more detail in the following chapter.

The concept of the *output-inflation transform* can serve to summarize the behavior of the economy, as represented by the model, in this regard. The output-inflation transform (OIT) is defined as the fraction of an induced increase in nominal GNP which represents real activity rather than inflation. The output-inflation transform shows the time profile of the output-inflation coefficient, which represents the division between real output and inflation of the multiplier effect created by any policy change. An output-inflation coefficient of one would represent the case where a measure of stimulus created only real output and no inflation, i.e., the traditional Keynesian case at underemployment. An output-inflation coefficient of zero would imply that the entire effect of the stimulus is inflation without any real output gains, the case of the strong versions of the rational expectations theory.

Fig. 1.6 shows the output-inflation transform of the DRI model for an increase of real government spending. It can be seen that the OIT starts out at unity, and drops to 0.6 after two years. In the subsequent years, the OIT drops rapidly, as the real output benefits disappear. By the sixth year, the OIT coefficient is zero.

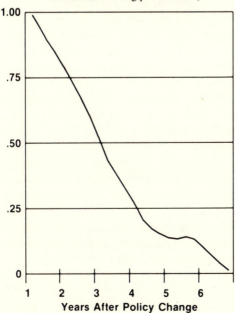

Figure 1.6
Output-Inflation Transform
(Sustained $10 billion increase in
government expenditures
Simulation starting point: 1966:1)

Years After Policy Change

The output-inflation transform will depend on the particular source of the economic stimulus as well as the particular historical circumstance. Supply-oriented fiscal measures, such as an investment tax credit, will boost potential GNP and productivity, and thereby partially offset the inflationary effects of increased activity. Such measures are discussed in more detail in Chapter 3, where it will be seen that the best of the supply-side measures seem to have a long-run OIT of 0.3 to 0.4, sufficient to provide major permanent benefits to the economy, but still showing some net inflationary effect. The output-inflation transform also will depend on the condition of the economy: when resource utilization is modest and unemployment exceeds the natural unemployment rate, the OIT will be higher, i.e., more favorable, than in an economy in a boom condition. The presence or absence of inflationary shocks will have a small effect as well, since there are some closed nonlinear loops within the wage-price block. Finally, the condition of the financial system has some independent influence: in a period of capital scarcity, the crowding-out created by stimulus will be greater, displacing some investment and reducing the supply-side benefits.

7. Forecasting Experience with the Third-Generation Model

The DRI Quarterly Model of the U.S. Economy is large and complicated, requiring twenty-five full-time professionals to develop, update and operate it for forecasting and policy analysis. It also uses computers at the top of the available scale. Thus, the project probably represents the largest private undertaking in macro forecasting history. Is there a reward of more accurate forecasts for this sizable investment of people and technology?

DRI has always left the evaluation of forecasts to third party scholars.[24] It is impossible for a forecasting organization to be utterly objective about its own work. But the following material will provide some insights.

First, in its initial years, the third-generation DRI model produced good forecasting results, substantially better than what could be found before. Forecasts prepared with second-generation models, including DRI's, failed to anticipate the full violence of the 1973-75 crisis, although the end of the previous boom was recognized in timely fashion, and strong warnings of the dangers in faulty policies were issued by the second quarter of 1973. But in the years 1976 to 1979, after the adoption of the new-generation model, the forecasting record was good by any reasonable standard. Adoption of a more

---

[24]The principal studies are by Stephen K. McNees in various issues of *The New England Economic Review*, published by the Federal Reserve Bank of Boston. The most recent study is "Recent Record of Thirteen Forecasters," *New England Economic Review* (September-October 1981), pp. 1-20.

rigid monetarist approach to monetary policy in October 1979 introduced a structural break by freeing interest rates from central bank control, which complicated the forecasting task once more. In 1980, the imposition of consumer credit controls produced the kind of exogenous shock which has been at the root of most of the larger forecasting errors. The 1981 recession was forecast, but the timing was premature. The effect of high interest rates took longer than anticipated.

Forecast users see the full record in the quarterly track record exercises published in the *Data Resources Review*, which show the forecasts made over the preceding several years for the particular quarter for two dozen of the most important variables. Table 1.2 is a summary of these track record exercises for the period from the third quarter of 1976 to the middle of 1981. The table shows that the average absolute percent error for the level of real GNP in the forecasts of the preceding eight quarters ranged from 0.4% for routine quarters during the upswing phase of this cycle to as large as 2.4% for the quarter of economic collapse in the spring of 1980 following the imposition of the consumer credit controls. The average error for all 20 quarters for real GNP is 0.91%. The errors for consumption are of the same general magnitude. Business fixed investment shows errors about two-and-a-half times as large, reflecting the somewhat greater cyclicality of this component of final demand. Residential investment shows larger errors still because of its extraordinary volatility in response to financial conditions. Forecasts for federal, state and local government purchases show middling errors, with the federal outlays, which are largely exogenous, the least predictable.

The forecasts for unemployment show an average absolute error for the 20 quarters of 0.42%, with relatively little variation among quarters. Unemployment responds relatively sluggishly to short-lived changes in output, and consequently is easier to predict.

Forecasts for inflation tend to be too low, with an average absolute error in the four-quarter forecasts of 1.2% during this particular time span. The eight-quarter forecasts show an average absolute error of 1.3%, indicating little worsening as the forecast interval is lengthened. Even the one-quarter forecasts showed an average absolute error of 1.1% in the inflation rate, though much of this error occurred during the quarters with OPEC surprises.

The accuracy of interest rate forecasts declined sharply after the adoption of monetarism in the fourth quarter of 1979. Prior to that date, forecasts of bond yields showed an average absolute error of just 32 basis points; the errors became much larger, 271 basis points in the first seven quarters after the change in monetary regime. Errors in short-term interest rates also became larger, though the contrast is not as extreme.

Table 1.2
Summary of DRI Track Records
Third Quarter 1976 to Second Quarter 1981
(Average percent error of previous forecasts for that quarter)

	1981		1980				1979				1978				1977				1976	
	II	I	IV	III	II	I	IV	III	II	I	IV	III	II	I	IV	III	II	I	IV	III
Real GNP and Components																				
Total	1.2	1.9	1.8	2.1	2.4	1.3	1.3	1.2	1.3	0.5	0.4	0.5	0.7	1.7	0.5	0.6	0.4	0.6	0.7	0.8
Consumption	1.3	1.8	1.6	1.7	2.4	0.9	1.1	0.9	1.2	0.5	0.7	0.5	0.5	0.8	0.6	1.1	1.2	1.1	0.9	0.9
Nonresidential Investment	2.3	3.2	3.5	2.4	3.0	2.0	1.3	1.1	1.2	1.5	1.8	1.9	1.9	1.6	1.3	1.6	2.0	1.7	2.2	2.9
Residential Investment	7.7	9.9	13.7	21.6	24.9	4.4	5.2	3.3	2.1	2.1	1.5	2.6	4.4	4.0	4.2	4.0	4.6	4.7	4.5	8.0
Inventories	68.6	144.7	NC*	142.6	222.9	NC*	140.4	23.5	47.1	14.8	54.0	25.3	8.6	26.0	58.4	24.1	39.9	38.8	38.2	56.6
Federal Purchases	2.8	3.8	3.3	4.0	4.8	3.5	2.3	3.8	3.8	2.8	2.4	2.3	5.2	2.7	3.2	5.4	2.8	0.9	1.8	11.5
State & Local	1.1	1.0	1.4	2.5	3.1	2.6	2.7	2.7	2.6	2.5	0.6	0.6	0.8	1.7	1.0	1.2	2.2	2.9	2.2	1.2
Average Absolute Error - Percentage Points																				
Unemployment Rate	0.4	0.5	0.5	0.6	0.7	0.4	0.5	0.4	0.5	0.4	0.4	0.3	0.4	0.3	0.3	0.3	0.3	0.3	0.5	0.4
AA-Utility Rate	4.14	3.35	2.88	1.75	1.95	3.16	1.78	0.44	0.62	0.63	0.44	0.28	0.13	0.13	0.44	0.63	0.56	0.41	0.58	0.38
3-Month Bill Rate	4.62	4.55	4.08	1.24	1.79	4.08	3.37	1.78	2.05	2.33	2.03	1.04	0.36	0.33	0.49	0.74	1.32	1.18	1.29	0.63
Absolute Error in Compound Annual Growth Rate																				
Real GNP																				
1 Quarter Forecast	2.3	7.4	3.7	5.2	4.2	2.0	2.4	3.9	6.7	1.9	3.5	1.5	1.3	5.1	1.0	1.2	0.3	3.5	1.3	2.8
4 Quarter Forecast	2.7	2.9	1.6	0.2	2.6	0.5	0.8	0.7	1.2	0.2	0.3	0.5	1.0	2.1	0.1	0.0	1.0	2.2	0.6	0.8
8 Quarter Forecast	0.8	1.7	1.8	2.9	3.2	1.8	1.3	1.3	0.6	0.9	0.2	0.1	0.4	1.3	0.2	0.3	0.6	0.5	0.1	1.2
Implicit Price Deflator																				
1 Quarter Forecast	3.7	3.3	0.3	1.1	0.3	0.2	0.6	0.0	1.4	1.8	1.3	0.7	2.9	1.1	0.8	0.1	0.9	0.0	0.0	0.4
4 Quarter Forecast	0.3	1.2	0.4	1.2	1.1	0.7	1.5	1.9	2.5	2.3	2.2	1.7	1.2	0.2	0.4	0.8	0.7	0.3	1.5	2.6
8 Quarter Forecast	0.6	0.8	1.7	2.1	2.4	2.6	2.8	2.5	2.2	1.5	1.5	1.7	1.0	0.1	0.4	1.0	0.1	0.4	1.2	0.6

Further perspective can be gained on the actual track record by comparing the forecast results with an experiment conducted over the last three years using the ARIMA, time-series analysis method. DRI developed optimal ARIMA forecasting formulas,[25] using an elaborate simulation exercise for a stratified sample of historical business cycle quarters, using only the data that were actually available at the time. These formulas have been applied each quarter to produce alternative one-quarter and four-quarter forecasts which were published alongside the DRI model forecasts.

Table 1.3 summarizes this experiment. It can be seen that the model forecasts generally were more accurate. For example, the errors in the four-

Table 1.3
Ratio of Root Mean-Square Errors of
Forecasts of DRI Model and ARIMA
(1977:4-1980:3)

	One Qtr. Ahead	Four Qtr. Ahead
Real GNP Components		
Gross National Product	0.83	0.64
Gross National Product (Nominal)	0.73	0.81
Consumption	0.77	0.56
Business Fixed Investment	0.71	0.94
Government Expenditures	0.91	0.86
State and Local Expenditures	0.69	0.76
Business Inventory Changes	0.72	0.94
Prices (Rate of Change)		
All Urban Consumer Price Index	0.85	1.04
Interest Rates		
Federal Funds	0.79	0.76
U.S. Government 3-Month Bills	0.69	0.69
High-Grade Corporate Bonds	0.84	1.11
Production and Employment Related		
Total Production Index (1967=1)	0.62	0.51
Capacity Utilization Rate	0.60	0.48
Unemployment Rate (%)	0.92	1.01
Housing Starts (Mil.)	0.36	0.87
Retail Automobile Sales (Mil.)	0.88	0.84
Other		
Aftertax Corporate Profits ($ Bil.)	0.87	1.12
Consumer Sentiment Index	0.78	0.93
Stock Prices (Standard & Poor's)	0.41	0.66
Money Supply (M1)	0.73	0.47

[25]See Stephen Chazen, "Macro Forecasting With ARIMA Models," *Data Resources Review* (October 1977), pp. 21-25.

quarter forecasts of real GNP produced by the model method were 0.64 as large as those produced by ARIMA. It should be emphasized that this experiment, unlike the experiments previously reported in the literature, is the first to report on a genuine forecasting test where both methods are applied on an ex-ante basis, with the projections published at the same time.

There are some surprises in the experiment. Model forecasts show a substantial advantage for common stock prices and short-term interest rates, both of which are associated with what are usually considered to be efficient markets, and where the ARIMA method should do very well. On the other hand, the ARIMA method did as well or better in forecasting such variables as the consumer price index and corporate profits, variables where one might expect the model to do particularly well.

ARIMA is inapplicable for longer forecast horizons. The optimal parameters produced by the data are always of low degree, implying that ARIMA is limited to extrapolation of existing trends. As the forecast horizon moves toward eight quarters, it begins to correspond to the length of the business cycle, and since ARIMA will not produce turning points, the method then is guaranteed to fail.

It must be recognized that much error remains in the forecasts, enough to preserve considerable humility and to be a warning to users against acting on univalued projections. Even in ex-post simulations, the model cannot calculate the timing or precise extent of the minor inventory cycles. It just takes too little to set off the speculative bubbles in which purchasing executives hoard inventories against imagined shortages, driving up production and utilization rates, and deteriorating vendor performance in a self-inflaming way.

The model also requires some major exogenous elements which are very difficult, if not impossible, to forecast. The OPEC price of oil has been the initiating source of two recessions. The Federal Reserve is the other major source of uncertainty and forecast error. Its monetarist behavior should be making its behavior more predictable, but the initial results have been the opposite: unparalleled fluctuations of interest rates. Truly exogenous factors, such as the weather or world political and military disturbances, remain as powerful as ever and act upon an economic system in which the cushions and margins are not what they were fifteen years ago. Finally, research on the modeling of the psychological-cum-expectational element in private decision making, another source of difficulty, is still in an early stage and will provide a continuing agenda for further work.

CHAPTER 2

ECONOMIC THEORY, ECONOMETRIC MODELS AND THE BEHAVIOR OF THE U.S. ECONOMY*

1. Introduction

The relation between the theoretical and empirical branches of economics has never been an easy one. Our discipline has not followed the model of the natural sciences in which theories are a response to previously unexplained phenomena and enter the body of accepted doctrine only after empirical testing. In economics, theory is treated as the property of the neoclassical school, deriving its principal ideas from Smith, Ricardo, Marshall and Walras. Fortunately, the impetus from Keynes' attempt to shift mainstream economics into different channels is not yet fully spent, and macroeconomic theory retains a role for psychological, expectational and disequilibrium elements in behavior.

Empirical economics, on the other hand, has resided mainly in the applied branches of the discipline. Such fields as public finance, international economics, labor economics, monetary economics and industrial organization have always considered empirical data their basic material for research and analysis. In recent years, these fields have assimilated the advances in econometric methods and have made intensive use of theory, creating a rapprochement between the two camps.

The development of macroeconometric models has created a new source of tension between the theoretical and empirical branches. The models are a check on the delivered doctrine of economic theory. They describe the behavior of the economic system and on some issues are an alternative theory.

*Stephen Brooks developed the crowding-out simulations and Frank Cooper conducted the rational expectations experiments. Roger Brinner, Jerry Green and Allan Meltzer commented on this chapter and improved it. The material was initially presented at the NBER-NSF Conference on Macroeconometric Models, Ann Arbor, Michigan, October 1978.

The writings of Robert Lucas[1] show that theorists are aware of this challenge. As government relies heavily on the macroeconometric models for policy analysis and as the models become an important source of expectations for both the private and public sectors, controversy must be expected.

The intellectual origins of macroeconometric models contained some anticlassical strands in economic thought. It is no accident that Jan Tinbergen is the father of both macroeconometric models and the theory of economic policy.[2] The development of models appeared to create the possibility of a high degree of intervention by the state: if the future could be calculated and the impact of instruments known, it should be possible to use the tools of government to achieve rather precise and numerous goals. While the neoclassical tradition of economic theory has most commonly served as an elaborate rationale for government inaction, the macroeconometric models appeared to be a foundation for interventionism.

The next three chapters put the current relation between economic theory and macroeconometric models, as illustrated by the DRI model, into a factual perspective. This chapter deals principally with these issues: (1) Are the micro foundations of the model consistent with economic theory? (2) In what ways has the model gone beyond delivered doctrine to incorporate aspects of the microeconomic world which have never received much attention from economic theory? (3) What are the principal behavioral characteristics of the economy as represented in the models with regard to such currently live theoretical matters as crowding out, rational expectations, errors-in-expectations, policy analysis and cyclicality? The next chapter examines the issues of aggregate supply. Chapter 4 explores the interaction between the real and financial systems, including the channels of monetary policy.

The disagreements between the DRI model and economic theory are quite narrow and are mainly due to the empirical necessities created by explicit representation of the dynamics of learning, expectations, errors and adjustment. Much of the apparent controversy is based on a distorted and obsolete picture of the nature of the models. Both theorists and econometricians are blown by the same winds: differences are related less to intellectual origins than to styles of research and choice of problems.

---

[1]Robert E. Lucas, "Econometric Testing of the Natural Rate Hypothesis," in Otto Eckstein, ed., *The Econometrics of Price Determination* (Washington, D.C.: Federal Reserve Board, 1972); and "Econometric Policy Evaluation: A Critique," in Karl Brunner and Allan H. Meltzer, eds., *The Phillips Curve and Labor Markets* (Pittsburgh: Carnegie-Rochester Series on Public Policy, 1976), pp. 19-46.
[2]Jan Tinbergen, *Business Cycles in the United States: 1912-1932* (Geneva: League of Nations, 1939); and *On the Theory of Economic Policy* (Amsterdam: North-Holland Publishing Co., 1952).

2. Micro Foundations

There is much agreement between the econometricians and the theorists on the micro foundations of the models. The wave of scientific innovations in the 1950s and the early 1960s, including Jorgenson's work on investment,[3] Duesenberry,[4] Modigliani-Brumberg and Ando-Modigliani[5] on consumption and DeLeeuw's formulation of a financial sector[6] for the Brookings Model, brought solid theoretical underpinnings to the model equations. Indeed, even the early Klein model[7] provided a microeconomic basis for its equations. Differences in emphasis remain, of course. Theory has mainly a micro-orientation and usually assumes price flexibility without lags, limiting the effect of random factors (white noise) to similar uncorrelated noise in prices and quantities. The models accept the time lags the data appear to imply and thereby leave room for random factors to affect the system's behavioral properties.

Table 2.1 shows the foundations of the principal behavioral sectors in the DRI model derived from economic theory, as well as some of the extensions which further economic theory, research, changing times and experience have added. While the principal equations are discussed more fully later in this volume, this overview illustrates that the day-to-day necessity of building and maintaining a workable model leads the researcher into modeling phenomena that economic theory does not emphasize. Ten years of data of increased variability produced by a shock-ridden economy have required some modifications in the representation of behavior. Demographic changes and stock-flow relations are of empirical importance. Spending decisions are affected by risks originating in the macro-economy. While theory has rushed to embrace a concept of rational expectations in which only unbiased expected values enter decisions, the model shows the effects of economy-wide errors in expectations and changing variances. The interplay of the financial and real sectors has become tighter as the economy's liquidity position has deteriorated. The representation of cost and supply factors has become more

[3]Dale W. Jorgenson, "Capital Theory and Investment Behavior," *American Economic Review, Proceedings* (May 1963), pp. 247-259.
[4]James S. Duesenberry, *Income, Saving and the Theory of Consumer Behavior* (Cambridge: Harvard University Press, 1952).
[5]Franco Modigliani and Richard Brumberg, "Utility Analysis and the Consumption Function: An Interpretation of Cross-Section Data," in K.K. Kurihara, ed., *Post Keynesian Economics* (New Brunswick: New Jersey, Rutgers University Press, 1954); Albert Ando and Franco Modigliani, "The 'Life-Cycle' Hypothesis of Saving: Aggregate Implications and Tests," *American Economic Review* (March 1963), pp. 55-84.
[6]Frank DeLeeuw, "A Model of Financial Behavior," *The Brookings Quarterly Econometric Model of the United States* (Chicago: Rand McNally, 1965), pp. 465-530.
[7]Lawrence R. Klein, *Economic Fluctuations in the United States: 1921-1944* (New York: Wiley, 1950).

Table 2.1
Economic Theory and Specifications in the DRI Model

Variable	Foundations from Standard Theory	Extensions
—Households Consumption	Utility maximization Temporary and permanent income, real and financial assets, relative prices, net worth	Variance of income, debt burden, demographic structure, consumer sentiment (modeled from macro risks of inflation and unemployment)
Labor Supply	Unemployment rate, real aftertax wages	Demographic composition of the labor force
Wages	Price expectations, unemployment rate	Short- and long-term price expectations
—Firms Fixed Investment	Profit maximization Rental price of capital, stock adjustment	Long- and short-term real sales expectations, surprises in actual sales, cost of capital by financial sources, debt burden, balance sheet instability, pollution abatement requirements
Inventory Investment	Stock adjustment to sales expectations	Errors in sales expectations, capacity utilization, delivery conditions, debt burden
Production	Variable coefficient input-output relations, supply from production functions including energy	Effects of several capacity constraints on output and price
Employment	Output, wage rates, productivity trends	Cyclical productivity swings
Pricing	Material cost, unit labor cost, demand-supply disequilibrium, exchange rate	Stage of processing approach, vendor performance
—Financial Institutions Portfolio Decisions	Return-maximizing portfolio behavior Balance sheet, expected own and alternative real, aftertax rates of return and opportunity costs	Flow-of-funds cycles Modeling of flow-of-funds of households, corporations, financial intermediaries
Interest Rates	Price expectations, supply and demand of liquidity, sector credit demands, monetary policy	Segmented short- and long-term markets, competitive returns and costs on various assets and liabilities, interrelated portfolio adjustment dynamics
—Central Bank	Exogenous in policy parameters	

—State and Local Government	Utility maximization for spending and taxes subject to budget constraint	Optimal revenue combination, demographic structure
—Federal Government		
Spending	Real full employment values as policy variables	Policy levers for major fiscal instruments
Taxes	Income distribution, activity levels	Rates as policy variables
—Rest-of-World		
Exports	Activity levels and relative prices abroad, exchange rate	World grain reserves, exchange rate response to balance of trade constraint
Imports	Relative prices, exchange rate, input-output relations	Capacity utilization, excess demand, real income

elaborate: price controls, a world food shortage and the energy revolution have made the management of production, which had been a solved problem for advanced industrial societies, a central concern and a force for inflation once more. The responsiveness of aggregate supply to policy changes has also become a major focus of the model.

3. Validation

The validation procedures developed in the last ten years help assure a general consistency between model and theory. A model may consist entirely of esthetically and scientifically pleasing equations which will act poorly in full model simulation. It may prove too sluggish, unable to reproduce actual business cycles, or oversensitive, triggering subsector loops that have not been observed. Multipliers may be inconsistent with the general body of knowledge; the Phillips Curve may be unrealistically flat; or the model may have invalid growth properties. A single equation appearing to be reasonable enough on every theoretical and statistical criterion can destroy the simulation properties of a model.

Besides the standard single-equation statistical tests, the validation procedures used in the annual respecification of the DRI model include the following:

(1) A full, dynamic, ex-post simulation for 15 years to assure successful simulation of the actual historical record. The quality of this simulation is measured by an historical error-cost function, E_h

$$E_h = \Sigma \alpha_i RMSE_i, \tag{1}$$

where $RMSE_i$ is the percent root-mean-square error in the full dynamic simulation for a particular variable i, and α_i reflects the importance of the variable in assessing the accuracy of the model. Because the economy is a single system, good simulation requires that all the principal elements, including final demands, production, aggregate supply, inflation and interest rates, show small errors and little bias in history. Consequently, the error-cost function is relatively insensitive to its relative weights.

(2) Tests of all policy levers. Counter-intuitive results, which are considered appealing in noneconomic models of social systems behavior, are treated as suspect in the econometric models and usually found to be inadvertent byproducts of eccentric specifications. Policy levers must show direct and indirect responses consistent with the academic literature.

(3) Tests of various other significant features of the economy. Are the effects of foreign exchange rates consistent with the price and income elasticities of exports and imports reported in the specialized literature? Does potential output react properly to variations in capital formation, and are the various productivity and capacity responses mutually consistent? Do income shares stay within historical ranges and display realistic elasticities? Are the Engel Curves consistent with long-term historical studies of consumer behavior? How does personal saving respond to various changes in the economy? These and other questions must be resolved through continuous testing. Heavy simulation use helps assure that the model be relatively free of anomalous properties.

(4) Ex-ante simulations, using conventional assumptions about exogenous variables, to assure the model can follow a balanced growth path well into the future. Labor force growth and factor productivity trends change over the decades, and the step-up of inflation can produce previously unobserved behavioral reactions, particularly in the financial system. But inexplicable breaks with the past are treated with suspicion.

(5) Destructive tests. Will the model produce hyper-inflations if shocks are large enough and monetary policy is accommodating? Will the model produce a real downturn if stimulus presses activity against the full-employment ceiling? Is a depression possible if fiscal and monetary policies react perversely to the initial declines? These tests also provide the opportunity to verify the detailed structural properties of the model, to make sure that the highly disaggregated demand, production, employment and flow-of-funds equations respond as economic theory and common sense would dictate.

One of the challenges to economists, both theorists and econometricians, is to define the full list of questions which they must be prepared to analyze. New issues have arisen with great rapidity, and the model builders have scrambled to include them in their work and to offer a serious treatment in time for the policy decisions that the society had to make. The list of test questions for validating the model is therefore never complete.

4. The Crowding-Out Coefficient

While there is a commonality of ideas, there are apparent disagreements between economic theory and econometric models about a number of critical issues. The remainder of this chapter treats several such cases. The next two chapters treat the particular issues of aggregate supply and of the interactions of the real and financial systems in fuller detail.

Does fiscal policy work? Or does the financing of deficits "crowd out" private activity? This has been one of the more durable controversies in macroeconomic theory, and is also reflected in the model counterparts. The purely "fiscalist" model must assume monetary policy to be fully accommodating so that the multiplier mechanism can occur without negative feedback from higher interest rates. The monetarist position, on the other hand, assumes that the financing of fiscal stimulus fully displaces private spending, leaving fiscal policy powerless regardless of the degree of resource utilization. As Brunner and Meltzer[8] have shown, the importance of assets to flow decisions is very much at the heart of the monetarist crowding out conclusion.

Like most empirical implementations of theoretical ideas, the DRI model requires some sharpening of the issue of "crowding out" and provides answers which are both conditional and variable. The amount of crowding out can be determined by comparing the stimulative effects of a fiscal policy in which monetary policy is nonaccommodating with one in which monetary policy is accommodating. At least four different degrees of monetary accommodation can be defined within the model. The least accommodating policy keeps the pattern of money supply growth unchanged. This policy requires the Federal Reserve to operate according to a model which allows it to calculate the effect of fiscal stimulus on the demand for money and to reduce the growth of nonborrowed bank reserves sufficiently to leave the actual amount of money in circulation unaffected. A looser definition of nonaccommodating monetary policy leaves the growth of nonborrowed bank reserves unchanged. The actual amount of money in circulation would be slightly higher in response to the fiscal stimulus because of the increased demand for money.

---

[8] Karl Brunner and Allan H. Meltzer, "Aggregative Theory for a Closed Economy," in Jerome L. Stein, ed., *Monetarism* (Amsterdam: North-Holland Publishing Co., 1976), pp. 182-205.

Another level of monetary accommodation increases bank reserves to leave real interest rates unchanged. A fuller accommodation leaves nominal short-term interest rates unchanged, a policy which could be defined to be over-accommodation since it would reduce the real cost of borrowing through the inflation created by the fiscal stimulus. Both of the interest rate criteria must be made specific in terms of a particular rate, since the fiscal stimulus will alter the relative rates between Treasury and private securities and between long- and short-term maturities.

To illustrate the empirical representation of crowding out in the DRI model, two sets of exercises were run using the 1981 edition of the model. The first exercise takes the economy in a normal period, well short of full resource utilization and with a stable history of inflation, and applies a sustained increase of $10 billion in real nonmilitary purchases of goods and services. Fig. 2.1 summarizes the results under the four monetary policies sketched above. In the polar fiscalist case, where nominal interest rates are left unchanged, nominal GNP grows without limit since the monetary aggregates and the price level will advance together. In real terms, however, the peak multiplier is reached after six quarters, at a value of 2.1. Thereafter, the damage of inflation, even with unchanged nominal interest rates, brings the multiplier down to 0.6 after five years. For the case of constant real interest rates, the multiplier is still large, peaking at 1.8 in year two and remaining a positive 0.3 after five years.

A policy of unchanged nonborrowed bank reserves shows a peak multiplier of 1.6 after six quarters. The early restraining effect is accentuated in the final case, where the nominal money supply is held unchanged: the multiplier reaches an immediate peak of 0.7, and fades to zero over four years.

The size of the crowding-out effect also depends upon the choice of fiscal instrument. For example, a reduction in corporate income tax rates directly enhances the liquidity of business. An investment tax credit, on the other hand, adds a strong stimulus to spending, thereby creating two opposing effects on business liquidity. Similar variations can be found among types of personal tax reductions and among spending programs.

Finally, the extent of crowding out depends upon the condition of the economy. When the financial situation is very strong, with households having large liquid savings and light debt burdens, business firms possessing strong balance sheets and local governments experiencing operating budget surpluses, crowding out will be less than in periods of financial stringency.

Crowding out develops through two channels: "financial" crowding out through higher interest rates and portfolio displacement effects created by increased public debt issues, and "real" crowding out from higher prices, wages and interest rates which reduce demands of businesses and households.

Figure 2.1
Fiscal Policy Multipliers Under
Different Monetary Policy Assumptions*

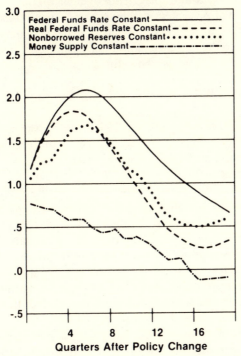

Federal Funds Rate Constant ———————
Real Federal Funds Rate Constant — — — — — ·
Nonborrowed Reserves Constant • • • • • • • • •
Money Supply Constant —·—·—·—·—·—·—·—·

Quarters After Policy Change

*In each of the simulations, real nondefense purchases of goods and services were increased by $10 billion from their baseline value. In the first, nonborrowed reserves were held constant. In the second, nonborrowed reserves were increased by enough to hold the nominal federal funds rate at its baseline value. In the third, nonborrowed reserves were changed enough to hold the real federal funds rate, the nominal federal funds rate minus the annual rate of increase in the GNP deflator, constant. In the fourth, nonborrowed reserves were adjusted to leave the nominal money supply unchanged.

Because some price effects occur at all levels of activity, real crowding out occurs even when the economy is far from the full-employment ceiling. The extent of crowding will depend upon the initial conditions of the economy in terms of inflation, the degree of resource utilization, the liquidity position of the financial system, the willingness of foreigners to buy government debt, particular shocks during the period of stimulus and other factors.

According to the traditional fiscalist position, real crowding out should not occur until the economy is near full employment. At that stage, it is generally recognized that public stimulus simply serves to displace other demands. But the empirical representation of the DRI model shows that the distinction between full employment and under-employment cannot be made rigidly. There are significant displacement effects even under conditions of substantial resource underutilization. Prices respond to demand in a continuous fashion, and not according to the presence or absence of an inflationary gap.

A crowding-out coefficient can be defined as

$$COC = 1 - \Delta GNP72'/\Delta GNP72'' = 1 - k'/k'', \tag{2}$$

where COC is the crowding-out coefficient, k' is the multiplier under nonaccommodating monetary policy and k'' with accommodation. A crowding-out function can be defined as the variation of COC with particular other economic variables.

Financial crowding out varies particularly with the extent of inflation before and during the period of stimulus. Therefore, the fiscal stimulus exercises were performed on twelve baseline simulations, each with a different underlying historical rate of wage inflation. The wage rate determines the price level through wage-price interactions, and this in turn determines the state of the financial system at the time of the fiscal stimulus. To minimize the effects of real crowding out, the simulations in this experiment were designed so that real activity was the same prior to the stimulus. During the simulation, however, inflation was allowed to affect real activity.

Twelve alternative histories were created going back three years, by varying the rate of wage increase from 4% to 10.5%. Applying the fiscal stimulus under the two alternative monetary assumptions yields twelve paths of crowding-out coefficients, shown in fig. 2.2 and table 2.2. These paths show that crowding out varies with the inflation rate. They also show that it takes about three quarters for half the crowding out to occur, and three years for it to approach its maximum. The crowding-out coefficients are compared after three years of stimulus across the twelve solutions. It can be seen that crowding out is as low as 0.6 when wage inflation is 4%, and is complete at 1.0 when wage inflation is as high as 10.5%. The particular values of the crowding-out coefficients depend on the specifics of the initial conditions, of course. For example, because the financial system adjusts to steady inflation, the coefficients depend partly on the change in the inflation rate. To an extent, therefore, worsened inflation creates a nonlinear crowding-out response, and produces the monetarist, full crowding-out answer if inflation moves 4% above the "core" rate to which the economy had adjusted.

The conclusions of the econometric model on this issue are probably closer to the monetarist than to the fiscalist position. Real crowding out occurs over

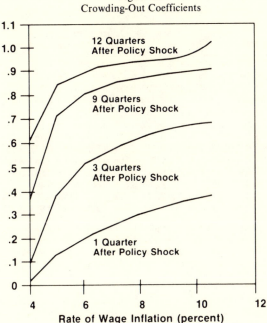

Figure 2.2
Crowding-Out Coefficients

a much broader range of resource utilization than the traditional Keynesian analysis would have suggested. Financial crowding out is sizeable even in the short-run so long as the central bank is not fully accommodating. Further, if the central bank is fully accommodating, the absence of financial crowding out is converted into real crowding out a year or two later. Thus, the DRI model, with its simultaneous real and financial sectors including flows of funds and balance sheets, and with its more sensitive responses of prices to variations in demand and supply, shows the power of fiscal policy to be quite circumscribed.[9] At the same time, the crowding-out coefficients derived from the model do not show the quick or simple results beloved by the true monetarist.

---

[9]For generally similar results using other models, see Franco Modigliani and Albert Ando, "Impacts of Fiscal Actions on Aggregate Income and the Monetarist Controversy, Theory and Evidence," in Jerome L. Stein, ed., *Monetarism* (Amsterdam: North-Holland Publishing Co., 1976), pp. 17-42; and Ray C. Fair, "The Sensitivity of Fiscal Policy Effects to Assumptions about the Behavior of the Federal Reserve," *Econometrica* (September 1978), pp. 1165-1180. The exact time lags and patterns of effects differ among the models, however, reflecting differences in model structures.

Econometric Models and the Economy

Table 2.2
Crowding-Out Coefficients*

Wage Increase in Base Period	1	2	3	4	5	Quarters 6	7	8	9	10	11	12
4.0%	0.008	0.029	0.070	0.115	0.155	0.204	0.252	0.296	0.350	0.421	0.502	0.601
5.0%	0.127	0.252	0.384	0.469	0.527	0.586	0.636	0.674	0.715	0.763	0.806	0.846
6.0%	0.204	0.367	0.511	0.594	0.648	0.702	0.746	0.777	0.808	0.842	0.872	0.899
6.5%	0.235	0.407	0.551	0.632	0.683	0.734	0.776	0.804	0.833	0.865	0.891	0.913
7.0%	0.262	0.440	0.582	0.659	0.709	0.758	0.798	0.825	0.853	0.882	0.905	0.924
7.5%	0.286	0.467	0.607	0.682	0.730	0.778	0.817	0.844	0.867	0.893	0.915	0.934
8.0%	0.307	0.490	0.627	0.700	0.747	0.794	0.832	0.857	0.877	0.901	0.923	0.941
8.5%	0.326	0.510	0.645	0.715	0.761	0.806	0.844	0.865	0.885	0.909	0.931	0.948
9.0%	0.341	0.526	0.658	0.726	0.771	0.816	0.853	0.873	0.892	0.917	0.938	0.955
9.5%	0.356	0.541	0.670	0.736	0.780	0.824	0.861	0.879	0.899	0.925	0.947	0.967
10.0%	0.369	0.554	0.681	0.745	0.787	0.832	0.867	0.886	0.907	0.934	0.960	0.987
10.5%	0.381	0.566	0.690	0.753	0.795	0.839	0.873	0.893	0.916	0.947	0.983	1.033

*Twelve baseline simulations were created, each with identical real activity in the preceding three years, but with different rates of wage growth as indicated, ranging from 4% to 10.5%. Nominal incomes, interest rates, prices, etc., were all different among these baseline simulations. A fiscal stimulus of a $10 billion sustained increase in real nondefense purchases was applied to each of the twelve baselines leaving nonborrowed reserves unchanged—the nonaccommodating case. A second set of twelve simulations combined the fiscal stimulus with changes in nonborrowed reserves sufficient to hold the federal funds rate at its baseline value. The simulations could also be run holding the money supply unchanged, a more rigorous definition of nonaccommodating policy, which would show larger crowding-out coefficients.

5. Rational Expectations?

The current gulf between the theoretical (mainstream) and empirical branches of economics appears to be greatest in the treatment of expectations and errors. The concept of rational expectations developed by Muth[10] and made central to macroeconomics by Friedman[11] was honed into a sharp critique of econometric models by Lucas[12]. Rational expectations are an extension of the theory of individual decisions of households and firms to include a specific pattern of behavior under uncertainty: the individual decision maker has a coherent (usually monetarist) view of the economic

[10]John F. Muth, "Rational Expectations and the Theory of Price Movements," *Econometrica* (July 1961), pp. 315-335.
[11]Milton Friedman, "The Role of Monetary Policy," *American Economic Review Proceedings* (May 1968), pp. 1-17.
[12]Robert E. Lucas, op. cit.

system and interprets all the information available to him without systematic bias in reaching his own decisions.

The rational expectations school has advanced four propositions that are pertinent to econometric models. They deal with the "natural" rate of unemployment, the definition of rationality, the learning rate in expectation formation and the potential of policy.

First, the economy possesses a "natural" rate of unemployment. This rate is determined by the normal period of search of individuals as they change from one job to another in a world of imperfect information. In the absence of policy disturbance, the economy moves toward the natural rate. There is no trade-off between inflation and unemployment in the long run, and it would require accelerating and surprising inflation to hold unemployment below its natural rate.

While this lack of trade-off, the absence of a permanent Phillips Curve, is the most commonly cited disagreement between theory and models, the DRI model has shared this long-term property for some time. The wage equation is "near-accelerationist" with a price coefficient near unity.[13] The remainder of the wage-price sector contains sufficient additional demand effects to gradually convert real stimulus into inflation, as fig. 2.1 showed. The noninflationary rate of unemployment is quite high in the model, though the precise estimate is dependent on initial conditions and assumptions for exogenous variables.

While the general conclusion in the DRI model has much similarity to the natural rate-rational expectations school, the mechanisms which produce the result are not the same. The difference lies mainly in the speed of adjustment. There are adaptative expectations mechanisms in individual equations, some of which reflect learning processes stretching over more years than a tough-minded rationalist would consider within the bounds of his definition of rationality. Both businesses and households learn only gradually from experience and form their expectations of the future principally from objectively observed conditions of the past.

The DRI model also rejects the definition of rationality which bases decisions only on the expected values of the variables, ruling out the higher moments of their distribution. The variance of income and other measures of macro and financial risk also affect spending decisions, introducing a bias

---

[13]Otto Eckstein and Roger Brinner, "The Inflation Process in the United States" (Washington, D.C.: Joint Economic Committee, U.S. Government Printing Office, February 1972), reprinted in *Parameters and Policies in the U.S. Economy*, Otto Eckstein, ed. (Amsterdam: North-Holland Publishing Co., 1976), pp. 99-158.

below expected values if uncertainty is great.[14] The data suggest that, in the aggregate, consumers and businesses are averse to risk.

The length of the period of adjustment is perhaps the biggest difference between the DRI model and the rational expectations viewpoint. The school looks for a quicker approach to the no trade-off condition because of the semantic problem created by its use of the concept of "money-illusion." Since learning processes are not treated explicitly nor a formal mechanism shown by which information modifies expectations, the quick adjustment of instant market-clearing is necessary to keep out the irrationality of money illusion.[15] But in the actual world, it takes years of experience to disentangle temporary from permanent changes and to assess in what ways the fundamental movements of the economy have been altered. A society which can assess its true state over a space of a few years is doing very well. Even after matters are understood, adjustment processes are slowed by the existence of long-term contracts including three-year wage agreements, by the bureaucratic pricing processess which characterize some concentrated, capital-intensive industries, by the regulatory lag for utilities, by slow turnover of portfolios, and other rigidities.

To test the potential role of a "quick rational expectations" approach in the DRI model, a wage equation was developed which embodies a quick price adjustment term and leaves only fleeting room for money illusion. The equation in the model, in contrast, applies two concepts of price expectations: a "permanent" expectation generated by a second order Pascal lag with an average lag of nearly two years, and a "temporary" price expectation based on the price increases of the last four quarters. These terms are combined with a demand measure, the ratio of actual to potential GNP, and with dummies for the mid-1960's guideposts, Phase I of the Nixon Controls, and the data break of 1964. The sum of the price coefficients in this equation is 0.88, or near-rational in the sense of being free of bias and money illusion in the long run. But because of the weight on the permanent price term with its long lag structure, the adjustment process is slow. This is the principal factor which creates the long lags between variations in real activity and the response of the price level.

---

[14]Some of the literature on rational expectations considers the case where higher expected moments affect decisions; see Edward C. Prescott and Finn Kydland, "Optimal Stabilization Policy: A New Formulation," Carnegie-Mellon paper, 1974. For a survey of the literature, see Robert Shiller, "Rational Expectations and the Dynamic Structure of Macroeconomic Models, A Critical Review," *Journal of Monetary Economics* (January 1978), pp. 1-44. Shiller concludes that most of the theoretical development requires the assumption that only the mean expectation matters.

[15]Benjamin Friedman, "Optimal Expectations and the Extreme Information Assumptions of 'Rational Expectations' Models," *Journal of Monetary Economics* (January 1979), pp. 23-42.

The "quick rational expectations" alternative uses only the last quarter's behavior as the basis for price expectations. In this experiment, an attempt was made to see if a statistically adequate equation could be derived with so brief a price expectations process, and whether the DRI model would show shorter adjustment periods if such a wage equation were substituted.

Since price expectations cannot be observed, an instrumental variable approach must be used.[16] Using theoretical harmony with the rational expectations-monetarist viewpoint as one of the criteria for choosing the instrumental variables, the increase in the money supply for each of the preceding three quarters and the level of the long-term interest rate on high quality bonds in the current and the preceding two quarters were used. The bond yields incorporate price expectations of the participants in the bond market which themselves may or may not be rational. The DRI model equation for bond yields has a high price coefficient, but its adaptive expectations process is also long, with an average lag of almost two years.

Table 2.3 presents several wage equations. Clearly, the statistical quality of the quick equation is inferior. This, in itself, is not a surprising result, since the earlier wage studies had explored in detail whether the lags could be shorter. But two other conclusions were more surprising. First, insistence on a quick formation of price expectations produces an equation in which the demand measure plays a smaller role and the price coefficient drops to 0.80, both weakening the response of inflation to stimulus. As a result, when this equation is embedded in the model, the dynamic simulation properties show a weaker response of the price level to a policy stimulus.

The substitution of the "quick" wage equation in the model also damages the historic simulation quality of the model. Table 2.4 shows the percent root-mean-square errors for the two versions of the DRI model in full historical simulation, 1966 to 1977. The difference in the errors for nominal GNP is not dramatic, but the difference is great in real terms. The increased error originates in the wage equation; its full system simulation error is greater by a factor of four, with a strong downward bias. This produces a negative bias for the whole wage-price sector which creates a positive bias in real activity.

To explore the territory of intermediate speeds of adjustment, a wage equation was developed with the most recent one-year change in prices as the basis for expectations, using the same instruments of bond yields and M1. The results are much better, but still inferior to the model (tables 2.3 and 2.4). The speeds of adjustment are fairly slow, so the distinctions become small.

---

[16]Bennett T. McCallum, "Rational Expectations and the Natural Rate Hypothesis: Some Consistent Estimates," *Econometrica* (January 1976), pp. 43-52.

Table 2.3
Wage Equations With Four Kinds of Price Expectations

Dependent variable: ln (w/w_{-1})

	Quick Expectations Coefficient	t-stat	Less Quick Coefficient	t-stat	M1 Expectations Coefficient	t-stat	Model Coefficient	t-stat
Constant	.007	7.12	.008	11.27	.004	6.35	.008	16.02
ln $(p_{-1}/p_{-2})^1$	.80	10.11	--	--	--	--	--	--
ln $(p_{-1}/p_{-5})^1$	--	--	.81	13.50	--	--	.444	6.59
PCEXP79^2	--	--	--	--	--	--	.441	4.71
MONEYEXP90^3	--	--	--	--	1.08	15.59	--	--
ln real GNP/ potential GNP	.019	1.63	.045	4.98	.013	1.76	.059	7.77
Controls dummy	.007	2.58	.006	2.92	.006	3.09	.006	3.34
Guidepost dummy	.0018	1.87	.0021	2.94	.0016	2.62	.0020	3.76
Data dummy (64:1)	-.0068	-2.15	-.0058	-2.44	-.0055	-2.54	-.0057	-2.95
R-bar squared	.645		.801		.802		.847	
DW	1.20		1.23		1.49		1.90	

^{1}The instruments are the bond yield (current, lagged once and lagged twice) and the growth in M1 (current, lagged once, twice and three times).
^{2}This is the second-degree Pascal lag on the deflator for consumer spending with speed of adjustment of 0.79 and an average lag of almost two years.
^{3}This is a second-degree Pascal lag on the growth of M1 with speed of adjustment of 0.9 and an average lag of four and one-half years.

Table 2.4
Percent Root-Mean-Square Errors of the
DRI Model with Four Wage Equations

	Quick	Less Quick	M1 Expectations	Model
Real GNP	1.30	0.96	1.10	0.86
Deflator	1.52	1.12	1.89	0.51
GNP	0.98	0.92	1.63	0.81
Wage Rate	2.16	1.47	2.47	0.59
Wholesale Price Index	1.09	1.15	1.45	0.75
Bond Yield	8.15	5.73	7.15	5.86

The above equations all use actual historical prices as the basis for price expectations. The instrumental variables employ the monetarist model to help estimate the relationship between price expectations and observed prices, but the monetarist mechanism is missing in simulation.

If price expectations are really derived from the behavior of M1, better results should be achieved by directly putting money in the wage equation, using a reduced form which short-cuts the nonobservable price expectations variable. Using past money growth as the measure for expected price growth, a wage equation was developed (table 2.3). Statistically acceptable results could only be obtained with long lag structures; correlations became similar to the intermediate case and demand variables turned perverse with short lags on money. The simulation results were generally inferior. This result is not conclusive, to be sure. Pure monetarism was applied to only one equation, and since M1 is not all-pervasive in the model, the wage-price loop becomes too weak if M1 replaces prices in the wage equation. The price level response to a given fiscal stimulus is shown in fig. 2.3 and seen to be largest under the model equation with its superior statistical quality.

Elsewhere,[17] results of other tests of the strong, i.e., quick, rational expectations hypothesis have been presented. These studies suggest that learning from actual price data slowed during the turbulent years after 1973, that the short-run record had a diminished influence in forming the price

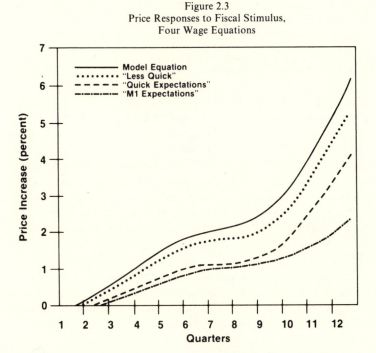

Figure 2.3
Price Responses to Fiscal Stimulus,
Four Wage Equations

---

[17]Otto Eckstein, *Core Inflation* (Englewood Cliffs: Prentice-Hall, 1981), ch. 9, pp. 72-85.

expectations underlying wage claims. Experiments on the price expectations in long-term interest rates generally confirmed the findings for wages: equations with quick learning show somewhat inferior statistical quality and relatively small price coefficients, too small to be consistent with the rational expectations hypothesis.

Rational expectations have arrived on the scene quite recently and will be tested in many equations of the model as they are re-estimated in future annual revisions. The "quick rational expectations" version is unlikely to score many victories in this contest of ideas. The three sets of equations with particularly long lags—wages, bond yields and business fixed investment—are not yielding readily to the new concepts. The data try to tell us that it takes workers, investors and businessmen several years to accept conditions of inflation or output growth as "permanent." Indeed, given the volatility of the variables which they confront, they would be irrational to take the evidence of short periods as sufficient indication of the future environment. The rational expectations school needs to specify the learning processes by which information enters decisions more explicitly, particularly to show how individuals form permanent expectations from temporary data and how they modify their behavior in response to changes in economic structure.

6. The Role of Errors-in-Expectations

While recent theoretical discussion has emphasized rationality under incomplete information, the highly cyclical behavior of the economy has produced quite a different line of empirical model research, seeking to identify how the expectations of businesses and households can be brought systematically into error. It is self-evident from postwar business cycle history that false expectations create decisions which produce incorrect stocks of fixed and variable capital and excessive employment. These errors are a critical ingredient in the process of recession. At several points in the postwar years, business and household expectations were in error, whether rationally arrived at or not, with events falsifying the assumptions on which decisions had been based.

The DRI model contains expectations mechanisms which can produce systematic error. This is clearest for the case of inventory investment. In the model's equations, the measure of sales expectations is based on a variant of the Metzler formulation,[18] in which future sales expectations are equal to a

---

[18]Lloyd A. Metzler, "The Nature and Stability of Inventory Cycles," *Review of Economics and Statistics* (August 1941), pp. 113-129, reprinted in Metzler, *Collected Papers* (Cambridge, Mass.: Harvard University, 1973).

short lag on actual sales, using a Koyck lag with a decay factor of 0.6 for a mean lag of less than two quarters. This formula can be used to calculate the systematic errors in sales expectations of business by contrasting its estimates with the sales that occurred (fig. 2.4). It can be seen that the actual errors in expectations are erratic for most of the interval, but at the critical turning points of the business cycle, sales expectations tended to be in error. For the period as a whole, serial correlation is small and errors apparently random, but in the periods of recession, the errors are large and systematically destabilizing.

Systematic error is also important in the determination of business fixed investment. While the Jorgenson theory is still serviceable as a general structure, the violence of the recent record produces two important modifications, a more elaborate treatment of business liquidity and the explicit introduction of systematic errors. For example, the model equation for producers' durable equipment contains a term which shows the surprise element in production, defined as the difference between actual production and a Koyck lag on past production which approximates an adaptive

Figure 2.4
Errors in Expectations:
Percent Difference Between Actual Sales and Expected Sales,
1960-1981

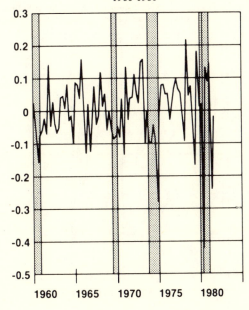

expectations process (fig. 2.5). The surprise—or error—elements are particularly destabilizing at moments of recession, but also seem to reinforce an occasional boom in unsustainable fashion. They are certainly far from the "white noise" assumption of the rational expectations theory. Similarly, fig. 2.6 shows the difference between actual and expected utilization rates used in the producers' durable equipment investment equation, using a Koyck lag with a decay factor of .10.

In the case of households, no systematic element of errors-in-expectations stretching beyond a quarter or two has been found. The reaction to risk is sufficient to create quick spending adjustments. The savings rate has leaped at the onset of macro difficulties. Apparently households are more sensitive than business, and can move more quickly. Of course, sharp changes in the economy do produce destabilizing stock adjustments in the household sector that would not occur if the future were foreseen correctly. Permanent income cannot be foreseen precisely, and hence financial and physical stocks will not be planned correctly.

Expectations processes capable of producing systematic errors are not in contradiction to the rational expectations theory. With incomplete information, external shocks, a stochastic economy, and unpredictable

Figure 2.5
Errors in Expectations:
Percent Difference Between Actual and Expected Output in
Equation for Producers' Durable Equipment

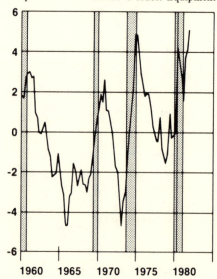

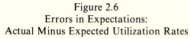

Figure 2.6
Errors in Expectations:
Actual Minus Expected Utilization Rates

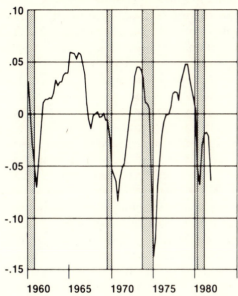

elements in policy all producing sizable surprises in the economic environment, even the most rational individual will make errors. But the model is closer to the older business cycle theories in its explicit modeling of errors that are critical to the economy's cyclic path as opposed to the theory's emphasis on bias-free expectations, certainty-equivalence that is derived from quadratic utility functions, and quick, market-clearing adjustments.

7. Policy Analysis

The rational expectations school has asserted that econometric models are unsuitable for policy analysis because the policies change the parameters of the economy.[19] This proposition has been specialized to become an argument against all demand management policies: the private sector, being rational and understanding the lack of permanent trade-off, recognizes that stimulus

[19]Robert E. Lucas, op. cit.

will be converted into inflation, will fail to create real gains, and therefore justifies no positive private spending response.

The empirical method of the large-scale econometric model puts this proposition in a quantitative perspective. Given that the "no trade-off" equilibrium is reached only after several years and that the business cycle moves more quickly, rational private decisions must consider the short-run impact of policy stimulus.

Whether short-term demand management yields a positive benefit is also an empirical question which can be assessed through stochastic simulations of the model, and through control-theoretic searches for optimal demand management.[20] The conclusions of studies with the DRI model suggest that the potential expected benefit is modest and its variance great.[21]

On the narrower issue raised by Lucas, it is an irrefutable theoretical proposition that policies will affect parameters. But the actual impact is an empirical question. Policy approaches have changed in the past, and deliberate policy moves have been among the major sources of variations in incomes, prices, interest rates, etc. The model's spending equations include the variability of incomes and the degree of leverage created by balance sheets, thus giving empirical expression to the effect of variability—whether from policy or other sources—on the behavior of the system.

If the approach to policy is changed so drastically that the economy operates under a new regime, the model may, indeed, cease to be applicable. But in this regard, policy is no different from any other major source of change. If the modelers are alert, they will quickly incorporate the changes in structure; if they are not, they will go astray. One of the biggest innovations in policy of the last thirty years was the imposition of wage and price controls in 1971. Although the DRI model was not built in anticipation of controls, this policy change was handled well, correctly calculating the effects on inflation rates and the short-term benefits to real activity.

Compared to such exogenous shocks as wars and the oil and food crises, the changes in policy approaches were small in the decade of the 1970s. The adoption of strict monetarism in October 1979 and its further strengthening in 1981 provide the opportunity for a fuller historical experiment. The initial data argue that learning has not been speeded up by the change in regime, that wage rates and bond yields are based on complete—but slow—learning from actual experience. Policy announcements still seem to be interpreted as carrying little or no information.

[20]Joseph Kelley, "Forecast Risk—A Stochastic Simulation Analysis," *Data Resources Review* (November 1977), pp. 17-30.
[21]Joseph Kelley, "Optimal Macroeconomic Policy: Some Control Theory Experiments," *Data Resources Review* (September 1978), pp. 9-23.

Policy is a source of stochastic variation, but no more so than other sources to which households and businesses must respond. There is no empirical basis to the assertion that the models are invalid beyond their usual stochastic risk bands because policies systematically change parameters. So far, the evidence suggests that changes in policy regimes are not among the principal causes of simulation error, that forecast error is largely created by other exogenous factors and the stochastic character of the economy.

8. Causes of the Business Cycle

Since the theoretical analysis of the business cycle reached its climax in the works of Hicks,[22] Duesenberry[23] and Matthews,[24] economic theory has advanced no strong hypothesis about the origins of cyclical behavior. Indeed, theory has always been uneasy in its treatment of the business cycle and has never placed it at the center of concern.

Econometric models, on the other hand, represent cyclical behavior and can be used to reach conclusions about the nature and origins of business cycles. The DRI model recognizes that cycles can originate from: (1) stock-flow or other nonlinear adjustment processes which can produce damped, repeating or explosive oscillations; (2) irregular exogenous shocks acting on a nonlinear system; (3) error terms of individual equations in a nonlinear system; (4) variations in public policies which are magnified in the private sector and which ultimately create reversing, hence cyclical, tendencies; and (5) in particular, responses of the financial system to monetary policy which create credit cycles that are transformed into real cycles.[25]

Various exercises conducted with the DRI model over the years yield some tentative conclusions about the relative importance of the five potential causes of the business cycle. First, the intrinsic structure of the economy, while embodying numerous stock-flow relationships, would yield sharply dampened, rather than repeating or explosive cycles. A typical exogenous disturbance boosting total demand, for example, creates a cumulative upward movement of the sort plotted in fig. 2.1, and runs its course over a year or two. The stock-flow adjustment processes do create a second cycle, but of much smaller magnitude, usually less than one-third as large as the

[22]John R. Hicks, *A Contribution to the Theory of the Trade Cycle* (Oxford, England: Oxford University Press, 1950).

[23]James S. Duesenberry, *Business Cycles and Economic Growth* (New York: McGraw-Hill, 1958).

[24]R. C. O. Matthews, *The Trade Cycle* (Cambridge: University Press, 1959).

[25]Allen Sinai, "Credit Crunches—An Analysis of the Postwar Experience," in Otto Eckstein, ed., *Parameters and Policies in the U. S. Economy* (Amsterdam: North-Holland, 1976), pp. 244-274.

original cycle. The reasons for the limited magnitude of the initial cycle lie in the various equilibrating forces in the model, including financial and real crowding out. The dampening in the succeeding cycles is partly due to the long lag structures on business fixed investment, the gradual working of inflationary forces, as well as the slow learning processes which modify various aspects of behavior. It is clear from the model simulations that if stock-flow adjustments and other nonlinear properties of the economy's structure were the only sources of the business cycle, the extent of cyclicality would be very small, much smaller than actually observed.

The stochastic elements in the model do produce cyclical behavior as they act on the nonlinear features of the economic structure such as the physical stock-flow adjustments and the portfolio effects.[26] Spectral analysis of the results of stochastic simulations of the DRI model discloses a cyclic pattern of output paths, though with a duration a few months shorter than in the actual record.[27] This analysis treats exogenous variables, such as real military outlays and the variation of bank reserves, stochastically. For the exogenous variables, the stochastic error distribution is calculated from the deviations of trend values; for the equations, the stochastic simulations are drawn from distributions of equation errors in the period of historical fit. These exercises confirm that the unpredictable elements in behavior interact with the relatively weak nonlinear elements of the economy to produce the kinds of moderate cycles which have been typical of the postwar period. It also provides some insight into causes of the difficulty of accurately predicting the timing of business cycle turning points: since downturns tend to be associated with the occasional exceptionally large error term, their timing becomes dependent on such error terms during the phases when the economy is particularly vulnerable to these effects.

When one views postwar business cycles in a more strictly historical perspective, it quickly becomes clear that exogenous shocks have been the biggest source of variation. The Korean and Vietnam Wars each dominated the economy's cyclical behavior for several years, and the world food price explosion and the OPEC revolution were the dominant features in additional years. Demand management policies added to instability at some times and helped moderate it at others, producing a net effect which was probably somewhat destabilizing[28] if one includes the Vietnam War in the test, but was

---

[26]Irma Adelman and Frank L. Adelman, "The Dynamic Properties of the Klein-Goldberger Model," *Econometrica* (October 1959), pp. 596-625.

[27]Joseph Kelley, "The American Business Cycle: Evidence from the DRI Model," *Data Resources Review* (September 1978), pp. 9-23.

[28]Otto Eckstein, "Instability in the Private and Public Sectors," *Swedish Journal of Economics* (January 1973), pp. 19-26; and *The Great Recession* (Amsterdam: North-Holland Publishing Co., 1978).

moderately stabilizing if this episode is excluded.[29] Variations in monetary policy, sometimes triggered by price shocks, have reinforced the business cycle, and on some occasions actually created it.

9. Concluding Comment

Economists, including modelers and theorists, share a common training and intellectual heritage. Econometricians emphasize the empirical representation of the economic process through dynamic structures with specific quantitative parameters and representation of the stochastic elements. Theorists represent the economic process that can be derived from a minimum of behavioral assumptions, but are willing to pursue logical ramifications a good deal further. Given these differences in method and attitude, it is not surprising that the conclusions are not always identical. However, both camps are subject to the same intellectual influences and respond to the same challenges in trying to understand the economy. The gap between the two views of the economy is quite small, far smaller than the simplistic contrast between an extreme, fiscalist-dirigiste viewpoint and an extreme monetarist-quick rational expectations position. The models do not argue for large multipliers, weak monetary effects, successful fine-tuning, or the predictability of the future. They do argue against quick responses to demand management and therefore low costs to disinflation, against the use of a simple monetarist rule to policy, against discontinuous jumps in aggregate supply and, indeed, against every form of economic magic. The five principal positive conclusions from the models as opposed to the dominant theory are these:

(1) Learning is slow, and it takes several years for the society to correctly assess the fundamentals of the economic environment in terms of inflation and long-term growth.

(2) The expected variance of output and prices matters to decisions along with the expected values. Businesses and households are risk-averters and consequently reduce their spending behavior when expected variance increases.

(3) Errors-in-expectations are an important element in the business cycle mechanism and must be modeled to account for inventory, employment and fixed investment cycles. Errors-in-expectations are not necessarily evidence of irrationality, but a correct theory must make room for the effects of errors.

---

[29]Robert Gough, "Fiscal Policy: The Scorecard Between 1962 and 1976" (Washington, D.C.: Joint Economic Committee, U.S. Government Printing Office, November 1978), pp. 11-60.

There is evidence that observed errors-in-expectations have sufficient autocorrelation to reject the "white noise" hypothesis.

(4) Detail matters even in macroeconomic modeling. Particularly in a world of exogenous disturbances, differential availabilities of industrial capacity and institutionally determined variations in the portfolio policies of different participants in the financial system and the mix of activity affect the behavior of the economy in major ways. Hence, the size of today's models is largely determined by the necessity to disaggregate sufficiently to take account of these financial, supply and stock adjustment effects.

(5) Money, credit and financial institutions matter greatly to the business cycle, with large effects on the real economy and the potential for limiting the impacts of other policies. Episodes of financial instability appear to be a regular and systematic part of the business cycle, indeed perhaps a necessary condition for recessions. Stop-go monetary policies and volatile interest rates create portfolio imbalances which can have drastic effects on real activity with varying lags. Sectoral financial risk, debt service and repayment burdens and wealth effects are further channels through which financial factors affect real spending decisions of businesses, households and local governments.

Models rub our noses in the day-to-day reality of empirical relationships. In today's environment, the models are playing much of the role traditionally played by economic theory, a perpetual warning against quick, cheap results, a constant reminder that there are, indeed, trade-offs which are worse than we would like.

CHAPTER 3

THE SUPPLY SIDE IN THE DRI MODEL

1. Introduction

The idea of supply is so pervasive in economics that over half of the 800 equations in the DRI model could be characterized as supply oriented. The entire price block is largely supply, i.e., cost-based; the financial sector models the supplies of various categories of funds to different purposes; business fixed investment and residential construction activity are heavily determined by supply elements; the level and composition of unemployment are derived from labor supplies; the amount of labor and its productivity are supply-based. Indeed, since the model is a representation of markets, it is quite impossible to isolate the relative importance of demand versus supply factors; the first principle of the market economy is that prices and quantities are determined simultaneously by the factors underlying both supply and demand.

The last decade has seen a revival of focus on the quantitative determinants of aggregate supply, both in terms of the long-run developmental forces of the economy including the normal tendency for the growth of the basic factors of production, as well as the impact of specific fiscal and monetary policies. While industrial investment, capacity and operating rates have a significant impact on detailed prices and quantities, the fundamental driving force of the long-run growth of the entire economy is the growth of aggregate supply, usually called potential GNP. The determination of potential GNP from its inputs—labor, capital, energy and technology—is the topic of this chapter. The relation of the tax system to potential GNP is an important sub-theme.

2. Return of Supply Economics

While supply antedates demand in the history of economic thought starting with the work of Adam Smith[1] and stretching to John Stuart Mill,[2] and always retained at least an equal share with demand in the field of microeconomics, it must be acknowledged that demand overshadowed supply in macroeconomic analysis since the Great Depression and the rise of Keynesian national income analysis.[3] In the serious academic literature, however, supply theory regained prominence rather quickly: the path-breaking growth model of Harrod[4] analyzed, at least in a primitive way, the need to match the growth of aggregate supply and aggregate demand, and the model of Domar[5] introduced these ideas into the American literature. The modern theory of growth initiated by Solow[6] revived the aggregate production function of Cobb-Douglas, showed its central role in the economy, and launched the search for better aggregate production functions. Even in the Keynesian years, the input-output analysis of Leontief[7] offered theoretical and empirical models which had a production and supply focus. Kendrick's[8] and Denison's[9] analyses of growth and productivity, Schultz'[10] and Becker's[11] work on human capital, and the large body of writings by Griliches, Jorgenson, Mansfield, and other scholars made the 1950s and 1960s the most fertile decades for the scientific study of the supply-side of the economy.

However, this body of work had little impact on the macroeconomics used for policy. Aggregate demand seemed to be the determining factor of output and the price level in the postwar decades. The growth of aggregate supply could be modelled adequately by the simplest productivity calculations, multiplying labor supply by a productivity trend derived by historical

[1]Adam Smith, *Wealth of Nations,* 1776, Modern Library Edition (New York: Random House, 1973).

[2]John Stuart Mill, *Principles of Political Economy* (London, 1848).

[3]John Maynard Keynes, *The General Theory of Employment, Interest, and Money* (New York: Macmillan & Co., Ltd., 1936).

[4]Roy F. Harrod, "An Essay in Dynamic Theory," *Economic Journal,* 1939, pp. 14-33.

[5]Evsey Domar, "Capital Expansion, Rate of Growth, and Employment," *Econometrica* (April 1946), pp. 137-147.

[6]Robert M. Solow, "A Contribution to the Theory of Economic Growth," *Quarterly Journal of Economics* (February 1956), pp. 65-94.

[7]Wassily W. Leontief, *The Structure of American Economy, 1919-1939* (New York: Oxford University Press, 1941).

[8]John W. Kendrick, *Productivity Trends in the United States* (Princeton: Princeton University Press, 1961).

[9]Edward F. Denison, *The Sources of Economic Growth in the United States and the Alternatives Before Us,* Supplementary Paper 13 (New York: Committee for Economic Development, 1962).

[10]Theodore W. Schultz, "Investment in Human Capital," *American Economic Review* (March 1961), pp. 1-17.

[11]Gary S. Becker, *Human Capital* (Washington: National Bureau of Economic Research, 1964).

extrapolation. Okun's law,[12] which was based at least implicitly on these productivity projections, seemed perfectly adequate to identify the gap between aggregate demand and aggregate supply, to estimate the unemployment rate, and to help set the gauges for fiscal policy. The great tax cut of 1964 was derived from Okun's law estimates of the "gap" between actual and potential output, divided by accepted estimates of the multiplier on personal tax cuts. Even in the immediate years after 1964, when demand became excessive and highly sophisticated methods for estimating aggregate production functions were available, the simpler methods seemed to suffice: taxes should have been higher, but it was not a shortcoming of economic analysis that made policy go wrong.

The large-scale econometric models which began to take over the tasks of policy analysis in the early 1970s did contain some supply-side elements: aggregate production functions, sophisticated equations for investment and capital stocks, detailed measures of industrial production and capacity, input-output tables, and equations for the availability of finance. But the production functions used were still relatively simple and unresponsive, following the Cobb-Douglas tradition in which the link of investment to potential output is relatively weak and slow, and the technology residual is exogenous and impervious to policy. Energy was not in the picture, of course.

The decade of the 1970s posed different and increasingly serious challenges to macroeconomic analysis. The worldwide boom of 1971-73 produced acute aggregate shortages of capacity in the materials-producing industries even though aggregate measures did not signal shortages. The OPEC revolution of 1973 and the subsequent surges of world oil prices had devastating effects on the economic performance of the entire industrial world. The virtual disappearance of productivity growth after 1973 and the resultant explosion of employment repealed Okun's law or any simple calculation of the productivity trend. It became increasingly evident that the renewal of productivity growth was becoming the main task of economic policy.

The new circumstances make the growth of potential output, or aggregate supply, one of the two or three most critical variables for the economy. Once the potential GNP trend is no longer a *deus ex machina* that drives the economy forward regardless of short-term policies or circumstances, the variables that determine the increase of potential again become the center of attention, as they had been through most of history. What are the critical determinants of the supplies of the factors of production? How do they combine to determine aggregate productivity? And how do fiscal and

---

[12]Arthur M. Okun, "Potential GNP: Its Measurement and Significance," *Proceedings of the Economic Statistics Section of the American Statistical Association* (Washington: 1962), pp. 98-104.

monetary policies affect them? These are the supply-side issues that need to be modeled.

3. Supply Features of the DRI Model

While the DRI model has long contained major aspects of the supply side of the economy, the 1980 version introduced new elements designed to have the model benefit from the growing body of scientific work on this topic. The innovations include some tax effects in the equations for the supply of labor and potential output, a more elaborate and more quickly adjusting equation for the determination of aggregate potential and a relation between real interest rates and personal saving.

DRI also revised its simulation methodology for supply-oriented policies in order to more clearly distinguish between the traditional Keynesian multipliers and the newer supply multipliers. In the past, DRI model solutions testing fiscal policies usually used an unchanged pattern of nonborrowed bank reserves as the definition of a "neutral" monetary policy. As a result, a large part of the initial effect of a supply-based tax change was to create extra activity through the Keynesian multiplier before the supply effects could be felt. While this made policies look very favorable in terms of the creation of employment and activity, it blurred the effects on inflation and supply because the extra stimulus produced a tighter economy. DRI now uses a definition of "neutral" monetary policy based on unchanged real short-term interest rates, and a policy of unchanged money supply for the nonaccommodating policy. The identification of supply effects of fiscal policy is now based on the "differential incidence" viewpoint, long identified in the public finance literature,[13] with offsetting changes in government expenditures or personal taxes introduced to keep the aggregate unemployment rate unchanged. These policy definitions allow a clearer distinction between aggregate supply and aggregate demand effects. This is not to foreclose the policy choice for aggregate demand: the government can decide how to divide the benefits of supply policies between higher real activity and lessened inflation. But the method leaves a clearer set of analytical conclusions and lets the supply effects be seen in relatively pure form.

The changes in the model create somewhat stronger supply effects than earlier versions but do not turn the conclusions upside-down. The economy's

---

[13]Richard A. Musgrave, *The Theory of Public Finance* (New York: McGraw-Hill, Inc., 1959), pp. 212-216.

ability to produce responds more positively to tax incentive changes. But the magnitudes are limited, and even with a more quickly responding measure of potential, the effects are slow and require much patience. Unless carefully offset by tighter money or fiscal moves, supply-oriented tax cuts initially boost demand more than supply, and thereby initially make inflation worse. The reduction of inflation comes later, and indeed not at all without some reinforcing demand management. The federal deficit is enlarged by tax reductions unless they are offset by reduced spending or increases of other taxes.

While realistic estimates of supply effects leave no room for miracles, they do indicate major opportunities for restoring productivity performance and partial recovery of long-term growth rates toward the historical norm. The decline in productivity performance is due to a considerable extent to the lack of improvement of the capital-labor ratio and to reduced investment in research and development. The capital stock is aging excessively and is using too much energy for current prices. Supply policies can reverse these factors.

The model also focusses on the imbalance between the supply of labor and the supply of industrial capacity. The changed historical relationship between the utilization rates of basic industries and national unemployment produces extra inflation. The deterioration of delivery conditions in industrial markets is measured by the critical vendor performance measure of the model and affects monetary policies and prices. High utilization rates also directly create inflation in specific industries. Hence, those supply-oriented tax measures which aim to stimulate the growth of industrial capacity improve price performance and make lower unemployment possible. Conversely, measures which do not affect industrial capacity tend to have more limited price benefits.

The DRI model adheres to the philosophy of seeking to build models that represent the behavioral characteristics of the economy as fully as possible. As Chapter 1 indicated, the macro models of the 1970s gradually incorporated several important new features that advancing understanding and a changing economic situation required. Earlier innovations, some of them based on the scientific work of the 1960s, included the use of a variable-coefficient input-output table as part of the model's simultaneous block to calculate industrial output and capacity utilization, an elaborate financial system representing the flows of funds of households and businesses, extensions of Jorgensonian investment equations to include flow-of-funds effects on capital formation, stage-of-processing pricing equations to carry particular cost increases more precisely into retail prices, a production-inventory-price loop, and an elaborate energy sector. The introduction of each of these innovations modified the basic behavioral characteristics of the model somewhat, with the aim of making the model reflect the current state of knowledge as found in the work not only of DRI, but of the academic and general research community. This approach is an alternative to pure "supply models." While models that exclusively are devoted to classical relationships among the factors of production may be appropriate for very long-term analysis, understanding of inflation and the business cycle requires representation of demand, finance, stock-flow adjustment processes, expectation formation, and other short-term elements. For analysis of the economy in the 1980s, whether for forecasting or policy purposes, purely supply-oriented models are inadequate. The current financial, energy, and business cycle situations are sufficiently far removed from equilibrium that the next decade will be heavily determined by the initial conditions and other short-run factors. Perhaps there is no long-run of such duration that these factors can be safely ignored.

DRI's approach—to add carefully derived estimates of tax and other supply effects to an already elaborate representation of the economy—should provide as good estimates for the policy options as it is possible to obtain at this time. It should be recognized, however, that the new territory of supply economics, encompassing both the intermediate-term tax issues and the longer range questions of demography, saving, and private-public sector relations, is a very large one and will take years to fully explore. The extensions of the DRI model are only a few steps along the road to a full econometric representation of supply. "Supply multipliers" in the current model deal with only limited issues. Some of them are not yet as seasoned as the demand multipliers and it will take several years of scientific debate before agreement begins to emerge. At least the point has been reached where supply economics is, and should be, making itself felt in the "mainstream" models.

The supply equations in the DRI model can be classified under the following headings:

(1) The Supply of Labor;
(2) The Supply of Physical Capital;
(3) The Supply of Energy;
(4) The Supply of Materials; and
(5) The Supply of R&D.

In addition, supply is also determined by the effectiveness with which the factors of production are combined, giving rise to these additional equations:

(6) The Aggregate Production Function;
(7) The Determination of Industrial Capacities; and
(8) The Efficiency of Energy Use for Household and Business Purposes.

This list is far from exhaustive, of course. Numerous other equations are a part of the supply analysis, including the several hundred equations represented by the input-output, stage-of-processing, energy, and financial sectors. However, the list above includes the more significant equations in which the supply economics issues come into focus.

The relation of the supply issues to tax policy is summarized in Table 3.1. As research continues and supply multipliers settle toward a scientific consensus, the list may become more elaborate and the parameters may change.

4. The Supply of Labor

The DRI long-term forecasts employ a set of eight equations for the principal working-age population groups. The participation rates depend on time trends, cyclical conditions as measured by the unemployment rate, real wages, and for a few categories, the personal tax burden as represented by the average effective personal tax rate plus the employee share of payroll taxes and the average effective benefit levels of particular transfer programs such as AFDC and Social Security. These equations are used to forecast the long-term labor supply under normal conditions. These forecasts are preliminary to the macro model solutions.

The macro model contains one equation for labor supply which relies on the working-age population aged 18 to 64, the share of the population represented by males aged 25 to 54, the national unemployment rate, real wages, a time trend to reflect the sociological changes in the participation rate, and the average effective personal and payroll tax rate (Table 3.2). This equation has simulation characteristics that are close to the properties of the eight-equation labor force model. It has an elasticity of supply with regard to real wages of 0.1, i.e., a 1% increase in real wages adds 0.1% to the number of workers, which at 1980 values would represent 100,000 individuals. The elasticity of the labor force with respect to the personal tax burden is -0.04, indicating that a 1% rise in the real tax burden discourages 0.04% of our workers from the labor force. Since 1965, the real tax burden has increased by almost 50%, driving 1.9 million people from the labor force according to the equation.[14]

5. The Supply of Physical Capital

The supply of aggregate physical capital is determined by equations for producers' durable equipment and nonresidential construction. These

---

[14]This estimate is consistent with the results of Fullerton's authoritative survey. Don Fullerton, "On the Possibility of an Inverse Relationship between Tax Rates and Government Revenues," Working Paper 467, National Bureau of Economic Research, April 1980.

Table 3.1
Summary of Tax Effects on Supply in the DRI Model

Tax	Equations	Results of Statistical Testing	Description of Tax Effects in DRI Model
Corporate income	Investment, macro and industries, R&D	Well-established effect using Jorgenson theory	Affects rental price of capital and cash flow.
Depreciation lives	Investment, R&D	Same	Same.
Investment tax credit	Investment on equipment, R&D	Same	Same.
Personal Taxes	Labor supply	Significant at 5% level, using average effective rate of personal income and personal payroll taxes. Transfer payments affect supply of workers over 65 and of women aged 25 to 44. Period of fit affects parameter. Value in model is typical.	Elasticity of labor with respect to tax burden is -0.04. Elasticity of labor with respect to tax-induced change in real wages is -0.20.
	Potential output	Average effective burden of personal and payroll taxes is significant at 5% level. Choice of period affects parameters, DRI model uses typical value obtained over various intervals and various specifications.	Elasticity of potential output with respect to personal tax rate is -0.05. Extra potential raises productivity and lowers inflation.
	Personal savings	Consumer spending affected by real interest rate, after tax.	
	Savings deposits and bond holding of households	Savings flows affected by disposable income and by aftertax interest return.	Principally affects mortgage market and residential construction.
	Wages	Payroll tax burden has impact on compensation per hour.	Higher compensation affects prices and core inflation.

62

Table 3.2
Labor Force

Ordinary Least Squares

Quarterly (1956:1 to 1979:4):—96 Observations
Dependent Variable: DEPVARLC

	Coefficient	Std. Error	t-Stat	Independent Variable
1)	5.91041	0.1680	35.18	Constant PDL(QRULESSRUADJ(-1), 1,4,FAR)
(-1)	-0.0559273	0.005050		
(-2)	-0.0419455	0.003787		
(-3)	-0.0279637	0.002525		
(-4)	-0.0139818	0.001262		
Sum	-0.139818	0.01262	-11.08	
Avg	1.00000	0.0		
2)	0.00701561	0.0001457	48.16	PARTIPTREND
3)	3.81471	0.1246	30.62	log(NM25@54/N16&)
4)	0.287908	0.03770	7.637	log((JAHEADJEA(-1)/ PC(-1)))-log(TP+TWPER)/ TAXBASE)

R-Bar squared: 0.9761
Durbin-Watson statistic: 0.5961
Standard error of the regression: 0.02543   Normalized: 0.015

DEPVARLC=log(LHSLC/(0.70-LHSLC)), the participation rate, fitted in logit form,
LHSLC is the civilian labor force as a percentage of the civilian population age 16 and over,
QRULESSRUADJ is unemployment minus a demographic adjustment,
PARTIPTREND is the time trend used in the equation for the civilian labor force,
NM25@54 is the total male population age 25 through 54 years,
N16& is the population age 16 and over,
JAHEADJEA is the index of hourly earnings of private nonfarm production workers, mix and overtime corrected,
PC is the implicit price deflator for personal consumption expenditures,
TP is personal tax and nontax payments,
TWPER is personal contributions for social insurance,
TAXBASE is the personal income taxbase.

equations, which are discussed fully in Chapter 7, follow the neoclassical Jorgenson theory which relies on a carefully calculated measure of the rental price of capital and on the level of expected output. The DRI model's investment equations have extended the Jorgenson approach by correcting the investment need for pollution abatement expenditures, by calculating the rental price of capital from the actual sources of corporate finance at any particular time as estimated from the flow of funds, by adding a debt burden variable which indicates the ratio of debt service to corporate cash flow, and by introducing a surprise element into output which contrasts actual output with what was expected.

This equation shows a quite considerable effect of changes in the rental price of capital on the rate of investment and therefore on the growth of the capital stock. For example, the mean elasticity of investment in plant and equipment with respect to the rental price of capital was found to be 0.7.

The same theoretical approach is used for the calculation of investment levels of 24 industries, including the two-digit manufacturing industries in such fields as utilities, communication, mining, and the various transportation industries. These equations serve as a check on the macro estimates.

6. The Supply of Energy

The supply of energy is largely exogenous to the DRI macro model. Both the quantity and the price of oil from foreign sources must be considered largely exogenous, though there are some loops from activity levels of the industrial world to OPEC pricing. Domestic pricing is partly exogenous because natural gas is still in the period of legislated decontrol price schedules. The supply of domestic energy is estimated endogenously in DRI's energy models, and the price of imported oil is derived from a model of the world oil market. These answers are entered into the macro analysis. The model does contain various simulation rules that represent the responses of energy prices and supply to changing macro conditions to permit fuller analysis of policies or other alternative scenarios, for to ignore such responses would attribute a stability to the economy that it does not possess. For example, the OPEC price responds proportionately to the domestic price level as represented by the GNP deflator. These simulation rules are not used in forecasting, where separate analyses determine these variables.

The model's energy sector serves three functions: to trace the effects of the exogenous energy prices to the retail stage, to provide a supply-demand check to see if available supplies can sustain particular levels of economic activity, and to determine the effects on potential GNP and productivity. The price effects are estimated by a series of equations which link the production and import prices of coal, natural gas, and oil through input-output coefficients to industrial wholesale and the pertinent consumer prices. The changed prices impact on real activity and the system as a whole, partly depending on the monetary policy response.

To test for the adequacy of energy supplies, the model calculates and cumulates the demand for energy by principal sources, including oil, gas, coal, and electricity. The total energy requirement is compared to the energy supply in particular model solutions. If supply falls short of demand and if prices are still controlled, an energy shortage develops which must be allocated. Consistency can be achieved by pulling down aggregate activity, by imposing allocations or rationing in specific markets, or by letting delivery conditions deteriorate and thereby creating some indirect inflation.

The effect on potential GNP is measured by energy's role in the production function. As higher prices lead to energy conservation, there is less energy input into the economy and therefore less output. Because the Cobb-Douglas function does not contain interaction terms, the effect may be understated.

7. The Supply of Materials

Because the DRI model takes the market approach, prices are the principal vehicle for supply conditions to affect the economy. A scarce supply of materials, such as steel, chemicals, oil, lumber, etc., is shown through high utilization rates, which increase finished goods prices through the stage-of-processing price equations. Besides the utilization effects, the model also contains a separate channel for vendor performance, the well-known measure of delivery conditions in industrial markets. Poor vendor performance acts in the model to raise industrial prices and to stimulate inventory hoarding.

In considering the determination of the supply of materials, processed materials must be distinguished from raw materials, The supply of processed materials is determined by the growth in capital stocks and by technology. An industry's capital stock is determined from equations explaining the level of investment. The supply of raw materials is modeled through prices: agricultural commodities and world oil are reflected in exogenous price variables; other raw materials prices are endogenous, moved by the strength of demand, and on the supply side by strike variables. DRI's micro models of industrial and agricultural commodities do model the availability and costs of supply very elaborately, and this work is an input to the materials price forecasts in the macro model.

8. The Supply of R&D

The DRI model incorporates the stock of technical knowledge, as measured by the cumulated research and development outlays of governments and private industry, as one of the inputs in the aggregate production function. Thus, the volume of R&D investment affects the growth of potential GNP.

The stock of R&D, which is treated analogously to the stock of physical capital, is assumed to depreciate over 10 years. In a competitive world, a society which does not advance its technology will lose its relative industrial position, and therefore its growth of potential will diminish. Thus, the stock of knowledge must be treated as a depreciating asset. Technology is also required to offset the decline in exhaustible resources. Investment in R&D is determined analogously to other investment decisions, using an equation embodying the Jorgenson approach.

9. The Aggregate Production Function: Potential GNP

Potential GNP, the supply measure of the economy's ability to produce goods and services, is estimated by an aggregate production function. The factors treated explicitly are capital, labor, energy, and the stock of research and development capital. Research and development is partly capital enhancing

Table 3.3
Potential GNP: Step 1

Ordinary Least Squares

Quarterly (1957:1 to 1979:1): —89 Observations
Dependent Variable: NEWLHSGNP72A

	Coefficient	Std. Error	t-Stat	Independent Variable
	1.39819	0.01486	94.12	Constant
1)	0.00151723	6.283E-05	24.15	TIME
2)	0.0481635	0.01035	4.652	log(DTFUELSALLB/
				EHHHOURSA)
3)	0.290869	0.005939	48.98	log(UCAPFRBM*KADJ(-1)/
				EHHHOURSA)

R-Bar squared: 0.9874
Durbin-Watson statistic: 0.4923
Standard error of the regression: 0.01012   Normalized: 0.005

NEWLHSGNP72A=log(GNP72/EHHHOURSA)-0.08*log(TOTALR&DSTOCK72(-1)/
EHHHOURSA),
GNP72 is gross national product in 1972 dollars,
TOTALR&DSTOCK72 is total stock =of research and development,
TIME is the time trend, 1947:1 = 1.0,
DTFUELSALLB is the demand for all fuels, total, all sectors,
EHHHOURSA is total worker hours,
UCAPFRBM is total manufacturing capacity utilization,
KADJ is the age-adjusted capital stock.

Table 3.4
Potential GNP: Step 2

Ordinary Least Squares

Quarterly (1957:1 to 1979:1): —89 Observations
Dependent Variable: LHSGNP72[1]

	Coefficient	Std. Error	t-Stat	Independent Variable
	1.28416	0.04866	26.39	Constant
1)	0.00189295	0.0001432	13.21	TIME
2)	0.336940	0.1432	2.353	log(HPM/HPM(-1))
3)	-0.000370151	0.0002303	-1.607	TIMEONE
4)	-0.00918571	0.005368	-1.711	TIMETWO
5)	-0.0518671	0.02302	-2.253	log((TP+TWPER)/TAXBASE)

R-Bar squared: 0.9497
Durbin-Watson statistic: 0.7874
Standard error of the regression: 0.009059   Normalized: 0.005921

LHSGNP72+log(GNP72/EHHHOURS)-0.08*log(TOTALR&DSTOCK72(-1)/
EHHHOURS)-0.05*log(DTFUELSALLB/EHHHOURS)-0.29*log(UCAPFRBM*
KADJ(-1)/EHHHOURS),
GNP72 is gross national product in 1972 dollars,
EHHHOURS is total worker hours,
TOTALR&DSTOCK72 is total stock of research and development,
DTFUELSALLB is demand for all fuels, total, all sectors,
UCAPFRBM is total manufacturing capacity utilization,
KADJ is age-adjusted capital stock,
TIME is the time trend, 1947:1 + 1.0,
HPM is weekly hours of manufacturing production workers,
TIMEONE is a time trend for potential GNP, 1967:1 = 1,
TIMETWO is a time trend for potential GNP, 1974:1 = 1,
TP is personal tax and nontax payments,
TWPER is personal contributions for social insurance,
TAXBASE is the personal income taxbase.

and partly labor enhancing. To reflect the influence of embodied technology further, the average age of the capital stock helps determined potential output. The cyclical influence on factor use is measured by the utilization rate of manufacturing capacity and by the change in average hours worked. The deleterious effect of the tax system on productivity is measured by the average effective rate of personal and payroll taxes.

Potential GNP is estimated in a two-step procedure which facilitates the introduction of the supply of energy and of the stock of research and development into the aggregate production function framework. Step 1 establishes a Cobb-Douglas production function which includes the four inputs—capital, labor, energy, and R&D. The average age of capital is introduced as an adjustment to the capital stock. The use of the capital stock in any period is determined by the utilization rate of manufacturing capacity. This equation is fitted in the form of the output-to-labor ratio in order to overcome the problems of multicollinearity (Table 3.3).

The coefficients derived from this Cobb-Douglas function are used to calculate an index of composite factor inputs which is then employed in a second equation shown in Table 3.4. This equation explains the "residual," the measure of change in the productivity of all factor inputs. This equation uses time trends to carry the effects of disembodied technology, with separate trends to reflect the breaks of productivity which occurred in 1967 and 1973. In addition, the equation contains a measure of the personal tax burden to reflect the tax effect on the efficiency of resource utilization as measured by total factor productivity.

Table 3.5
Productivity

Least Squares with First-Order Autocorrelation Correction

Quarterly (1962:1 to 1979:1): —69 Observations
Dependent Variable: LHSJQ%MHNF

	Coefficient	Std. Error	t-Stat	Independent Variable
	-2.10402	0.04946	-42.54	Constant
1)	0.00150552	0.0001594	9.442	TIME
2)	0.00800536	0.003455	2.317	1/(1.1-UCAPFRBM)
3)	-0.0349436	0.02103	-1.662	log(TP+TWPER)/TAXBASE)
4)	-0.432759	0.1056	-4.097	log(QSTAR/LETOUTPUTPABE)
5)	-0.0614098	0.01932	-3.178	log((WPI05(-1)/PC&I&G(-1))/
				(WPI05(-5)/PC&I&G(-5)))
	0.716376	0.09638	7.432	RHO

R-Bar squared: 0.9540
Durbin-Watson statistic: 2.3156
Standard error of the regression: 0.005594   Normalized: 0.003043

LHSJQ%MHNF=log(JQ%MHNF)-log(GNP72FE/(52.0*0.001*HPMFE*
((1.0-.01*RUFE)*LC))),
JQ%MHNF is the index of output per hour of all persons in the nonfarm business sector,
GNP72FE is the full-employment level of real gross national product,
HPMFE is weekly hours of manufacturing production workers—full employment,
RUFE is the unemployment rate at full employment,
LC is the civilian labor force,
TIME is the time trend, 1947:1 = 1.0,
QSTAR is the expectations variable for real output,
LETOUTPUTPABE is real output factored up by the PABE (pollution abatement expenditures by U.S. business on capital account) ratio,
WPI05 is the wholesale price index for fuels and related products and power,
PC&I&G is the implicit price deflator excluding the foreign trade sector,
RHO is the first-order autocorrelation correction parameter.

The aggregate production function contains an implicit estimate for high-employment labor productivity. To estimate actual productivity, it is necessary to estimate its short-run variation around this potential trend (Table 3.5). The equation uses the utilization rate of manufacturing capacity and the "surprise" component in expectations for real GNP to explain the cyclical swings. Short-run productivity is also adversely affected by increases in the price of energy.

To measure potential output, the cyclical variables are set at their full employment values, which for this purpose are defined to be a manufacturing workweek of 40-3/4 hours, a full-employment unemployment rate following the Council of Economic Advisers' definition, and a utilization rate of manufacturing capacity of 87%. The resultant series is still too volatile and therefore is smoothed by a second-order Pascal lag with a decay factor of 0.7.

10. Industrial Capacity and Other Supply Effects

Shortages of industrial capacity in materials industries proved to be an effective supply constraint in 1971-73 and 1978-79. The DRI model estimates the capacities of manufacturing, materials, primary processing, and advanced processing industries from the investment estimates of the pertinent two-digit manufacturing industries. Through the embedded input-output table, the model calculates production for these sectors of manufacturing, which are then combined with the capacity estimates to calculate the utilization rates.

The impact of utilization rates on the economy is felt through several channels: first, they are the demand variables in several of the price equations in the stage-of-processing sector of the model. Second, utilization rates are important determinants of vendor performance, a measure of delivery conditions in industrial markets. Vendor performance, in turn, has important effects on industrial prices as well as on inventory policies which, in turn, strongly affect the demand for industrial output. Thus, there is a significant sub-loop in the model from industrial capacity to prices to inventories and back to prices. Finally, utilization affects profitability and productivity, and thereby affects the economy as a whole.

Among other supply-oriented features of the DRI model, the supply of finance should be singled out. The behavior of the mortgage market, which itself is mainly moved by the supply of personal saving and the partly policy-determined structure of interest rates, strongly affects the housing industry. Nonresidential fixed investment is also affected by the supply of finance, mainly through disequilibria in the balance sheets of the corporate sector. Consumer purchases of durable goods are affected by real interest rates and the balance sheet position of households.

11. Supply Multipliers

Aggregate supply responds more slowly than aggregate demand to changes in fiscal policy, but the impact on potential GNP can be quite sizeable. Furthermore, there are large differences in the aggregate supply effects of the various fiscal instruments.

The concept of a supply multiplier can be used analogously to the traditional demand multiplier. Model simulations can estimate the ratio of the change in potential GNP to the change in the value of the fiscal instrument, a measure of the supply multiplier.

Table 3.6 summarizes the model response to a real government spending increase, using the period beginning in 1966 as the test, and assuming monetary policies to be accommodating by holding nominal interest rates unchanged. Real GNP is boosted quickly because of demand effects. Increased income boosts consumption, and the higher level of activity induces some extra investment. However, by the fourth year, investment is reduced because the government deficit and the inflation rate boost interest rates to produce some crowding out. The supply multiplier reaches a peak of 0.58 after 15 quarters, but then declines because of the diminished investment. Inflation worsens, with the peak in the third year. Core inflation worsens over a longer period.

The supply multiplier of an increase in investment tax credits is substantially larger. Because the direct effect is through the investment decision, which takes over a year to be converted into investment spending, the first-year effects are negligible. But thereafter, the direct stimulus to investment directly boosts the capital stock and potential GNP, and indirectly reinforces these effects by creating a stronger economy. By the 24th quarter, the supply multiplier is 1.47, making the increase in potential GNP larger than the tax reduction. In later years, the supply effects continue to expand as the economy develops on a more capital-intensive path. The core inflation rate is lowered by as much as 0.91% after one year because of the reduced cost of capital, but some of the improvement is gradually lost due to a tighter economy and lower unemployment.

A reduction in the corporate tax rate has weaker supply effects because the change in the rental price of capital is small and it is mainly the cash flow stimulus through which the economy is affected. After 24 quarters, the supply multiplier reaches 0.52. The boost in the capital stock is considerable, but only half of the gain under the investment tax credit. The core inflation rate is temporarily lowered by 0.53% because of the reduction in the trend cost of capital, and unemployment is lowered somewhat because of the stimulus to the economy.

Table 3.6
Model Responses to a Real Government Spending Increase
(Unchanged nominal federal funds rate,
Test period: 1966-1971)

	\multicolumn{7}{c}{Quarters after Policy Change}
	1	4	8	12	16	20	24
Real GNP (Demand Multiplier)	1.18	1.93	2.01	1.45	0.95	0.64	0.44
Business Investment (% change)	0.09	0.18	0.21	0.11	-0.03	-0.15	-0.25
Consumption (% change)	0.11	0.46	0.50	0.35	0.16	-0.01	-0.09
Residential Construction (% change)	0.01	0.04	0.09	-0.03	-0.10	-0.10	-0.15
Potential GNP (Supply Multiplier)	0.00	0.04	0.26	0.51	0.58	0.45	0.28
Capital Stock (% change)	0.02	0.09	0.21	0.27	0.24	0.15	0.02
Labor Supply (% change)	-0.00	0.10	0.32	0.30	0.14	0.04	0.02
Productivity (% change)	0.29	0.49	0.43	0.14	0.04	0.03	-0.02
Government Surplus or Deficit (% change)	-0.54	-0.17	0.00	-0.05	-0.20	-0.28	-0.33
Unemployment Rate (change)	-0.07	-0.28	-0.33	-0.20	-0.10	-0.05	-0.02
Actual Inflation Rate	-0.01	0.32	0.50	0.60	0.41	0.26	0.15
Core Inflation Rate	0.00	0.06	0.23	0.40	0.51	0.51	0.47
Output-Inflation Transform	1.00	0.83	0.61	0.36	0.21	0.13	0.08

Table 3.7
Model Responses to a Real Increase in Investment Tax Credits
(Unchanged nominal rates,
Test period: 1966-1971)

	\multicolumn{7}{c}{Quarters after Policy Change}
	1	4	8	12	16	20	24
Real GNP (Demand Multiplier)	-0.02	0.16	1.59	1.52	1.04	1.60	2.33
Business Investment (% change)	0.00	0.16	1.13	1.14	0.88	1.26	1.63
Consumption (% change)	-0.01	0.02	0.26	0.33	0.28	0.43	0.77
Residential Construction (% change)	0.00	-0.01	0.02	-0.02	-0.07	-0.08	-0.12
Potential GNP (Supply Multiplier)	0.00	0.00	0.10	0.46	0.64	0.95	1.47
Capital Stock (% change)	0.00	0.08	0.75	1.60	2.35	3.30	4.27
Labor Supply (% change)	0.00	-0.00	0.09	0.31	0.22	0.10	0.12
Productivity (% change)	-0.01	0.16	0.92	0.67	0.63	0.97	1.27
Government Surplus or Deficit (% change)	-1.01	-0.98	-0.44	-0.40	-0.70	-0.62	-0.55
Unemployment Rate (change)	0.00	-0.02	-0.26	-0.30	-0.19	-0.24	-0.26
Actual Inflation Rate	-0.02	0.09	0.48	0.54	0.39	0.27	-0.05
Core Inflation Rate	-0.08	-0.58	-0.82	-0.31	-0.18	-0.10	0.15
Output-Inflation Transform	0.77	0.91	0.76	0.54	0.45	0.49	0.51

Table 3.8
Model Responses to a Real Corporate Tax Cut
(Unchanged nominal rates,
Test period: 1966-1971)

	Quarters after Policy Change						
	1	4	8	12	16	20	24
Real GNP (Demand Multiplier)	-0.01	0.12	0.44	0.47	0.65	0.80	0.53
Business Investment (% change)	0.00	0.12	0.27	0.30	0.44	0.55	0.41
Consumption (% change)	0.00	0.03	0.15	0.20	0.31	0.38	0.29
Residential Construction (% change)	0.00	-0.02	-0.02	-0.04	-0.10	-0.14	-0.16
Potential GNP (Supply Multiplier)	0.00	0.00	0.04	0.14	0.34	0.54	0.52
Capital Stock (% change)	-0.00	0.10	0.50	0.96	1.41	1.84	2.18
Labor Supply (% change)	0.00	-0.00	0.07	0.19	0.15	0.08	0.05
Productivity (% change)	-0.02	0.13	0.43	0.36	0.34	0.46	0.50
Government Surplus or Deficit (% change)	-1.01	-0.99	-0.90	-0.88	-0.87	-0.89	-1.00
Unemployment Rate (change)	0.00	-0.02	-0.17	-0.19	-0.15	-0.13	-0.04
Actual Inflation Rate	-0.03	0.07	0.23	0.31	0.22	0.11	-0.08
Core Inflation Rate	-0.06	-0.42	-0.53	-0.36	-0.17	0.07	0.21
Output-Inflation Transform	0.84	0.95	0.77	0.59	0.51	0.47	0.41

A personal tax cut shows a peak supply multiplier of 0.54 after 16 quarters, before beginning to decline. Lower personal tax rates quickly stimulate consumption and thereby lift the whole economy. Labor supply is increased both because of better job opportunities and a modest stimulus to the willingness to work created by a lower tax burden. The busier economy also stimulates investment and thereby augments the capital stock. Compared to the government spending results, the personal tax supply multiplier takes somewhat longer, but retains more of its value in the long run. Government spending boosts GNP more quickly because there is no initial savings leakage, and the stronger economy draws forth a larger supply of capital and labor. But inflation and higher interest rates gradually crowd out some of these benefits in the government expenditure case and ultimately lower the level of investment. In the personal tax case the demand effects are smaller, but there is the direct boost to labor supply which is permanent.

The simulations show that measures tailor-made to boost aggregate supply are a lot more powerful than general measures. The investment tax credit drastically changes the rental price of capital and creates a permanent incentive for higher investment, with all of its benefits on productivity and potential GNP. The government spending increases, personal tax cuts and

Table 3.9
Model Responses to a Real Personal Tax Cut
(Unchanged nominal rates,
Test period: 1966-1971)

	Quarters after Policy Change						
	1	4	8	12	16	20	24
Real GNP (Demand Multiplier)	0.18	1.19	1.43	1.10	0.79	0.56	0.55
Business Investment (% change)	0.03	0.14	0.21	0.15	0.07	-0.01	-0.05
Consumption (% change)	0.19	0.89	0.97	0.92	0.84	0.70	0.72
Residential Construction (% change)	0.00	0.03	0.08	0.01	-0.05	-0.05	-0.07
Potential GNP (Supply Multiplier)	0.01	0.07	0.22	0.43	0.54	0.51	0.41
Capital Stock (% change)	0.01	0.07	0.23	0.35	0.39	0.35	0.27
Labor Supply (% change)	0.11	0.13	0.34	0.39	0.24	0.13	0.10
Productivity (% change)	0.04	0.49	0.57	0.26	0.10	0.10	0.09
Government Surplus or Deficit (% change)	-0.95	-0.55	-0.32	-0.35	-0.47	-0.54	-0.57
Unemployment Rate (change)	-0.01	-0.17	-0.31	-0.21	-0.10	-0.04	-0.02
Actual Inflation Rate	0.04	0.31	0.47	0.59	0.45	0.30	0.13
Core Inflation Rate	-0.01	-0.08	0.07	0.31	0.47	0.52	0.49
Output-Inflation Transform	0.91	0.82	0.63	0.40	0.25	0.16	0.14

corporate rate reductions all show rather modest supply multipliers, peaking near 0.5, though differing in the degree of permanence of the gains.

The economic conditions under which the fiscal stimuli are applied make a big difference to the supply multipliers. The results shown so far were drawn from simulations of the late 1960s, when the economy was in the neighborhood of full employment and inflation was quite moderate. The simulations were rerun for a hypothetical test period beginning in 1984, with the economy assumed to be near equilibrium or somewhat below it, and unemployment rates typically between 6% and 7%. This test period also was free of the particular disturbances of the late 1960s, including the periods of extreme credit stringency and large variations both in personal and corporate taxes. Table 3.10 contrasts the peak supply multipliers for the four fiscal instruments as well as their terminal values in the 24th quarter. It can be seen that the supply multipliers tend to be somewhat more favorable in a slacker economy because fiscal stimulus leads to less crowding out of private spending. On the other hand, the lower inflation rate of the earlier period partially offset this tendency.

The reaction of monetary policy to the fiscal stimuli also has a large effect on supply multipliers. Under a strict monetarist regime, where the central bank assumes that the growth of the money supply is left unchanged, the

Supply Side in the DRI Model

Table 3.10
Supply Multipliers Under Different Economic Conditions,
Peak Values

	1966-71	"1984-89"
Government Purchases	0.58	0.72
Personal Tax Cut	0.54	0.67
Corporate Tax Cut	0.54	0.63
Investment Tax Credit	1.47	1.58

Table 3.11
Supply Multipliers Under Different Monetary Policies,
Peak Values,
Test Period: 1966-1971

	Unchanged Nominal Interest Rates	Unchanged Money Supply
Government Purchases	0.58	0.12
Personal Tax Cut	0.54	0.16
Corporate Tax Cut	0.54	0.27
Investment Tax Credit	1.47	1.11

supply multipliers are smaller because the aggregate demand effects are kept small and brief. Table 3.11 contrasts the supply multipliers under the two monetary regimes. For the general measures, the differences are great because they depended mainly on the supply effects created by a tighter economy. The investment tax credit remains powerful because it acts largely through a relative price change which is little affected.

12. The Output-Inflation Transform

The concept of the Output-Inflation Transform (OIT) was presented in Chapter 2, and defined as the ratio of the real increase in GNP to its nominal increase in response to a change in a fiscal policy instrument. The OIT concept can also be used to illustrate the relative supply-side effects of different fiscal instruments.

Fig. 3.1 shows the output-inflation transform for the four fiscal changes, contrasting the tax policies with the OIT of the government spending change. Using the latter as the baseline, the shaded areas in the figure show the benefits created for this important tradeoff through the supply-side aspects of the various measures. Government spending has no direct supply-side effects

Figure 3.1
Output-Inflation Transforms for Four Fiscal Changes,
Test Period: 1966-1971

Investment Tax Credit
Versus Federal Purchases

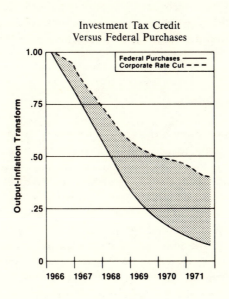

Corporate Tax Rate Cut
Versus Federal Purchases

Personal Tax Cut
Versus Federal Purchases

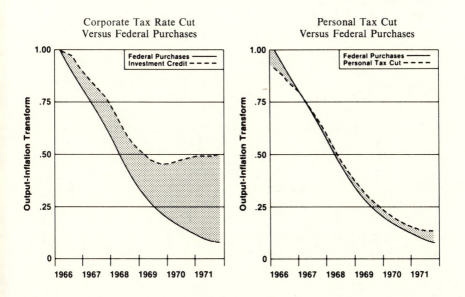

according to the production function used in the DRI model, and since the demand-induced boosts to supply show little difference among the fiscal instruments tested, the differences in the OIT curves can be attributed to the supply-side effects.

It can be seen that the improvement in the output-inflation transform is much the largest for the investment tax credit, the selective device designed to stimulate aggregate supply. Personal and corporate rate reductions show rather similar effects which are measurably positive but quite modest.

13. Concluding Comment

This chapter has shown that a large-scale, econometric model based on the traditional national income account concepts and including elaborate representation of the demand effects can assimilate supply-side ideas quite easily. For serious analysis, there is no possible choice between demand and supply models: both sides of markets must be modeled.

The tax effects on the supply of labor and on personal saving and their subsequent effects on the growth of potential GNP are relatively new econometric topics and the conclusions of the scientific community are not yet as settled as in other areas. Thus, it will be important to continue to focus research on these particular parameters. The evidence at hand shows that supply-side effects are sizeable but take several years, while demand effects tend to be quicker but fleeting.

CHAPTER 4

MODELING THE FINANCIAL SYSTEM[1]

1. Introduction

The financial factor has assumed increasing importance in the short-run behavior of the U.S. economy over the last three decades. While the early postwar years saw questioning of the role of money in the determination of real output and prices, the pendulum has now swung to the other extreme and the financial factor is recognized as the most important determinant of the short-run situation.

There are various methods for representing the financial factor in macroeconomic models. The monetarist models rely on reduced forms linking the money supply and nominal GNP. The earlier macroeconomic models relied principally on interest rates to affect real spending, with monetary policy, through its control of bank reserves, largely determining short-term interest rates.

The availability of the Federal Reserve's measures of the flows-of-funds for the various major sectors of the economy opens up the possibility of more explicit modeling of the financial system. Total sources and uses of funds of businesses, households, and financial institutions are determined, in an accounting sense, by their expenditures, incomes and net financial investments. But in the behavioral sense, decisions about real and financial matters are made as part of a broader set of choices designed to maximize the unit's economic welfare. Modern portfolio theory provides the logical underpinning for this behavior and shows how these units react to real flows, rates of return and capital costs, and to the risks created by balance sheet

---

[1]The financial system of the DRI model was developed under the direction of Allen Sinai. A full account of the structure, simulation properties and policy analyses will be presented in a separate, companion volume. For an earlier account of this work, see Allen Sinai, "The Integration of 'Financial Instability' in Large-Scale Econometric Models: Theory, Practice, Problems," Paper presented at the meeting of the Midwest Economic Association, April 1975, and Allen Sinai "Financial Instability in the U.S. Economy: A Discussion," in A. Sametz and E. Altman, eds., *Financial Crises: Institutions and Markets in a Fragile Environment* (New York, Wiley, 1977), pp. 187-203.

allocations of assets and liabilities among different financial instruments and physical assets.[2] The DRI model implements these concepts by equations which determine the flows-of-funds, the resultant asset and debt changes, and the effects of these financial factors on real spending for consumption and investment.

The representation of household and business flows-of-funds leads to several innovations in macroeconomic modeling. Most important, flows-of-funds and the resultant balance sheets become explanatory variables in the equations explaining final demands and incomes. Along with interest rates, these movements in flows-of-funds and balance sheets are the principal channels of interaction between the real and financial systems. The modeling of flows-of-funds also allows the projection of many detailed long- and short-term interest rates, permitting more effective integration of supply and demand considerations in capital markets with the fundamental forces underlying interest rates such as price expectations and monetary policy.

The equations for the flows-of-funds must reflect the changing pattern of regulation. The increasing trend toward competition among financial institutions and the removal of interest rate ceilings has meant that the particular media in which the public holds its assets are undergoing major shifts.

2. The Credit Cycle and the Real Cycle

The necessity to incorporate financial modeling in the macro structure is principally due to the decisive effects which monetary policy and the resultant credit cycle have had on the real cycle. Every recession since 1950 has been preceded by a period of credit stringency. While some of the recessions had other underlying causes, the turning point and the process of contraction were usually determined by the occurrence of credit rationing and peak interest rates.

In earlier DRI work,[3] a credit crunch was defined as having the following characteristics: (1) an extraordinary increase in the federal funds rate; (2) high net borrowed reserves by the commercial banking system; (3) rate

[2]Earlier flows-of-funds models include W.H.L. Anderson, *Corporate Finance and Fixed Investment* (Cambridge: Harvard University Press, 1964), and Barry Bosworth and James S. Duesenberry, "A Flow of Funds Model and its Implications," *Issues in Federal Debt Management* (Boston: The Federal Reserve Bank of Boston), June 1973, pp. 39-149. Also see Patric Hendershott, *Understanding Capital Markets, Volume 1: A Flow of Funds Financial Model* (Lexington, Mass.: Lexington Books, 1977).
[3]Otto Eckstein and Allen Sinai, "Crunch Monitor," *Data Resources Review*, August 1973, pp. 47-50, and Allen Sinai, "Credit Crunches—An Analysis of the Postwar Experience," in Otto Eckstein, ed., *Parameters and Policies in the U.S. Economy* (Amsterdam: North-Holland Publishing Co., 1976), pp. 244-274.

inversion, with short-term interest rates exceeding long-term interest rates; (4) weakening cash flow of business creating a rapidly expanding demand for short-term credit; (5) a deterioration in business balance sheets, with short-term liabilities becoming large in relation to such other balance sheet measures as total liabilities and short-term assets. Table 4.1 lists the periods of credit crunch and compares them to the periods of recession. Of the seven recessions, six were preceded by credit crunches, with only the 1953 recession preceded by tightened credit conditions that fell short of a crunch. The seven credit crunches helped produce six recessions, with only the 1966 crunch's effects limited to a growth recession because of the Vietnam War boom.

The credit cycle permeates the entire economy. On the business side, as measured by balance sheet conditions, finance is relatively strong during the periods of early upswing, when cash flow rises rapidly and spending commitments are still modest. As an expansion ages, cash flow slows down and commitments keep rising. During the credit crunch, interest rates rise sharply and surprisingly in response to tighter policy at a time of increased credit need, increasing the burden of interest payments and sometimes leading to credit rationing. As the economy weakens and ultimately turns down, business cash flow falls sharply while commitments are still high and unwanted inventories require costly financing. In response, business expectations finally are lowered sharply, commitments are reduced and employees are laid off. As the recession proceeds, business decumulates inventories and cuts back on commitments for people and fixed capital, allowing the business balance sheet to be at least partially restored through reliquefication. Credit demand may continue strong in the early stages of recession as business finds itself with disappointing internal cash flows and

Table 4.1
Periods of Credit Crunches and Recession,
1950-1982

Credit Crunch[1]	Recession[2]
	1953:2 - 1954:2
1955:4 - 1957:4	1957:3 - 1958:2
1959:2 - 1960:2	1960:2 - 1961:1
1966:1 - 1966:4	
1969:1 - 1970:1	1969:4 - 1970:4
1973:3 - 1974:3	1973:4 - 1975:1
1979:4 - 1980:1	1980:1 - 1980:3
1980:4 - 1982:2	1981:3 - 1982

[1]Based on criteria discussed in text.
[2]National Bureau of Economic Research definition of contractions.

obsolete, excessive commitments. But as the recession proceeds, credit demand dries up as the inventory and general commitment correction occurs, setting the stage for the next upswing.

The household credit cycle has a somewhat different timing and is less acute. While the debt burdens of households rise with the accumulation of consumer durables in the rapid phases of the business cycle expansion, consumers become cautious early and curtail their spending on durables either before the credit crunch begins or quickly thereafter. Nonetheless, consumers also go through a period of reliquefication during the recession downswing and enter the recovery with strengthened balance sheets.

Financial institutions reinforce the credit cycle. During a period of upswing they accommodate business and household demands for credit, also taking on an increasing volume of future commitments. When the turn in the credit cycle comes and interest rates go much higher, financial institutions find their commitments excessive in relation to shrinking inflows. Insurance companies suffer from a large volume of policy loans and banks are confronted by a dramatically higher cost of purchased funds. Even pension funds, which have among the most stable patterns of funds inflows, may encounter diminished company pension allocations once the profits fall. As financial institutions experience the funds squeeze, they cease to be active buyers in the bond and stock markets, creating sharp declines in stock and bond prices.

The Federal Reserve typically strongly reinforces the credit cycle. During recession the Federal Reserve is usually easy, providing a large volume of reserves to the banking system and thereby making the economy highly liquid. During the period of rapid upswing, the Federal Reserve is still accommodating and so real interest rates may be near zero or at low levels. But once the expansion ages and its side effects become visible with prices getting into more rapid motion, the Federal Reserve sharply limits the growth of the monetary base, credit tightens, and ultimately produces the erratic phenomena of the credit crunch.

The credit cycle is also the vehicle through which external shocks, such as world oil prices, create recessions in the economy. The rise in prices produced by the shock ultimately triggers the Federal Reserve into restrictive action. As the transactions demand for the higher-priced materials adds to the demand for money and credit at the same time that the Federal Reserve is curtailing their supply, interest rates are pushed to record levels, the credit crunch occurs and recession begins.

This integral role of flows-of-funds and real interest rates in the business cycle creates the need to build an elaborate financial sector into a macro model. While the process can be represented by various reduced form methods such as the traditional use of the differential between long- and short-term interest rates as a proxy for crunches, a more precise modeling can be obtained by explicitly representing the financial behavior of households and businesses.

3. Theoretical Underpinning of Flows-of-Funds Modeling

The modern portfolio model developed by Markowitz,[4] Friedman[5] and Tobin[6] derives portfolio behavior from investors' utility-maximizing behavior in the face of a choice of assets yielding different returns and associated with different risks. Markowitz is concerned with a choice among different stocks and seeks to define an efficiency frontier for portfolios. A point on the frontier has the characteristic that it is the highest rate of return that can be obtained for any given degree of risk. The actual optimization process consists of processing the cross-correlations among the risks of different stocks to derive optimal diversification. Friedman, on the other hand, was concerned with the demand for money which he treated as a capital good yielding productive services. The demand for money will vary with total wealth, including human, physical and financial wealth. This wealth may be held in the form of money, bonds, equities, physical goods or human capital. For each form of asset, an expected rate of return is defined, with the demand for money depending upon the relative expected rates of return and total wealth measured by permanent income.

Tobin produced the most explicit model of portfolio choice derived from utilities and analyzed the cases of individuals who are either risk-averters or risk-lovers. In his model the only choice is between money and bonds, with the risk associated with the return on bonds. Consequently, a larger bond holding will always be associated with both a larger return and a larger risk. A risk lover may choose to put all of his assets into bonds. A risk averter is more likely to find an optimal point where he sacrifices some expected return in order to reduce risk.

None of these cases fully covers the needs of flows-of-funds modeling in which the asset choice is among various kinds of physical goods, several kinds of short- and long-term debt securities, common stocks and money. In addition, households and businesses have to choose among several different forms of debt, which have corresponding risk patterns associated with them,

[4] Harry Markowitz, "Portfolio Selection," *Journal of Finance,* March 1952, pp. 77-91.
[5] Milton Friedman, "The Quantity Theory of Money: A Restatement," in Milton Friedman, ed., *Studies in the Quantity Theory of Money* (Chicago: University of Chicago Press, 1956), pp. 3-21.
[6] James Tobin, "Liquidity Preference as Behavior Towards Risk," *The Review of Economic Studies,* February 1958, pp. 65-86.

with long-term debt having a lesser risk of nominal interest cost but a higher risk in relation to future opportunity borrowing costs. Further, adjustment costs must be introduced to motivate a gradual adjustment process: businesses cannot adapt their balance sheet portfolios fully in response to changing financial, product and factor market conditions.

These basic ideas motivate equations which have a very general form:

$$A_{it} = f(A_{1,t-1}, ..., A_{i,t-1}, ..., A_{m,t-1}, D_{1,t-1}, ..., D_{j,t-1}, ... D_{h,t-1},$$
$$r_{1,t},..., r_{i,t},..., r_{m,t}, c_{1,t},..., c_{j,t},..., c_{h,t}) \tag{1}$$

where A_i is an asset type, D_j is a typical debt, r_i the rate of return on i and c_j the borrowing cost of j.

The above theory is a static theory of adjustment to equilibrium and does not, by itself, display any particular cyclical characteristics. To produce the mechanism of the credit cycle, additional elements must therefore be found in actual history. They are essentially of two forms: first, the central bank acts in a pro-cyclical manner by changing the supply of bank reserves in response to changing output and price behavior with a destabilizing lag. Since it takes some months for the effects of Federal Reserve policy to be felt in the financial system and additional months to affect real activity, the nonoptimality of the resultant monetary policy can be quite extreme and fundamental to the credit cycle. Second, the resultant surprising deviations from price and sales expectations trigger variations in private credit needs, and the desired balance sheet composition changes substantially. Since the majority of firms tend to be in a similar position, their attempt to correct balance sheets moves the rates of return and borrowing costs in the capital markets. Whether these markets have a tendency to "overshoot" is an open question, but casual evidence suggests this tendency. The credit cycle, with its crunch at the peaks, is the result of the policy and nonfinancial forces acting to produce desired portfolio adjustments that strain capital markets and produce large changes in their prices.

4. The Loci of Interaction

Flows-of-funds variables play a particular role in the DRI model as part of the simultaneity of the real and the financial sectors. While these variables have a smaller explanatory power of final demands than such traditional variables as incomes and relative prices, they are significant and play a destabilizing role at cyclical turning points. They intensify the responses of final demands to cyclical fluctuations and play a role in explaining the business cycle itself.

4.1 Consumption

Besides such variables as income, relative prices and associated stocks of consumer capital, the household sector's net worth affects expenditures for consumer durables, clothing and shoes, and other nondurables.[7] Household net worth is a comprehensive balance sheet measure, reflecting both physical and financial assets as well as various kinds of liabilities. In the short run, the series is moved by variations in the value of common stocks owned by households, but in the longer run the series also reflects fundamental saving trends. While the measure does not fully approximate Milton Friedman's measure of household wealth by omitting human wealth, it is otherwise comprehensive.

Consumer confidence, as measured by the Michigan Index of Consumer Sentiment, also affects all categories of durable goods consumption as well as outlays for other consumer services, household operations and transportation. Consumer confidence, in turn, is determined by several real variables, including the GNP gap, employment and energy prices, but is also affected by two financial variables, the Treasury bill rate and common stock prices. Thus, an increase in short-term interest rates or a decline in common stock prices reduces consumer confidence, and thereby reduces consumer expenditures for the more sensitive categories of outlays.

A third channel of influence of financial factors on consumption is via real aftertax interest rates which affect some categories of durables. Automobiles are also affected by interest rates through their effect on the rental price of cars. In the historically derived equations, this factor is still playing a rather small role and is confined to just a few categories of consumption. However, this variable only took on extreme magnitudes in recent years, and so its role in the equations is likely to rise in the future.

The opposite linkage—from consumer behavior to the financial system—is quite transparent. Consumption helps determine the demand for currency and thereby affects the entire financial system. Durable goods consumption affects such variables as bank loans to individuals, various kinds of savings deposits and other financial assets, the extension of consumer credit, the growth of physical assets, and virtually the entire household balance sheet. Consumer expenditures and incomes also affect total available savings flows. The distribution of inflows into various financial institutions is determined by relative rates of return and initial balance sheet positions; it affects the supply of mortgages for housing and the structure of interest rates.

[7]This variable played an important role in the FMP model. See Franco Modigliani, "Monetary Policy and Consumption: Linkages by Interest Rates and Wealth Effects in the FMP Model," *Consumer Spending and Monetary Policy: the Linkages* (Boston: The Federal Bank of Boston, 1971).

4.2 Business Fixed Investment

The important role of financial factors in equations for business fixed investment has long been established and was formalized in the work of Jorgenson.[8] While his work relied on one interest rate to represent the cost of financial capital, later data and research suggest that a weighted cost of capital should be substituted, relying on short- and long-term debt capital as well as equity. The modeling of the nonfinancial corporate flows-of-funds provides the weights to be introduced into the composite cost of capital. In addition, financial factors also make themselves felt through the burden of interest costs on corporate cash flow. Thus the ratio of interest expense to the gross internal funds of nonfinancial corporations is also of importance in the equations.[9] These financial terms are found in the equations for producers' durable equipment, nonresidential construction, as well as the investment equations of individual two-digit industries.

The reverse relationship, from investment to the financial sector, affects the total uses of funds of the nonfinancial corporate sector, the book value of depreciation and thereby cash flow, the volume of bank loans and commercial paper, bonds issued, deposits, new equity issues and other short-term assets, as well as various minor variables.

4.3 Residential Construction

Variations in housing activity are clearly dominated by financial considerations, and all short-term econometric models have long recognized this condition. In early models, the variations in the supply of mortgage money were modeled by a proxy variable defined as the differential between long- and short-term interest rates. During periods of rate inversion, when short-term rates exceeded long-term rates, money would be drained out of the thrift institutions and life insurance policy loans would surge, thereby depriving housing of its normal mortgage supply. The MPS model was the first to represent the mortgage market explicitly and to show its relation to housing activity.[10] The DRI model traces the flows-of-funds from individual and business saving through the portfolio behavior of the pertinent financial institutions into the mortgage market, with decisions governed by competing

---

[8]Dale Jorgenson, "Capital Theory and Investment Behavior," *American Economic Review*, May 1963, pp. 247-257.

[9]Cash flow considerations have also long been recognized in investment equations. See, for example, John R. Meyer and Edwin L. Kuh, *The Investment Decision* (Cambridge: Harvard University Press, 1957).

[10]See Edward M. Gramlich and D.M. Jaffe, *Savings Deposits, Mortgages and Housing* (Lexington, Mass.: D.C. Heath, 1973).

rates of return and existing balance sheet conditions. The equations for housing starts, in addition to relying on such factors as demography, incomes, the ratio of sales prices to construction costs, consumer confidence and other variables, tends to be driven in the short run by the availability of mortgages, which in turn are influenced by the structure of interest rates. At least until the business cycles of 1980 and 1981, the dominant variable seems to have been the ability of the housing industry to attract mortgage money, which was mainly a question of the balance sheet conditions of the pertinent financial institutions and the competitive rates of return being offered. Thus, for example, under some circumstances, an increase in mortgage rates would expand housing activity despite the relative price effect on ownership costs, because high mortgage rates, other things equal, would attract more funds to the sector. On the other hand, high short-term interest rates are very damaging because they drain away the funds from the mortgage sector to other uses. The experience of 1980-82 shows, however, that when mortgage rates are deep in double-digit territory, they do have a severe effect on the rental price of housing and create a "nonaffordability" condition for a large percentage of all households which is as devastating for housing activity as the previous elements of rationing of mortgage money created by disintermediation.

Mortgage commitments are a key variable linking the financial sector to housing activity. For single-family starts it is the commitments of savings and loan associations and mutual savings banks that matter; for multi-family starts the mortgage commitments of life insurance companies must be added.

4.4 Governments

The expenditures of state and local governments are affected by their budget position and by the cost of their debt capital. When the accumulated deficits of state and local governments are large, they must curtail their spending because they operate under a long-term budget constraint.

Federal spending is defined to be an exogenous variable, at least at high employment levels. Thus, no direct financial effect from the federal budget position to spending is assumed. Unfortunately, this assumption seems to be confirmed by the historical record.

The opposite relationship is important for the federal sector, however. Large government deficits raise both short- and long-term interest rates. This is the principal mechanism by which government deficits crowd out private spending.

5. Other Aspects of the Financial Sector

In other regards, the financial sector generally elaborates the methods developed in earlier models, using the general approach pioneered by DeLeeuw.[11] The bank reserve mechanism is modeled, with nonborrowed reserves the fundamental exogenous variable and borrowed reserves determined by interest rate differentials and disequilibria between required and nonborrowed reserves: the gap between the discount rate and money market rates affects the decision whether to borrow reserves at the discount window.

Short-term interest rates are determined partly by the volume of borrowed reserves, by recent money supply behavior which affects expectations about future Federal Reserve policy, as well as the relation between the real monetary base and real GNP, a summary measure of Federal Reserve policy and of the overall state of liquidity of the economy. Fifteen short-term interest rates are modeled, including three Treasury bill rates, federal funds, the discount rate, Eurodollars, commercial paper, the prime rate, large CDs, money market funds, the auto installment loan rate and the rates on various kinds of savings deposits. No one rate is the pivotal rate determining all others, with several of the rates simultaneously interdependent. In addition, factors affecting particular rates create differentials. Thus, for example, the Treasury bill rate is not only affected by the federal funds rate and the monetary policy variables, but also by the size of the federal deficit. The commercial paper rate is partly determined by the Treasury bill rate, but also by corporate cash flow in relation to commitments. Bank loan behavior impacts the rates paid on the large CDs required to finance these loans. The simultaneity of rates is dictated by the portfolio-theoretic approach: if the need for a particular form of short-term credit is particularly large for market reasons, lenders must be offered an extra return to produce the needed reallocation of assets.

Long-term interest rates follow the approach developed by Feldstein and Eckstein,[12] which relies principally on long-term price expectations based on an adaptive learning process and a measure of policy-controlled liquidity of the economy, the ratio of the real per capita monetary base to real per capita GNP. This approach has been extended by adding various flows-of-funds and portfolio considerations. Thus, the volume of nonfinancial corporate bonds

[11]Frank DeLeeuw, "A Model of Financial Behavior," in James S. Duesenberry, Edwin I., Kuh and Lawrence R. Klein, eds., *The Brookings Quarterly Econometric Model of the United States* (Chicago: Rand Econometric Model." *Federal Reserve Bulletin,* January 1968, pp. 11-40.

[12]Martin Feldstein and Otto Eckstein. "Fundamental Determinants of the Interest Rates." *Review of Economics and Statistics,* November 1970, pp. 363-375.

to be issued affects the new AAA corporate bond rate. The expected return on common stocks also enters the equation, for a strong stock market competes with the bond market for investor funds. There is less simultaneity among long-term interest rates, with the ten long-term interest rates largely driven by the estimate for the new AAA bond rate, modified by factors peculiar to each market.

The previous paragraphs give a very summary account of the financial sector, which in fact encompasses nearly 200 equations, or about one-quarter of the model. There are equations for bank loans of various types, for M1, M2, M3 and their numerous components, and other financial magnitudes. But a full account of these matters will have to await the publication of the volume on the financial system in the DRI model by Allen Sinai.

6. Effects of the Financial System on the Real Economy:
   A Simulation Exercise

To illustrate the workings of the model, two simulations have been run which differ in the tightness of the supply of nonborrowed bank reserves, the central exogenous variable of the financial sector. The results are summarized in table 4.2. Tighter bank reserves raise the federal funds rate immediately and keep it high for the first year. But the rise in this rate diminishes in the second year because of the reduced demand for money created by lower real activity. Treasury bill rates respond only slightly more sluggishly. Long-term interest rates, on the other hand, show only a very small increase in response to the tighter bank reserves, and this only for a few months. By the end of one year, bond rates are actually no higher with tighter bank reserves and then turn lower because the weakened economy has reduced the inflation rate and cut the supply of bond issues. Mortgage rates, on the other hand, are slightly higher and remain that way, principally because sharply higher short-term interest rates make savers reallocate their funds away from the thrift institutions which are the main source of mortgage money. The smallness of the effects on long-term rates is due to the large role of rationing—now that this effect is gone, the rate response will be larger. Stock prices fall for about one year due to lower earnings growth and higher interest rates, but by the second year this decline is reversed as lower long-term interest rates offer less competition in portfolio choices, and by year three stock prices are actually higher.

Turning to real final demands, the effect on consumption can also be seen. Lower stock prices cut household net worth. Consumer confidence is reduced by higher interest rates and higher unemployment. Real disposable income is

Table 4.2
Effects of Tighter Financial Conditions on the Real Economy
(Percent differences in levels unless otherwise indicated,
Test period: 1975:2-1979:1)

	Quarters				
	1	4	8	12	16
Financial Variables					
Nonborrowed Reserves (cut $2 billion)	-5.8	-5.8	-5.8	-5.5	-5.0
Federal Funds Rate*	346	464	364	275	236
3-Month T-Bill Rate*	237	361	307	239	202
New AAA Bond Rate*	28	1	-54	-70	-61
Mortgage Commitment Rate*	11	29	17	10	39
Stock Prices	-0.5	-8.2	-5.5	3.1	8.4
Consumption	-0.7	-2.3	-3.2	-2.3	-1.5
Real Disposable Income	-0.4	-1.6	-2.0	-1.2	-0.5
Consumer Confidence	-10.4	-19.0	-17.0	-9.5	-6.1
Household Net Worth	-0.8	-4.1	-3.6	-2.0	-1.0
Cost of Car Operation	0.7	1.7	3.6	5.2	5.1
Residential Construction	-3.7	-16.4	-20.6	-14.7	-8.6
Savings Deposits at S&Ls	-1.3	-5.0	-8.2	-8.8	-8.8
New Mortgage Commitments at S&Ls	-9.3	-39.7	-31.8	-27.6	-23.8
Single-Family Housing Starts	-6.9	-22.7	-25.7	-15.8	-7.0
Business Fixed Investment	-1.0	-4.1	-6.6	-5.7	-3.5
Average Effective Interest Cost*	22	40	56	59	77
Interest Cost as Percent of Cash Flow (change in percent)	2.2	4.6	4.6	2.9	2.2
State and Local Government Purchases	-1.1	-2.0	-2.5	-2.6	-2.4
Real GNP (aggregate demand)	-0.9	-3.1	-4.2	-3.2	-2.0
Potential GNP (aggregate supply)	0	0	-0.2	-0.6	-0.8

*change in basis points

cut by the economy's decline, and all these factors combine to produce a significantly lower consumption. The more volatile categories respond more strongly, of course. Consumer expenditures on autos and parts show a very dramatic response, though this effect, like most effects of tighter money, shrinks by year three.

The effect of tight money on the housing sector is also illustrated in table 4.2, particularly the effects channeled through the savings and loans industry. Deposits are cut very substantially by the increased competition from money market instruments, and this deposit decline produces a considerable decline of new mortgage commitments. The commitments, in turn, slash single-family housing starts. Similar channels run through mutual savings banks and the financial system as a whole, and the figures for multiple housing starts are similar to those shown for singles.

In the case of investment, the principal effect is through lower output expectations created by the weaker economy. The interest cost of capital rises only moderately because long-term bond yields are a little lower. The net effect is significantly negative, however, because investment remains highly responsive to actual and expected output.

Table 4.3 shows the effects of tighter monetary policy on the various components of final demands in absolute and percentage terms, and then shows the composition of the cut in final demand. Because consumption is the largest final demand component, the biggest effect of tighter money accrues in this sector. Residential investment is second, inventory investment is third, nonresidential investment fourth and state and local government purchases fifth. Federal purchases are set exogenously and therefore show no effect. The demand effects peak at the end of eight quarters, and after four years are cut in half.

Expressed in percentage terms, the response is much the greatest for residential investment and automobiles. Nonresidential investment and nonauto durables show a second level of responsiveness. Consumption as a whole and state and local spending are less responsive still because of the role

Table 4.3
Response of Final Demands to Tighter Financial Conditions
Peak Response Period: Eight Quarters After Reserve Policy Change

	Decline in $1972 Billion	Percent Decline	Percent of Total GNP Decline
Consumption	-27.0	-3.2	47.6
Autos and Parts	-9.0	-14.7	15.9
Other Durables	-4.2	-5.8	7.4
Residential Investment	-11.7	-20.2	20.6
Business Fixed Investment	-9.1	-6.6	16.0
Producers' Durable Equipment	-6.6	-6.7	11.6
Nonresidential Construction	-2.4	-6.1	4.2
State and Local Government	-4.3	-2.5	7.6
Federal Government	0	0	0
Inventory Investment	-7.4	n.m.	13.1
Net Exports	2.7	n.m.	-4.8
Total GNP	-56.7	-4.2	100.0

of services. Federal government purchases are not affected at all, and net exports improve because of the weaker economy. Thus the model confirms recent observations that housing and automobiles are the main interest-sensitive sectors.

CHAPTER 5

CONSUMER SPENDING

1. Introduction

The micro-theory of consumer behavior determines spending from household preferences, the level of income which determines the budget constraint, and relative prices. Macro-theory has added several propositions: Keynes[1] elevated the consumption-income relationship to the very center of the economy's behavior. Haberler,[2] Pigou,[3] Patinkin[4] and Zellner[5] argued that assets mattered to consumption outlays, shifting the consumption-income relation upward. Duesenberry[6] and Modigliani,[7] observing the long-run constancy of the saving-income ratio, showed that cultural pressures in a society raised the "need" to consume in proportion to the rise in average incomes. They also found that these pressures, as reflected by previous peak income, would tend to maintain consumption during the temporary income declines of recessions. Modigliani,[8] with Brumberg and Ando, found that individual provision against lifetime fluctuations in income, including the need to provide for income in retirement, could account for much of saving

[1]John M. Keynes, *The General Theory of Employment, Interest, and Money* (New York: Harcourt, Brace and World, 1936), chs. 8-10.
[2]Gottfried Haberler, *Prosperity and Depression* (Geneva: League of Nations, 1937), pp. 242, 389, 403, 491-503.
[3]A.C. Pigou, "The Classical Stationary State," *Economic Journal* (December 1943), pp. 343-351.
[4]Don Patinkin, *Money, Interest, and Prices*, 2nd ed. (New York: Harper & Row, 1965).
[5]Arnold Zellner, "The Short-Run Consumption Function," *Econometrica* (October 1957), pp. 552-567.
[6]James S. Duesenberry, *Income, Saving and the Theory of Consumer Behavior* (Cambridge, Mass.: Harvard University Press, 1949), chs. 1- 3, 5, 7.
[7]Franco Modigliani, "Fluctuations in the Saving-Income Ratio: A Problem in Economic Forecasting," *Studies in Income and Wealth* (New York: National Bureau of Economic Research, 1949), pp. 337-441.
[8]Franco Modigliani and Richard Brumberg, "Utility Analysis and the Consumption Function: An Interpretation of Cross-Section Data," in *Post Keynesian Economics*, ed. K. Kurihara (New Brunswick: Rutgers University Press, 1954); Albert Ando and Franco Modigliani, "The Life Cycle Hypothesis of Saving: Aggregate Implications and Tests," *American Economic Review* (May 1963), pp. 55-84.

behavior. Friedman[9] showed that consumers act on "permanent" income, that is, their expectations of long-term economic position as measured by wealth or by an extended period of experience in receiving income or wealth.

These theoretical and empirical advances were sufficient to account for aggregate consumer behavior in the more placid years of the postwar period and for the remarkable constancy of the saving-income ratio in this century. These theories also showed an increasing absorption of the micro-theoretic assumptions of consumer behavior, including the rational adjustment of consumption to a lifetime economic situation.

The theories offered more limited ideas to account for the short-term business-cycle behavior of consumer spending. The Duesenberry-Modigliani theory showed that the saving ratio would fall in recession because of adherence to consumption standards set by previous peak income. The later Modigliani and Friedman theories also produced this conclusion, and applied it to show that transitory variations in income created by fiscal policy would produce only a very partial response in spending.

The experience of the last fifteen years, with the return to a more violent business cycle and the creation of a more uncertain macro environment, made the older theories inadequate. On at least eight occasions, variations in consumer spending propensities played a critical, independent role in reinforcing the business cycle, counter to the conclusions of the previous theories. In the 1970 recession, consumption did not play its usual stabilizing role, but accentuated the downswing through a jump in the savings rate to record levels. In the 1971 upswing, consumption rose at extraordinary rates on apparent real income gains made possible by price controls, reinforcing the investment and financial excesses of that boom. In early 1973, consumption faded despite growing incomes, as households began to sense the onset of a major economic disturbance. In early 1974, consumption fell more violently than incomes, as the oil embargo created near-panic. Wild inflation and a financial collapse set back spending again the fall of that year. Inflation-anticipatory buying became a significant factor once double-digit inflation was experienced beginning in the mid-1970s. In 1980, tight money and consumer credit controls created a collapse of consumer spending that created a brief but deep recession. The consumer credit controls of 1980 created the sharpest one-quarter GNP decline of the postwar years, and the 1981-82 recession was led by the collapse of auto sales. This record suggests that an adequate theory of consumption must include a fuller treatment of the role of an uncertain economic environment on consumer spending.

[9]Milton Friedman, *A Theory of the Consumption Function* (Princeton: Princeton University Press, 1957), chs. 1-3, 6, 9.

2. Theory of Consumer Spending: The Effect of Macro Risk

In the DRI model, the expected risks of income and personal finance are added to the inherited theory of consumption[10] and identified in the equations representing the empirical data. Suppose a household plans its spending on the basis of its known current income, y_1, its expected normal income in the future period, y_2, its net worth or asset-debt position, and the uncertainty surrounding the second-period income. The household maximizes a two-period expected utility function,

$$E(u) = u(c_1) + E(u(c_2)),\qquad(1)$$

where $u(c_1)$ and $u(c_2)$ are the same. If there is no time preference or return on saving, the budget constraint is

$$c_1 + c_2 = y_1 + y_2 + a_1 + a_2 - d_1 - d_2,\qquad(2)$$

where a is the return including amortization on the household's financial assets, and d is normal debt service including scheduled repayments. The same utility function is assumed to apply in both periods. In the absence of uncertainty, the household's optimal spending plan would require

$$\partial u(c_1)/\partial c_1 = \partial u(c_2)/\partial c_2,\qquad(3)$$

and

$$c_1 = c_2 = (y_1 + y_2 + a_1 + a_2 - d_1 - d_2)/2.\qquad(4)$$

To introduce uncertainty in the future period, we define an alternative state (y'_2, a'_2, d'_2), a clearly defined contingency which drastically changes the household's economic situation. The loss of job by the head of the household is the most common such contingency. Job loss not only affects income, but also may make it impossible to renew outstanding debt, thereby raising the debt service burden (including repayment). The death or disablement of a wage earner is an even greater contingency, though one not related to the general economy. Surprisingly tight credit conditions or the loss of overtime are smaller contingencies.

[10]The earliest known treatment of this problem, generally reaching the present conclusions, is Irving Fisher, *The Theory of Interest* (New York: Macmillan, 1930). Other treatments include Hayne E. Leland, "Saving and Uncertainty: The Precautionary Demand for Saving," *Quarterly Journal of Economics* (August 1968), pp. 465-473; Agnar Sandmo, "The Effect of Uncertainty on Saving Decisions," *Review of Economic Studies* (July 1970), pp. 353-360; Jacques H. Dreze and Franco Modigliani, "Consumption Decisions Under Uncertainty," *Journal of Economic Theory* (December 1972), pp. 308-335; and Frederic S. Mishkin, "Illiquidity, Consumer Durable Expenditures and Monetary Policy," *American Economic Review* (September 1976), pp. 642-654. The present theoretical treatment follows the Mishkin approach in its use of a contingency state.

The secondary loss of effective purchasing power beyond the direct income reductions will rise with the debt to be serviced and fall with the available assets. In other words, a consumer with past spending patterns that produce a highly exposed financial position will suffer a greater consumption loss if a serious contingency develops.

Let the resultant shortfall of consumption be

$$L_c = c_2 - c_2' = (y_2 - y_2') + (a_2 - a_2') - (d_2 - d_2'), \tag{5}$$

and

$$u(L_c) = u(c_2) - u(c'_2). \tag{6}$$

If the contingency state has an expected probability of occurrence p, then the expected utility function becomes

$$E(u) = u(c_1) + (1 - p)\, u(c_2) + pu(c_2'), \tag{7}$$

or

$$E(u) = u(c_1) + u(c_2) - pu(L_c). \tag{8}$$

The optimum spending behavior in this uncertain situation is defined by maximizing (8). Taking the derivative with respect to first-period consumption (which is the only choice in the model),

$$\partial E(u)/\partial c_1 = \partial u/\partial c_1 + (\partial u/\partial c_2)(\partial c_2/\partial c_1) - p(\partial u/\partial L_c)\, \partial L_c/\partial c_1 = 0. \tag{9}$$

Since $\partial c_2/\partial c_1 = -1$ due to the budget constraint,

$$\partial u/\partial c_1 = \partial u/\partial c_2 + p(\partial u/\partial L_c)\, \partial L_c/\partial c_1. \tag{10}$$

Thus, c_1 will be less than c_2, with the difference depending on the probability of the contingency, the size of the contingency consumption loss, and the resultant loss of utility. First-period marginal utility will be larger, consumption smaller, and saving larger, the greater the probability of the contingency, the effect of the contingency on second-period purchasing power, and the associated loss of utility. It should be noted that the expected level of consumption in the second period, $(1-p)c_2 + pc'_2$, varies with p in this formulation.

L_c can be decomposed into its three sources: the loss in income, the loss of asset yield, and the rise in debt service,

$$L_c = L_y + L_a + L_d. \tag{11}$$

Two of the three components probably have positive relationships with c_1, i.e.,

$$dL_d/dc_1 > 0, \text{ and } dL_a/dc_1 > 0. \tag{12}$$

The case is clearest for debt. High first-period consumption raises the debt burden in period two, requiring a larger commitment of income to debt service. If the contingency develops, debt service costs will rise because the lender's risk on this debt will be greater and refinancing will be more difficult. The contingency loss of return on assets also varies positively with first-period consumption: lower assets leave less room for portfolio adjustments to sustain consumption in the event of income loss. The third source of contingency consumption loss, the second-period income decline, has no transparent association with first-period consumption—indeed, the high-consumption person may have a greater incentive and effectiveness to stave off the contingency income loss that might be created by the economy.

Eq. (10) showed that the incremental saving to hedge against future uncertainty depends on the probability of the contingency and the utility of the consumption loss due to decreased income and asset yield and increased debt service. The losses, particularly on debt service and asset return, depend on the consumption behavior which creates the existing portfolio position of assets and debts. Thus, the consumption function can be written as

$$c_1 = f(y_1, a_1, d_1, y_2, a_2, d_2, p, L_y, L_a, L_d). \tag{13}$$

In the actual circumstance, households must act on their expectations, and these expectations in turn are the vehicle through which macro uncertainties affect behavior. These expectation hypotheses can be summarized as follows, with all left-hand variables to be interpreted as expectations:

$$y_2 = g(y_1, y_0, ..., y_{-n}, U, \dot{P}), \tag{14}$$

i.e., expected income is based on past income, transitory and permanent as indicated by prior experience, and by macroeconomic risk based on the reported unemployment rate (U) and inflation $(\dot{P})$.

The expected probability of the occurrence of the contingency depends on the current unemployment and inflation situations, and on the observed variability of income, σ_y.

$$p = h(U, \dot{P}, \sigma_y). \tag{15}$$

Both the expected asset return and its expected contingency shortfall depend on the real value of financial assets (A). The total of financial assets includes money, deposits, bonds and the market value of equity. Therefore, stock price behavior (a_s) and interest rates (a_r) affect the expected asset return,

$$a_2 = a_2(A_1, a_{2,s}, a_{2,r}), \tag{16}$$

and

$$L_a = L_a(A_1, a_{2,s}, a_{2,r}).$$ (17)

Both the expected debt service burden and its expected contingency impact depend on the volume of debt, interest cost and repayment schedule, all taken in relation to current income, i.e.,

$$d_2 = d_2(d_1/y_1),$$ (18)

and

$$L_d = L_d(d_1/y_1).$$ (19)

Compressing these functions into an empirically verifiable consumption function, we obtain,

$$c_1 = f_1(y_1, y_0, ..., y_{-n}, a_1, A_1, a_s, a_r, d_1/y_1, U, \dot{P}, \sigma_y),$$ (20)

i.e., consumption is a function of past and present income, the return and level of financial assets, the current debt-service burden, stock price behavior, and the three measures of macro-risk: unemployment, inflation and variability of income.

3. How Do Consumers Form Expectations?

As shown in Section 2 above, consumer spending depends critically upon household evaluation of their economic prospects. To some extent, expectations can be measured directly from consumer attitude surveys, and the DRI model does include the Consumer Sentiment Index of the Survey Research Center, University of Michigan, as an endogenous variable which affects several categories of the more volatile consumer spending categories. The Consumer Sentiment Index (see fig. 5.1 for its role in the model) is explained by an equation which includes the four-quarter changes in employment, oil prices, payroll tax rates and stock market levels, along with the one-quarter rate of inflation and the levels of Treasury bill rates and the full-employment gap. This equation provides some evidence that consumer expectations are formed from data of the preceding year and to a degree from the data of the current quarter. Lengthening the lags on the variables deteriorates the statistical quality of the equation.[11]

---

[11]The study by Michael C. Lovell finds similar short lags. See Michael C. Lovell, "Why was the Consumer Feeling so Sad?," *Brookings Economic Papers*, 1975, no. 2, pp. 473-479.

Figure 5.1
The Role of Consumer Sentiment

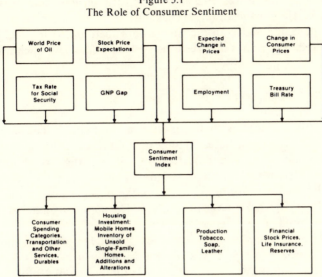

The process by which consumers form expectations can also be identified by the particular concept of income which serves as the most effective explanation of spending behavior. Consumer theory, and also the DRI model, emphasize the distinction between permanent income and transitory income, with the former setting fundamental consumer expenditure levels, and the latter affecting the more volatile investments of consumers in durable goods.

While the definition of permanent income seems to imply a very gradual formation of income expectations, the empirical results point to a relatively quick formation process. Permanent income is defined by a Pascal lag on disposable income with a decay factor of 0.1. This implies a mean lag of nine quarters. The difference between actual and permanent disposable income defines transitory income, and this variable also has a significant role in various consumer spending equations.

The relatively rapid learning process by which consumers form their expectations and their considerable ability to quickly modify behavior helps to explain the volatility of consumption. Whereas consumer spending was viewed as a stabilizer in earlier business cycles and in earlier writings,[12] it has actually played a destabilizing role at the upper turning point of recent business cycles, has reinforced the depths of the declines, but then has also

[12]See the works of Duesenberry, Modigliani and Friedman, cited in footnotes 6 to 9.

proved instrumental in creating the lower turning point and leading the upswing. As the financial factor has also become more important to consumer behavior under an increasing debt load and rising real interest rates, the credit cycle has reinforced the cyclical behavior of spending.

4. The Role of Demography

The above theory applies to the individual household. The number of households and the age structure change over time, reflecting past variations in birth rates, immigration and death rates. These changes come slowly but make a big difference to consumer spending patterns. In the postwar years, the mid-1960s were a turning point, when the postwar population growth began to affect the working-age population. The increasing number of older persons also has a large influence.

The DRI macro model uses only a few highlights of the demographic picture, in contrast to DRI's Age-Income Model which makes this aspect central to consumption analysis. But even the limited use of demography has important implications for the model's behavior. The use of population variables partially deemphasizes income variables, somewhat limiting multipliers.

Particular categories of consumer spending are strongly affected by elements of population structure. Automobile purchases depend on the number of individuals of driving age, who are the pool of potential car buyers. Health-related spending depends on the number of people age 65 or over because of the greater incidence of illness.

Population structure could affect the aggregate saving rate since there is a strong lifetime pattern to saving behavior. However, the population changes actually observed in the postwar period were too limited and too gradual to produce empirically identifiable variations in the saving rate.

5. Empirical Implementation

All of the equations determine consumer spending in terms of 1972 dollars. Real disposable income and relative prices are important in each equation, along with the other determinants, as shown in figs. 5.3, 5.4 and 5.5. The functional forms of the equations were determined from the dynamic simulation properties of the model, both inside and outside the sample period, using the resulting saving rate and income and price elasticities as criteria. Specifics of the consumption equations are given below.

5.1 Automobiles

The determination of the consumption of automobiles reflects a stock-adjustment process: for a given economic situation, there is a desired stock of cars in relation to the number of people of driving age. The actual stock of cars is determined by past sales and decisions on scrappage. Once the consumption of motor vehicles and parts is determined, total unit sales and the split between imported and domestic units are calculated from behavioral equations reflecting relative prices. Economic conditions determine the rate at which the gap between the desired and actual stock is closed.

Permanent and transitory income are important determinants of consumption of motor vehicles and parts. The decision to spend is modified by the Consumer Sentiment Index, the relative price of operating a car and the driving-age population. The income elasticity for automobiles and parts in full-model dynamic simulation is 2.1 in the first year, as shown in table 5.4. The stock of cars determines the sale of parts.

One of the major determinants of consumption of motor vehicles and parts is the cost of car ownership which is defined parallel to the "rental price" of capital goods. The cost of ownership depends on the original purchase costs as seen in the implicit deflator, the price of operating the car as reflected in the gasoline price and the cost of automobile installment loans. The elasticity of purchases with regard to ownership cost is -0.46.

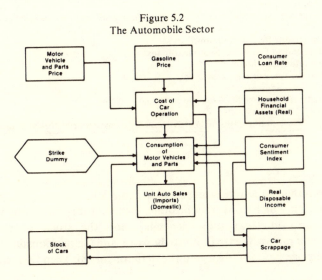

Figure 5.2
The Automobile Sector

Table 5.1
Equation for Real Consumption of Motor Vehicles and Parts

Two-Stage Least Squares

Quarterly (1959:1 to 1981:4): 92 Observations
Dependent Variable: log(CDMV&P72/N18@64)

	Coefficient	Std. Error	t-Stat	Independent Variable
	-6.98790	1.809	-3.863	Constant
1)	3.02987	0.7771	3.899	*log(YDPERM72/N18@64)
2)	2.83881	0.7636	3.718	*log(YD72/YDPERM72)
3)	-0.552503	0.1114	-4.960	log(.6*JCOSTCAR/PC+.4*
				JCOSTCAR(-1)/PC(-1))
4)				PDL(LNJATTC,1,2,FAR)
(-0)	0.298616	0.05413		
(-1)	0.149308	0.02706		
Sum	0.447924	0.08119	5.517	
Avg.	0.333333	0.0		
5)	-1.45027E-05	2.617E-06	-5.541	DMYSTR371
6)	-1.26724	1.016	-1.247	log(KREGCARS(-1)/N18@64)

* marks the two included endogenous variables

R-Bar squared: 0.9451
Durbin-Watson statistic: 1.1310
Standard error of the regression: 0.05715   Normalized: 0.5454

Excluded exogenous variables: RESFRBNB, RESFRBNB(-1), GF72, GF72(-1), EX72, EX72(-1), ZB72, ZB72(-1)

CDMV&P72 is real consumer spending on autos and parts,
N18@64 is the population aged 18 to 64,
YDPERM72 is real permanent income,
YD72 is real disposable income,
JCOSTCAR is the cost of operating a car, including purchase price, interest rate, gasoline and repair prices,
PC is the price deflator for consumption,
JATTC is the Michigan Consumer Sentiment Index,
DMY371 is an auto strike dummy,
KREGCARS is the stock of registered cars,
RESFRBNB is nonborrowed reserves,
GF72 is real federal purchases of goods and services,
EX72 is the real volume of exports,
ZB72 is real profits excluding adjustments for inventory valuation or historical depreciation.

The automobile equation is presented in table 5.1. The equation which converts consumer expenditures on motor vehicles and parts into unit car sales depends upon the stock of cars, the unemployment rate, strikes in the auto industry, and the relationship between the average price paid for a car and the deflator for this spending category.

5.2 Consumer Expenditures on Durables Other Than Autos

The equations for nonauto durables have income elasticities that are strongly affected by risk variables, reflecting the ability to defer these expenditures. The equation for furniture and appliances is shown in table 5.2.

Table 5.2
Equation for Consumption of Furniture and Appliances

Two-Stage Least Squares

Quarterly (1962:1 to 1981:4): 80 Observations
Dependent Variable: log(CDFURN72/N)

	Coefficient	Std. Error	t-Stat	Independent Variable
	-4.16339	0.1872	-22.24	Constant
1)	1.09453	0.1007	10.87	*log(YDPERM72/N)
2)	2.00825	0.2602	7.719	*log(YD72/YDPERM72)
3)	-0.573168	0.1080	-5.305	log(.6*PCDFURN/PC+.4* PCDFURN(-1)/PC(-1))
4)				PDL(logJATTC,1,2,FAR)
(-0)	0.0428127	0.01865		
(-1)	0.0214064	0.009324		
Sum	0.0642191	0.02797	2.296	
Avg.	0.333333	0.0		
5)	0.393490	0.08221	4.786	log(HHNETWORTH(-1)/PC)/N)
6)				PDL(RMCICCBNSREAL,1,2, FAR)
(-0)	-0.00755354	0.001278		
(-1)	-0.00377677	0.0006392		
Sum	-0.0113303	0.001918	-5.909	
Avg.	0.333333	0.0		

* marks the two included endogenous variables

R-Bar squared: 0.9953
Durbin-Watson statistic: 1.2952
Standard error of the regression: 0.01812   Normalized: 0.01092

Excluded exogenous variables: RESFRBNB, RESFRBNB(-1), GF72, GF72(-1), EX72, EX72(-1), ZB72, ZB72(-1)

CDFURN72 is real consumer expenditures on furniture and household equipment,
N is population,
YDPERM72 is real permanent income,
YD72 is real disposable income,
PCDFURN is the deflator for consumer expenditures on furniture and household equipment,
PC is the deflator for consumer expenditures,
JATTC is the Michigan Consumer Sentiment Index,
HHNETWORTH is real net worth of the household sector as measured in the flow-of-funds,
RMCICCBNSREAL is the real interest rate on consumer installment credit,
RESFRBNB is nonborrowed reserves,
GF72 is real federal purchases of goods and services,
EX72 is the real volume of exports,
ZB72 is real profits excluding adjustments for inventory valuation or historical depreciation.

Figure 5.3
Equations for Durables Other Than Automobiles

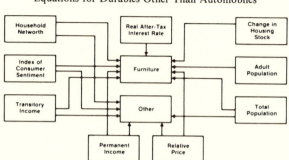

The equation for furniture and appliances per person depends on permanent income with an elasticity of 1.1 and transitory income with an elasticity of 2.0. Relative prices also play an important role in the equation. The price of furniture and appliances in relation to the consumer expenditure deflator has an elasticity of -0.58.

Financial factors enter the equation in two ways. First, household net worth per capita affects spending, reflecting the accumulation of personal savings and the growth of debt as well as the movements of the stock market. Second, the real aftertax interest rate affects spending. It is measured by the prime interest rate corrected by the personal tax rate, adjusted by the increase in the consumer price deflator for the preceding four quarters.

Finally, the Consumer Sentiment Index affects spending for this volatile category. Since expectations also operate through the income and financial variables, the equation portrays consumer spending in this category as subject to highly volatile responses to changes in economic and financial conditions. The structure of the equation is shown in table 5.2 and fig. 5.3.

The equation for other durables is similar in structure. It includes the population below age 16 to reflect its role in toy purchases, records, baby equipment and other child- and youth-oriented items.

5.3 Nondurable Consumption

Clothing and shoes are categorized as nondurables although the equation captures the fact that these items are actually semidurables. True nondurables include food, gasoline, oil and others. For these categories the income elasticity is lower than for the durables and semidurables.

Table 5.3
Equation for Real Consumption of Clothing and Shoes

Two-Stage Least Squares

Quarterly (1962:1 to 1981:4): 80 Observations
Dependent Variable: log(CNCS72/N)

	Coefficient	Std. Error	t-Stat	Independent Variable
	-2.51096	0.1728	-14.53	Constant
1)	0.719269	0.05107	14.08	*log(YDPERM72/N)
2)	1.26189	0.2848	4.430	*log(YD72/YDPERM72)
3)	-0.712965	0.03108	-22.94	log(.6PCNCS/PC+.4* PCNCS(-1)/PC(-1) N))
4)	0.0672558	0.02742	2.453	log(H HNETWORTH(-1)/PC)/N)

* marks the two included endogenous variables

R-Bar squared: 0.9913
Durbin-Watson statistic: 0.8398
Standard error of the regression: 0.01608   Normalized: 0.01221

Excluded exogenous variables: RESFRBNB, RESFRBNB(-1), GF72, GF72(-1), EX72, EX72(-1), ZB72, ZB72(-1)

CNCS72 is real consumer expenditures on clothing and shoes,
N is population,
YDPERM72 is real permanent income,
YD72 is real disposable income,
PCNCS is the deflator for consumer expenditures on clothing and shoes,
PC is the deflator for consumer expenditures,
HHNETWORTH is the net worth of the household sector as measured in the flow-of-funds data,
RESFRBNB is nonborrowed reserves,
GF72 is real federal purchases of goods and services,
EX72 is the real volume of exports,
ZB72 is real profits excluding adjustments for inventory valuation or historical depreciation.

Although food consumption is a necessity, there are many possibilities of switching among types of food consumption as the economy does better or worse. Consumers can buy fewer red meats and eat fewer restaurant meals. The income elasticity is kept down by the inclusion of population. Relative prices are also important. Economic risks are reflected by consumer sentiment.

Gasoline and oil consumption is largely determined by the stock of cars on the road and the miles per gallon obtained by those cars. Decisions to drive more or fewer miles depend upon real income modified by the installment-debt liquidation burden and the unemployment rate. When unemployment is low, more miles are driven to get to and from jobs, and consumers are more likely to travel farther for leisure. Relative prices are also critical, especially in determining leisure mileage.

Clothing and shoes consumption is a semidurable category which generally reflects the pattern exhibited for durable outlays. Spending behavior out of permanent and transitory income is affected by household net worth and relative prices. The equation is shown in table 5.3.

In the equation for other nondurables other than fuel oil, which includes paper goods, nondurable toys and sport supplies, semidurable house furnishings and drug preparations, the short-run income elasticity is less than one, partly the result of the inclusion of population as a separate variable.

Fuel oil consumption, which is separated to permit identification of energy demand, depends on the stock of housing, relative prices and consumer sentiment.

Figure 5.4
Equations for Nondurable Consumption

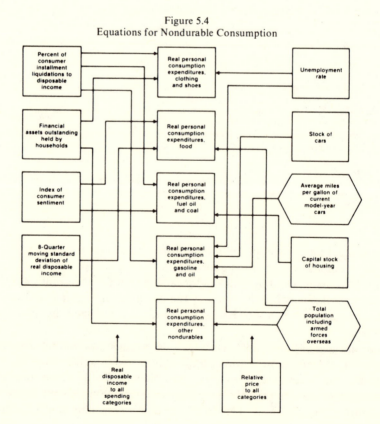

Figure 5.5
Equations for Consumer Services

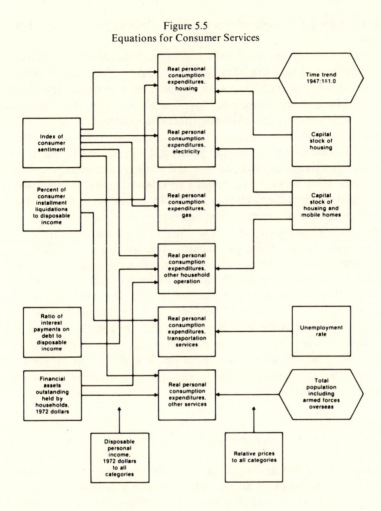

5.4 Services

The equations for consumer services are specified to capture the nature of the recorded data along with the fundamental economic factors.

Housing services are actual and imputed rent on the stock of housing. The equation for housing services depends heavily on the stock of housing and a time trend to reflect growth in real value of a housing unit. This is modified by current income with a low elasticity, relative prices with low elasticity and the Consumer Sentiment Index. The more volatile variables mainly reflect the influence of current conditions and attitudes on decisions to establish and maintain separate households on the part of young people, the retired and "singles."

Consumer outlays for other household operations include sanitary services and telephones. These are heavily determined by the stock of houses. In addition, there is some impact from income, relative prices, the Consumer Sentiment Index and income volatility. Telephone use is one of the channels through which short-run conditions affect these outlays.

Consumer outlays for natural gas and electricity are estimated with individual equations based on the housing stock, relative prices, consumer sentiment and financial assets as part of the energy demands.

Transportation services are mainly two kinds of items: automobile repair and public transportation. The purchases of these services are determined by income and relative prices. The unemployment rate is important in determining the purchases of public transportation and the mileage driven (and thereby the need for car repair). The inclusion of volatile airline transportation also makes the short-run variables important.

Other services, largely health care, have low income and relative price elasticities because so much of the purchase of these services is paid by insurance programs. Because of the government's willingness to pay a larger portion of the health care services performed on the elderly and their greater incidence of sickness, the population age 65 and over is weighted double in the population variables that enter this equation. In addition, the consumption of other services is affected by the financial asset positions of households, disposable income and income volatility.

6. The Dynamics of Consumption: Simulation Tests

To illustrate the dynamic properties of the consumer sector of the model, a set of dynamic simulations was run. They show the variety of reactions for different categories, as well as the sensitivity of the sector as a whole.

6.1 The Impact of Income

Real disposable income is the most important determinant of consumer spending. Categories with high income elasticities, those classified as "easily postponable purchases," suffer most when the ability to finance consumption deteriorates and benefit most when it recovers. A dynamic model simulation was run over history to show the complete-system income elasticities of each income category (table 5.4).

Table 5.4
Effect on Consumption of an Autonomous Increase in Income,
Full-System Income Elasticity[1]
(Percent change in real consumption of each category
for each 1% change in real disposable income)

	Quarters after change				
	1	4	8	12	16
Total Personal Consumption	0.329	0.874	0.778	0.752	0.773
Durable Goods	0.773	2.125	1.718	1.591	1.651
Nondurable Goods	0.258	0.654	0.591	0.577	0.580
Services	0.255	0.661	0.624	0.607	0.621
Autos and Parts	0.915	2.614	1.948	1.710	1.737
Furniture and Household Equipment	0.647	1.629	1.474	1.469	1.512
Other Durable Goods	0.719	1.956	1.715	1.691	1.747
Clothing and Shoes	0.315	0.843	0.643	0.595	0.580
Fuel Oil	0.139	0.332	0.307	0.283	0.257
Gasoline	0.221	0.646	0.793	0.926	1.056
Other Nondurable Goods	0.275	0.748	0.651	0.619	0.624
Transportation	0.248	0.706	0.769	0.844	0.936
Household Operation	0.398	1.036	0.977	0.975	1.020
Other Services	0.434	1.101	1.041	1.025	1.048

[1]These elasticities were calculated on the 1981 version of the DRI model.

The most highly volatile consumption categories are the durables—motor vehicles and parts, furniture and appliances, and others. Purchases of these items can most easily be postponed when income declines. The income elasticity of all durables reached 2.1 in the second quarter (i.e., for each 1.0% rise in real disposable income, a 2.1% rise in durable consumption results). This high elasticity response is not sustained, however, with the impact declining to 1.65 after twelve quarters. Other volatile consumption categories include clothing and shoes, other nondurables, transportation services, and other services. Each of these categories contains items termed necessities with low income elasticities, but also items for which purchases can be postponed.

The stable-consumption categories include food and gasoline consumption and the housing services. The elasticity of all nondurables begins at 0.26 and stabilizes near 0.6. The elasticity of services shows a similar pattern. The timing differences result partly from the impact of stocks on the consumption categories. There are major differences in elasticities and in timing in the subcategories of these aggregates. Some of the services, for example, do not reach their peak effects until the stock of houses and the stock of cars have expanded as a result of the increased income.

6.2 *The Impact of Own-Price Elasticities*

Price elasticities vary considerably in the consumption sector. Postponable goods have a high elasticity while necessities and imputations of rent have low price elasticities. To investigate the effect of an own-price increase, separate simulations were performed in which each implicit deflator was raised by 10%, raising the relative price.

Several categories have substantially higher elasticities in the first quarter than later on. These include autos and parts, clothing and shoes, food and beverages, transportation services and other services. For these categories, trend behavior resumes after much of a price "shock" has worn off.

Table 5.5
Percent Change in Real Consumption Outlays for
Each 1% Change in Own-Price, Full-System Price Elasticity

	Quarters from Initial Price Change							
	1	2	3	4	5	6	7	8
Autos and Parts	-0.21	-0.30	-0.41	-0.47	-0.47	-0.43	-0.39	-0.37
Furniture and Household Eq.	-0.86	-0.83	-0.88	-0.91	-0.90	-0.85	-0.80	-0.78
Other Durable Goods	-1.03	-1.04	-1.04	-1.05	-1.03	-1.01	-0.98	-0.95
Clothing and Shoes	-0.68	-0.68	-0.71	-0.72	-0.72	-0.71	-0.69	-0.68
Food and Beverages	-0.71	-0.50	-0.51	-0.51	-0.48	-0.46	-0.46	-0.46
Gasoline and Oil	-0.78	-0.31	-0.31	-0.31	-0.31	-0.31	-0.31	-0.31
Fuel	-0.21	-0.40	-0.41	-0.41	-0.41	-0.41	-0.41	-0.41
Other Nondurable Goods	-2.01	-2.02	-2.04	-2.08	-2.13	-2.14	2.12	-2.09
Housing	-0.29	-0.29	-0.32	-0.32	-0.32	-0.31	-0.30	-0.31
Household Operation—Electricity	-0.14	-0.14	-0.14	-0.14	-0.14	-0.14	-0.14	-0.14
Household Operation—Gas	-0.45	-0.46	-0.46	-0.46	-0.46	-0.46	-0.46	-0.46
Other Household Operation	-0.78	-0.79	-0.79	-0.80	-0.80	-0.79	-0.79	-0.79
Transportation	-0.11	-0.10	-0.10	-0.10	-0.10	-0.10	-0.09	-0.09
Other Services	-0.89	-0.07	-0.07	-0.04	-0.04	-0.03	-0.03	-0.03

Some other spending categories have price elasticities which increase after the first quarter because consumers take time to adjust their spending patterns. They include furniture and household equipment, other durables, and other nondurables.

The highest long-run price elasticities are for furniture and household equipment and other durables. The lowest long-run price elasticities are for other services, transportation services, housing, and food and beverages.

6.3 Impact of Stocks of Houses, Cars, and People

Spending is affected by the existing stock levels of automobiles, housing, and population. The automobile-related consumption categories include consumption of motor vehicles and parts, and indirectly, transportation services. The presence of a large stock of cars depresses automobile sales, but implies a need for greater gasoline consumption. The housing-related categories include furniture and household equipment, housing services and household operations, with the stock measure exerting a positive influence on consumption outlays. The categories of consumer spending driven to a large extent by population include food and the service categories, particularly other services (including medical care).

To show the effect of stocks of houses, cars, and people on consumer spending, simulations which increased each of these stocks were run. The housing stock was increased by 1.0 million units and then excluded from further adjustment in the simulation. This resulted in $2 billion of total consumption: housing services increased $1.1 billion and household operations $0.7 billion.

Similarly, the automobile stock was increased by 9.6 million units, leading to a first-year reduction of 2 million unit car sales, a reduction of $5 billion in consumer expenditures on motor vehicles and parts, and an increase of $1 billion of gasoline outlays.

Population was increased by 1 million while the other demographic variables were increased proportionately. This led to total consumption increasing by $3 billion, with services increasing $1.5 billion, nondurables $0.9 billion, and durables $0.6 billion. Within these categories, the large increases were on household operations which increased $0.7 billion, other services $1 billion, and food $0.5 billion.

6.4 Reaction to Consumer Boom

A dynamic simulation was developed to demonstrate the built-in adjustment mechanisms of the model to a period of heavy consumption outlays. Real consumption of each of the eight most volatile consumption categories was raised by 20% for four quarters. The mechanisms of the model brought spending abruptly down afterward.

The stock of cars per person had risen to a high level, with a subsequent downward movement forced by the stock-adjustment mechanism of the model. Household debt had been built up significantly to finance the four quarters of high spending. Service of this debt then cut the amount of

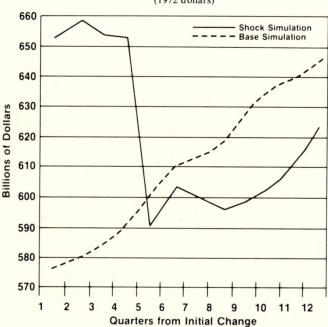

Figure 5.6
Effect of a Consumer Boom on the Economy
(1972 dollars)

disposable income available for spending. In a similar fashion, the excess debt liquidations forced by the higher spending also took away from consumption outlays later. Finally, the consumer sentiment index began to worsen after several quarters—the result primarily of higher inflation. Fig. 5.6 shows the results.

A separate simulation was developed to study the impact of a drop in the consumer sentiment index alone. If the index was moved down by five points, total real consumption dropped 0.6%, with the maximum negative impact not realized for five quarters. Durable outlays were hurt most, declining 1.7%. Nondurables and services both fell 0.4%.

7. The Personal Savings Rate

One of the most striking phenomena of consumer behavior over the last decade has been the sharp decline of the personal savings rate. The 1970s began with the highest peacetime savings rates of the modern statistical era, with rates rising to 8-1/2% by mid-decade. The 1970s concluded with a personal savings rate in the neighborhood of 5%, at least on the pre-1982 vintage data. This decline has been interpreted in various fundamental ways, including the hypothesis that at least one traditional puritan virtue was lost, with the willingness to save dissolved in a sea of excess consumer credit. Another interpretation blames the decline on the development of inflation, or very powerful effects created by the negative real interest rates which prevailed during most of the period of high inflation.

The highly detailed structure of the DRI model explains the decline in the personal savings rate in simpler terms. There is no equation for the personal savings rate, of course, but rather a set of 14 equations for the components of consumer spending. Personal saving is derived from the identity which defines disposable income as the sum of consumption, transfer payments to foreigners, interest paid to business and personal savings, with savings determined as the residual. The personal savings rate is determined by the structure of the consumer spending equations and therefore reflects their underlying theory.

The causes for the decline of the personal savings rate can be identified from model simulations of the 1970s in which some of the extraordinary circumstances of that decade are removed from the historical record, with the economy simulated to calculate the personal savings rate that would have occurred in that circumstance. The principal changes that were explored were the decline in the growth rate of real disposable income and the surge in relative energy prices. An income slowdown might lower the savings rate because other variables such as demography and the need to service stocks of housing and cars might keep consumption growing at higher rates. Energy outlays are a special case of this phenomenon: the initial consumer reaction to the exploding energy prices was to devote a rapidly rising share of income to energy, an increase from 6.0% in 1973 to 9.0% in 1980. Indeed, the rising share of energy in the consumer budget directly accounts for the entire decrease of the personal savings rate, raising the question why consumers took the entire bulge of energy outlays out of saving and none out of other consumption.

A simulation which removes the extraordinary rise of energy from the historical record but leaves real income near the historical levels through personal tax variations shows that the largest part of the decline in the personal savings rate was, indeed, due to the energy factor. Energy outlays have low short-run elasticities both with regard to income and relative price, certainly much less than unity, thereby converting high energy prices into a rising budget share. Other consumer outlays have an aggregate elasticity with regard to real income which is also less than unity, implying that the reduction of real income created by high energy prices does not produce sufficient reductions of other expenditures.

Other forces were also at work in the decade to reduce personal savings, but they appear to be quite small in comparison to the energy factor. The share of disposable income going to transfer payments rose from 13.1% in 1973 to 16.2% in 1980, probably inducing a reduction in the personal savings rate of two or three-tenths of a point. Poor performance of the stock market and the rapidly rising personal tax burden must have had additional effects. The decline of the real interest rate to negative values reduced savings, but according to the equations so far identified, this factor could not have accounted for more than a few tenths of a point.

8. Conclusion

The DRI model represents the consumer sector as considerably less stable than previous theories and models. The model's equations are based on the theory that families are risk-averse and therefore reduce their outlays in times of economic uncertainty. Consumer confidence, which is largely determined by the degree of uncertainty in the economic environment, explicitly affects spending. This factor allows exogenous, confidence-destroying events, such as oil shocks, wars, and political difficulties, to have an effect on consumer behavior and therefore on the economy as a whole.

Consumer spending is also shown to be heavily affected by the volatile financial positions of households. An excessive debt burden has a strong depressing effect. Changing wealth, which is affected by the stock market, requires portfolio adjustments of physical assets and leads to spending variations for durables, nondurables and services.

The physical stock position of households also accentuates cyclical behavior. There are elements of the traditional accelerator, stock-flow adjustments. After years of high automobile, other durable or housing sales, spending will be held down. Changes in economic circumstance which lower the desired stocks of durables have a magnified effect on outlays and help produce high short-run income elasticities. Changing stocks have further magnifying effects on the outlays for the associated service flows for repairs and operation. Real aftertax interest rates also affect spending.

There also are some important stabilizing elements in the consumer equations. The emphasis on demographic factors relates spending partially to predetermined variables that are independent of the economy in the near and intermediate term. The financial and physical stock elements have a self-correcting character. Consumers have been both alert and rational in correcting emerging excesses. If the environment itself were stable, consumers might very well be following an expenditure pattern of balanced growth. Unfortunately, history has provided no periods in which this proposition can be tested.

In summary, the DRI model shows a nervous consumer, subject to the risks of an unstable environment acting on an exposed financial position, forming "permanent" expectations rather quickly and acting to a considerable degree in response to short-term changes. This is a far cry from the viewpoint that treated consumption as passively responding to income, or from the life-time, permanent income theories of stable spending.

CHAPTER 6

HOUSING

1. Introduction

Housing activity is the result of demographic forces, financial market conditions, the population of household-formation ages, the economic situation of households and the profitability of building.[1] Its representation in the DRI model is quite complex. Supply and demand are modeled separately rather than in reduced form. The mortgage market, a sector of the model's financial system, is a critical influence both on builders and households. Incomes, relative prices, household net worth and macro-risks also affect demand. Disequilibrium is modeled both as short-run phenomena in home and mortgage markets and as a long-term stock-adjustment process of the housing stock.

The changes in the financial system are affecting the behavior of housing activity. The increased competition among financial institutions and the phasing out of statutory interest ceilings have cost the housing industry its previous captive supply of mortgage financing. The DRI model does not yet

---

[1]The classic econometric study of housing demand remains Charles F. Roos, "Factors Influencing Residential Building," in his *Dynamic Economics,* Cowles Commission Monograph No. 1 (Bloomington: Principia Press, 1934), pp. 69-110. Sherman Maisel launched the modern revival; see "A theory of Fluctuations in Residential Construction Starts," *American Economic Review* (June 1963), pp. 359-384. The work for the Federal Reserve-MIT model included explicit treatment of the financial flows which convert personal saving into supplies of mortgages and made disequilibrium in the housing market explicit. See John K. Kalchbrenner, "A Model of the Housing Sector," in *Savings Deposits, Mortgages and Housing,* Edward M. Gramlich and Dwight M. Jaffee, eds. (Lexington: D.C. Heath & Co., 1972), pp. 209-234; and Ray Fair and Dwight Jaffee, "Methods of Estimation for Markets in Disequilibrium," *Econometrica* (May 1972), pp. 497-513.

For the development of the more explicit linkages of mortgage flows and housing activity used in the DRI model, see, Gary Fromm and Allen Sinai, "A Policy simulation Model of Deposit Flows, Mortgage Sector Activity and Housing," paper presented at the Econometric Society Meeting, San Francisco, 1974.

A comparison of models as of 1973 can be found in Gary Fromm, "Econometric Models of the Residential Construction Sector: A Comparison," in *National Housing Models,* R.B. Ricks,ed. (Lexington, D.C. Heath & Co., 1973), pp. 125-156.

capture these structural changes fully, and it will take some time before sufficient data are available to identify the new equations.

2. Theoretical Foundations

Investment in housing has long been recognized to depend on the availability of financing as well as such demand factors as income, wealth, household formation, and relative prices. Because housing is a stock that takes time to produce, the demand for housing will not be met precisely on a continuous basis, and the investment rate will be partially determined by the disequilibrium between the desired and the existing stock.

The DRI model's housing sector has four major groups of decision makers: *households* who demand ownership or rental of housing units and supply funds to savings institutions; *builders* who combine finance with labor, materials, and equipment to produce, hold, and sell housing units; *financial intermediaries* who provide the mortgages and construction loans; and *government agencies* which add to financing and subsidize low-income housing. In addition, there are several indirect participants that affect housing activity. They include the *government housing agencies* which supplement the financing of housing in periods of tight money and help provide subsidized housing for particular groups; the *central bank* which controls the overall supply of credit, a particularly important factor in the housing industry which is a near-residual credit user; *producers of building materials* as well as *construction labor* who help determine the relative cost of housing; and finally, *individual savers* who determine much of the overall flow of long-term capital and who allocate their personal savings between housing-oriented financial intermediaries and the open capital market. An adequate model of housing must represent the decisions of each of these groups, since their actions are important and are heavily affected by the macroeconomic environment.

2.1 The Demand for Housing

The demand for housing is a special case of the general theory of consumer spending. Consumer outlays depend upon expectations of income and its variance, relative prices, household net worth and the population structure. Expectations are partly formed by household assessments of the macroeconomic risks.

The consumer demand for housing is specialized in three ways. First, it is an exceptionally large, discrete decision. Purchase of an initial single-family home or upgrading by moving into a larger home or to a better neighborhood is associated with large expenditures for interest, taxes, amortization, maintenance, associated transportation costs, as well as a large initial transaction cost. The house-purchasing decision is a commitment of outlays for many years. The decision to establish a new household and enter the market for rental units also is an exceptionally large one. Young adults setting up their first housing unit and older individuals retaining separate units are making a costly economic decision which is predicated on their expectations of real income and wealth. For these reasons, the demand for housing is modified by household assessments of the macroeconomic risk.

Second, the financial risk associated with the demand for housing takes a particular form. Financing is long term, thus the risk of losing access to credit in the future is less pertinent. But because of the size and duration of the credit embodied in a mortgage, the initial availability is an important consideration. Lenders assess a household's income and balance sheets, and will make loans in accordance with their own ability to attract funds and the relative profitability of mortgage lending. Thus, the demand for housing is affected by the household's ability to obtain mortgage financing, itself a variable highly responsive to the economy's credit conditions.

Third, the demand for housing depends upon the age structure of the population. Demand for single-family homes is determined by the growth of the adult population over age 22. The demand for multifamily units is particularly affected by the increase in the population in the 21-to-28 and over-65 age brackets.

The demand for housing services can be formally summarized as follows, using small letters for micro variables, capital letters for macro variables.

For a typical household, actual or potential, i, the desired level of housing services $c_h^*{}_i$ can be written

$$c_{hi}^* = f(age_i, y_i, U, P, w_i, P_h/P_c, f_i), \tag{1}$$

where age is the age of its head, y_i is the household's expected income, U and P are the macro-risks of unemployment and inflation, w_i is the household's net worth position, P_h is the price of housing services, P_c is the price of consumption as a whole, and f_i is the household's current ability to qualify for a mortgage. Each of the variables in (1) has its own determinants, some specific to the household, others the result of the macroeconomic situation and policies. In particular, P_h/P_c depends on tax policies, mortgage interest rates, energy costs, building costs, and disequilibrium in the housing market. f_i depends on i's income and balance sheet, and macro-financial conditions.

The demand for housing services varies among households according to age. Thus, in aggregating individual housing-service demand for the economy, the age distribution must be given a weight so that

$$C_h^* = F(Y, W, U, P, P_h/P_c, F, AGE_1, ..., AGE_T),$$ (2)

where $AGE_1, ..., AGE_T$ is the age distribution.

2.2 Supply

The desired stock of housing (K_H^*) is proportionate to the desired quantity of housing services, i.e.,

$$K_H^* = bC_h^*.$$ (3)

The level of housing starts, the usual behavioral measure of housing production activity, represents the partial adjustment of the actual to the desired housing stock and depends on the profitability of building. This profitability depends on price-cost relations including interest rates and taxes, the expected level of demand at expected prices, the current disequilibrium in the housing market, and the builder's ability to obtain financing. Thus,

$$I_h = \alpha(K_h^* - K_h) + \beta S_h + \gamma(P_h/P_{cost}) + \delta MTG,$$ (4)

where I_h is the level of housing starts, K_h is the actual stock of housing, and $K_h^*-K_h$ is the long-term disequilibrium in the housing market. S_h is the observed measure of short-term disequilibrium. P_h/P_{cost} is a measure of the profit margin in building. Output prices, such as the median sales price on new homes and a rent index, reflect revenue from housing production. Cost indexes and interest rates on construction loans and mortgages measure the cost side for the builder-developer. Depreciation rules and other tax provisions should also affect activity but are not yet modeled.

MTG is the availability of mortgage or construction financing, as seen in the decision to make new mortgage commitments and enlarge total mortgages outstanding. It is mainly a macro-variable reflecting the absolute size of deposit inflows to various kinds of institutions, the relative rates of return open to them on mortgages and bonds, and the existing structure of their balance sheets. It can be represented in eq. (5):

$$MTG = a(D + R) + bL + cR_m - dR_b - eR_e,$$ (5)

where D is deposit inflows, R is mortgage repayment flows, L is the lenders' portfolio position, R_m is the mortgage rate, R_b is the yield on competing debt and R_c is the cost of funds to the lenders.

2.3 Short- and Long-Term Disequilibria

Disequilibrium in the housing market can be viewed at several different levels of abstraction. In the long run, it is the difference between the desired housing stock and the actual housing stock. For the short run, there are several empirical measures including vacancy rates of rental units and the number of houses offered for sale and sold. These are sensitive measures and important sources of information, and the model includes equations which explain them. The vacancy rate and the number of single-family homes sold are affected by the demand variables. The number of homes for sale is determined by past production and sales. The resultant estimates for these disequilibrium measures enter the supply equations which reflect builder decisions: when the vacancy rate is high and the number of units for sale is large, builders will expect to hold their constructed units for a longer period before sale or rental, and the prices they can charge will be weak. They will therefore build less.

Long-term disequilibrium can be calculated from the relationship between the existing stock of housing and the size of the pertinent age groups of the population. When the stock of housing is large vis-a-vis the population, housing activity is held down; when the population is large in relation to the existing housing supply, housing activity becomes great. The trend in the number of housing units is mainly created by population growth. Their size depends on per capita income.

3. Empirical Implementation

The housing sector is divided into two components—single-family and multifamily—to reflect important differences between the two markets. Purchasers of multi-unit structures are more likely to be investors than owner-occupants, although the investment element has also become more important for the single-family buyer. Financing and taxes also differ between the two groups. Finally, the two types of housing cater to different age groups, multifamily housing being more attractive to the young and old, single units to the middle-aged.

Mobile home purchases and the remaining components of residential construction activity—alterations and repairs, brokerage fees, and the net value of used home purchases—are treated separately in equations of simpler structure.

For each component, there is a demand equation, explaining the number of units sold for single-family units, the number occupied for multi-units. These equations are the empirical counterparts to eq. (2). The supply equations contain the supply element corresponding to (4), including the long-term relation between stocks of housing and the pertinent population segments. The relations among the concepts of housing activity are shown in fig. 6.1.

Figure 6.1
Residential Fixed Investment

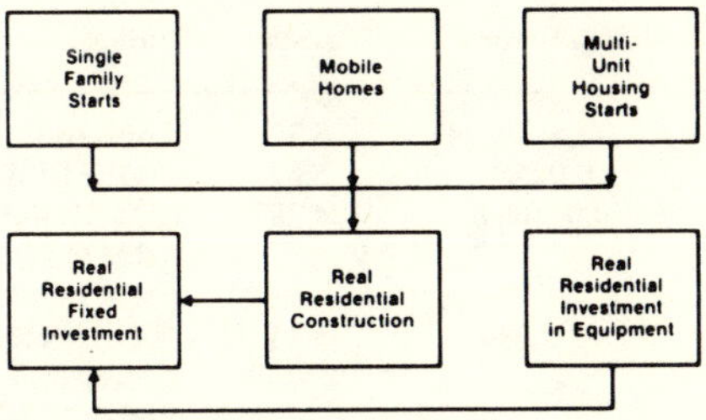

3.1 Single-Family Market

For the single-family market, demand is mainly defined as the number of new single-family homes sold. (Some units are not built for sale but are put up by their initial owners.) Demand is determined by real disposable personal income, consumer confidence, the interest burden of owning a home, and the size of the population most likely to live in single-family dwellings—those between the ages of 22 and 65. Real disposable personal income affects housing demand relatively quickly. Income change is an indicator of new information that affects expected permanent income. Thus the current level of income is the income variable with the closest statistical association with new home sales.

The financial burden of buying a home also has a strong present-period influence and is one of the most important forces influencing the home-buying decision. It is specified as the cost of purchase and financing relative to personal disposable income.

Given the level of homeowning ability, demand is strongly influenced by changes or perceived changes in macroeconomic events. Consumer confidence is an important component of housing demand and carries a significant positive coefficient in the sales equation. The final fundamental determinant of demand—population—helps establish the trend in the number of housing units needed.

The housing starts equation (table 6.1) shows how supply responds to changes in the cost and availability of mortgage money (with a distributed lag

Table 6.1
Equation for Supply of Single-Family Housing Starts

Ordinary Least Squares

Quarterly (1964:1 to 1981:4): 72 Observations
Dependent Variable: HUSTS1

	Coefficient	Std. Error	t-Stat	Independent Variable
	15.0199	2.793	5.377	Constant
1)	0.143262	0.02569	5.578	1/OFFER@SOLD
2)	0.00458102	0.001069	4.287	(PMHU1NSOLD/27.6)/ ((RMMTGCOM2575NS/7.596)* PICR)*(N22&—N65&)
3)	-30.6077	5.739	-5.333	(KQHUSTS1(-1)/(N22&(-1)— N65&(-1))
4)				PDL(MTGCOMNEW%PICR(-1), 2,5,FAR)
(-1)	0.00411021	0.001022		
(-2)	0.00306704	0.0003037		
(-3)	0.00213443	0.0002945		
(-4)	0.00131239	0.0004621		
(-5)	0.000600912	0.0003701		
Sum	0.0112250	0.0007687	14.60	
Avg	1.21842	0.2901	4.200	
5)	-0.154971	0.05091	-3.044	DMYWINTER77&78
6)	-0.144200	0.03605	-4.000	PCSHHOPEN

R-Bar squared: 0.9205
Durbin-Watson statistic: 1.3430
Standard error of the regression: 0.06595   Normalized: 0.06519

HUSTS1 is single-unit housing starts,
OFFER@SOLD is the ratio of homes for sale to homes sold,
PMHU1NSOLD is the median sales price of homes sold,
RMMTGCOM2575NS is the effective mortgage commitment rate with a 25% downpayment and a 25-year life,
PICR is the implicit price deflator for private residential construction,
N22& is population 22 years old or older, N65& is population 65 years or older,
KQHUSTS1 is the stock of single unit homes,
MTGCOMNEW%PICR is the real level of new mortgage commitments,
DMYWINTER77&78 is a dummy for extraordinarily harsh winter quarters,
PCSHHOPEN is the composite price deflator for electricity and natural gas.

Figure 6.2
Single-Family Housing Starts

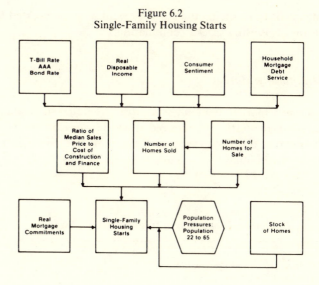

reflecting the time required to initiate housing construction), to the disequilibrium between existing and desired housing, and the rental price equivalent of new homes. The mortgage market exhibits characteristics of rationing. Therefore, changes in the real volume of mortgage commitments have an important role.

After financial market conditions, the rental price of housing is the most important factor affecting purchaser decisions. The price-cost relationship is specified in the equation as the ratio of the median sales price of new single-family homes to the cost index of residential construction and the mortgage rate.

Disequilibrium between existing and desired housing is included in the starts equation in two ways. First, the level of new single-family home sales relative to the inventory of homes to be sold measures short-term disequilibrium. Builders' production decisions are strongly influenced by the size of their unsold inventory relative to their rate of sales because inventory determines their expectation of the speed of sale and the price likely to be realized. The equation for inventory disequilibrium relies on the previous history of housing starts, recent disposable income, consumer confidence and an availability measure for financial markets.

The long-term measure of supply and demand is the relationship of adult population aged 22 to 65 to the stock of single-family houses. This measure reflects the long waves in building activity and population. It is also an effective means of introducing the stock-flow adjustment created by recent past variations of housing stock accumulation.

3.2 The Multifamily Market

In the multifamily market, demand-side forces are reflected in equations for the desired stock of units. This desired stock depends on the population, permanent income, transitory income with a negative coefficient and the relationship between building costs and rents (table 6.2).

Table 6.2
Equation for the Desired Multiunit Housing Stock

Ordinary Least Squares

Quarterly (1960:1 to 1980:4): 84 Observations
Dependent Variable: KQHUSTS2&/N

	Coefficient	Std. Error	t-Stat	Independent Variable
	0.0583648	0.001401	41.67	Constant
1)	0.0109099	0.0006014	18.14	YDPERM72/N
2)	-0.00718857	0.002581	-2.785	YDTRANS72/N
3)	-0.00446380	0.002935	-1.521	PICR/PCSHOUS

R-Bar squared: 0.9617
Durbin-Watson statistic: 0.0649
Standard error of the regression: 0.001317   Normalized: 0.01409

KQHUSTS2& is the stock of multiple units per capita,
N is population,
YDPERM72 is real permanent disposable income,
YDTRANS72 is real transitory disposable income,
PICR is the implicit price deflator for private residential construction,
PCSHOUS is the deflator for housing services, a measure of rent.

The low Durbin-Watson ratio is to be expected since it is the purpose of the equation to identify the disequilibrium of the actual housing stock from the desired (trend) stock.

On the supply side, many of the forces affecting builder decisions in the single-family market also apply. Builders are assumed to supply starts in response to the disequilibrium between the desired and actual housing stock, with an adjustment coefficient of 0.17. The availability of mortgage money is also important, along with the mortgage rate. The extent of government subsidized units also plays a role.

3.3 Other Elements in Modeling Residential Construction

Several other equations are needed to complete the calculation of real residential fixed investment. The conversion of starts into construction activity is represented by equations which reflect time profiles close to those used by BEA in its estimates. Because each start has a greater real value as living standards rise, real disposable income is an additional explanatory variable.

The number of single-family units for sale is calculated by a fitted near-identity linking starts and previous sales. Residential investment in equipment is derived from the housing stock and recent starts. Mobile home shipments are modeled in an equation partly reflecting multiunit activity, partly representing a consumer durable purchase process.

Table 6.3
Supply of Multiunit Housing Starts

Least Squares with First-Order Autocorrelation Correction

Quarterly (1960:1 to 1980:4): 84 Observations
Dependent Variable: HUSTS2&

	Coefficient	Std. Error	t-Stat	Independent Variable
	0.514414	0.1405	3.660	Constant
1)	0.173293	0.07025	2.472	(KQHUSTS2&NSTAR—
				KQHUSTS2&(-1))
2)				PDL(REALHUDSUB5&(-2),2,4,
				FAR)
(-2)	0.165842	0.2029		
(-3)	0.449554	0.1452		
(-4)	0.516484	0.1577		
(-5)	0.366633	0.1191		
Sum	1.49851	0.4841	3.095	
Avg	1.72332	0.4736	3.639	
3)	-0.0383532	0.01377	-2.785	RMMTGCOM2575NS
4)	0.00381655	0.0008587	4.444	REALMTGCOMNEW(-1)
	0.460311	0.05825	7.897	RHO

R-Bar squared: 0.9327
Durbin-Watson statistic: 2.0157
Standard error of the regression: 0.05473   Normalized: 0.1001

HUSTS2& is the number of multiunit housing starts,
KQHUSTS2&NSTAR is the desired multiunit housing stock as estimated by the equation in table 6.2,
KQHUSTS2& is the stock of multiunit housing,
REALHUDSUB5& is the number of units assisted by the Department of Housing and Urban Development,
RMMTGCOM2575NS is the effective mortgage commitment rate with a 25% downpayment and a 25-year life,
REALMTGCOMNEW is the real level of new mortgage commitments.

4. Simulation Properties

The performance of the equations is good, given the volatility of housing. The average size of the residuals, an indication of the predictive power of the equations, is quite small and compares favorably with similar estimates reported for other housing models.[2]

Single-equation tests, however, are only one measure of an equation's performance in the context of a structural model. Dynamic simulations are also important for assessing the performance of the sector, with feedback effects between the housing sector and other areas of the economy allowed to occur. For the housing equations, full dynamic-solution errors exceed single-equation errors substantially. The increase is due less to specification problems in the housing sector than to the complexity of forces acting on housing, particularly financial conditions. The errors shown for the full historical solutions are typical of actual forecasting results.

The dynamic properties and the stock-flow adjustment process as a source of cyclical variation are illustrated by some policy simulations.

4.1 Fiscal Policy Effects

To assess the impact of stimulative fiscal policy, two tests were performed. Personal taxes were reduced by $10 billion per quarter relative to a dynamic solution of the model over the period 1966:1 to 1977:4. In a separate simulation, nondefense government expenditures were increased by the same amount. In both cases, the response of housing shows an extended but moderate cyclical swing (table 6.4). Housing, however, is aided in the near term only in the case of the tax cut. The income stimulus raises the desired stock of housing. Deposit flows to commercial banks and thrift institutions rise, mortgage credit becomes more ample, the volume of housing starts is enhanced, and the adjustment of the actual to the desired housing stock is accelerated. With interest rates allowed to move with market forces and with unchanged bank reserves, mortgage rates are 11 basis points lower after two quarters, and the volume of housing activity rises: housing starts are 15,000 units higher in the first year. Thereafter, the enlarged housing stock and upward pressure on interest rates create a small loss of housing activity. The cumulative result is a decrease of 62,000 units for the three years.

In the case of the expenditure increase, the rise in income leads immediately to an increase in housing demand. However, the greater deficit financing

[2]Fromm, ibid.

Table 6.4
Impact of Stimulative Fiscal Policies
on Housing Activity[1]

	\$10 Billion Cut in Personal Taxes					
	Year 1		Year 2		Year 3	
	Change	% Change	Change	% Change	Change	% Change
—Billions of Dollars						
Personal Disposable Income	19.0	2.9	26.5	3.9	29.9	4.2
Personal Savings	7.5	21.1	7.0	18.1	8.3	22.1
New Mortgage Commitments	-0.5	-2.0	-2.6	-10.9	-5.1	-18.9
Residential Construction	0.3	0.8	-0.2	-0.5	-1.2	-2.9
—Millions of Units						
Housing Starts	0.015	1.2	-0.016	-1.3	-0.061	-4.0
	\$10 Billion Increase in Nondefense Purchases					
—Billions of Dollars						
Personal Disposable Income	8.0	1.2	11.3	1.7	11.9	1.7
Personal Savings	2.5	7.2	3.1	7.9	3.9	10.4
New Mortgage Commitments	-0.6	-2.8	-2.3	-9.4	-4.0	-14.5
Residential Construction	-0.1	-0.2	-0.8	-2.2	-1.6	-3.7
—Millions of Units						
Housing Starts	-0.007	-0.6	-0.049	-3.9	-0.084	-5.5

[1]These and the following simulations were performed on the 1978 edition of the DRI model.

partially crowds out housing. Higher short-term interest rates cause a loss of deposits, a drop in mortgage activity, and a cumulative loss of 140,000 units after three years.

4.2 Monetary Policy Effects

As housing activity is highly sensitive to the availability of credit, a simulation in which the monetary authorities inject an additional and sustained \$1 billion of nonborrowed bank reserves through open market operations shows a housing response which is both dramatic and quick (table 6.5). Mortgage activity rises sharply with the easing of monetary policy. New and outstanding mortgage commitments increase with the higher deposit flows. After some lags, mortgage acquisitions and outstanding mortgages rise. Mortgage rates decline as part of the easier credit situation.

Table 6.5
Impact of Monetary Policy on
Total Housing Activity

	$1 Billion Increase in Nonborrowed Reserves					
	Year 1		Year 2		Year 3	
	Change	% Change	Change	% Change	Change	% Change
—Billions of Dollars						
Money Supply	3.9	2.2	5.3	2.8	5.1	2.6
New Mortgage Commitments	6.3	27.3	4.8	20.0	1.4	5.3
Residential Construction	4.1	10.4	4.1	11.5	0.4	1.0
—Percent						
Federal Funds Rate	-1.66	—	-0.38	—	-0.11	—
Mortgage Rate	-0.12	—	-0.07	—	0.04	—
—Millions of Units						
Housing Starts	0.210	17.0	0.133	10.7	-0.026	-1.7

Figure 6.3
Change in Housing Starts as a Result of a
$1 Billion Increase in Nonborrowed Reserves
(Millions of units)

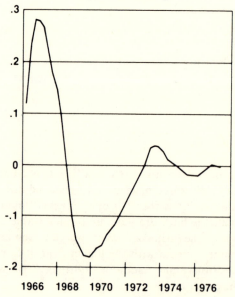

Housing starts respond sharply to the increased supply of mortgages and lower mortgage rates: the peak of the response occurs after four quarters, when total housing starts are almost 300,000 units above the base solution. After eleven quarters, the larger housing stock and the stock-adjustment process bring new housing starts below the base path. But the long-term cumulative effect of easy money is a modest net increase in housing.

4.3 Agency Activity

The impact of additional mortgage market support from the housing agencies, FNMA, GNMA, and from FHLMC was tested in two separate simulations. In each case, $1 billion of additional advances (annual rate) was assumed for each quarter. In both cases, the advances have a moderately positive impact on the supply of mortgages. In the near-term, advances by FNMA and GNMA have a larger impact on housing starts than those from FHLMC, in part due to the fact that mortgages purchased by FNMA and GNMA are purchased from all institutions whereas those by FHLMC are

Table 6.6
Impact of Secondary Mortgage Market Support
on Total Housing Activity

	A $1 Billion Increase in FNMA and GNMA Mortgage Advances					
	Year 1		Year 2		Year 3	
	Change	% Change	Change	% Change	Change	% Change
—Millions of Units Housing Starts	0.019	1.6	-0.007	-0.6	-0.004	-0.3
—Billions of Dollars Residential Construction	0.5	1.2	-0.1	-0.4	-0.1	-0.2
	A $1 Billion Increase in FHLMC Mortgage Commitments					
	Year 1		Year 2		Year 3	
	Change	% Change	Change	% Change	Change	% Change
—Millions of Units Housing Starts	0.012	1.0	0.008	0.7	0.004	0.2
—Billions of Dollars Residential Construction	0.2	0.6	0.2	0.7	0.1	0.3

purchased only from savings and loan associations. The FHLMC also deals primarily in single-family housing. In the case of FNMA and GNMA purchases, the impact in the first year is about 26,000 starts (table 6.6) or $500 million of extra construction activity.

5. Concluding Comments

The modelling of housing activity is a particular challenge because this sector is affected so heavily by long-term forces of population growth, by short-term disequilibria created by income and confidence swings, and by extreme variations of financial conditions.

The housing industry remains the principal channel for monetary policy to make itself felt on the economy. In Chapter 4 it was shown that housing accounts for significantly more than half of the total direct impact of monetary policy on aggregate demand, a remarkable condition, considering that housing is only about 5% of GNP. Clearly, the fiscal policy simulations reported in Chapter 2 show that housing is the final demand that is typically crowded out by measures of fiscal stimulus. Whether the current structure of the housing industry, with these vulnerabilities, is sufficient to create an improvement in housing standards along with rising real incomes remains to be seen, but the econometric study of the housing sector seems to produce mainly negative implications.

CHAPTER 7

BUSINESS FIXED INVESTMENT

1. Introduction

The modern econometric theory of business fixed investment, developed by Dale Jorgenson,[1] provides the framework for the investment equations in the DRI model. The events of the fifteen years since Jorgenson's basic work have required some refinements and extensions, to be sure. These include: (1) a broader approach to the calculation of the cost of capital; (2) recognition of variations in macroeconomic and financial risk; (3) a more elaborate treatment of the process of formation of expectations including elements of surprise and error, and (4) modeling of the investment requirements for environmental improvement through pollution abatement.

The DRI model focusses on two macro concepts of investment, producers' durable equipment and nonresidential construction, both in real terms. Near-recursive blocks contain equations for twenty-two individual industries, three categories of nonresidential building construction, and for light and heavy trucks.

2. Theory

The Jorgenson theory defines the capital stock that business would desire in order to produce its expected stream of future output. This desired capital

[1]Dale W. Jorgenson, "Capital Theory and Investment Behavior," *American Economic Review, Proceedings* (May 1963), pp. 247-259; also Robert E. Hall and Dale W. Jorgenson, "Tax Policy and Investment Behavior," *American Economic Review* (June 1967), pp. 391-414; Robert E. Hall and Dale W. Jorgenson, "Application of the Theory of Optimum Capital Accumulation." in *Tax Incentives and Capital Spending,* ed. Gary Fromm (Washington, D.C.: Brookings Institution, 1971), pp. 9-60.

For an earlier account of the DRI model's modifications of the Jorgenson approach, see Andrew F. Brimmer and Allen Sinai, "The Effects of Tax Policy on Capital Formation, Corporate Liquidity and the Availability of Investable Funds: A Simulation Study," *Journal of Finance* (May 1976), pp. 287-308, and Allen Sinai, "Tax Expenditures and Business Capital Spending," Testimony presented at Hearings on Tax Expenditures, House Committee on Ways and Means, March 17, 1979, pp. 353-381.

stock depends on the firm's production function and on factor prices. In particular, the factor price for capital is its rental price which depends on the interest rate or a broader cost measure for financial capital, the depreciation rate, and tax parameters which reflect both the rate structure and special features such as investment tax credits or special depreciation allowances. Thus

$$K^* = pQ^e/c, \qquad (1)$$

where K^* is the desired capital stock, p is the price level, Q^e is expected output, and c is the rental price of capital in nominal terms. Eq. (1) is derived from the optimal output-capital ratio Q^e/K^*, which must equal the ratio of rental price of capital to output price as a condition of profit maximization.

In the original Jorgenson formulation, Q^e was estimated from a distributed lag formulation on past output. After the more violent business cycles of the recent past, expectations are affected more strongly by current conditions as business shortens its planning horizons, discounts its views of the future with a larger risk premium and attaches more information value to present evidence from the market. As a result

$$Q^e = \alpha_1 Q_L^e + \alpha_2 Q_S^e, \qquad (2)$$

where Q_L^e is the long-term, or normal, expectation of future output, based on an adaptive expectation process, and Q_S^e is the short-term expectation based on observed current output behavior. Whether Q^e meets the criterion of rational expectations, defined both in terms of unbiased expectation of future output and variability around its mean, is an empirical question.

The rental price of capital has also evolved into a more sophisticated measure, utilizing the submodel of nonfinancial corporate flow-of-funds behavior as the determinant of the amounts of finance from different sources. The weighted interest rates and equity rates of return constitute the unit cost of financial capital, which is combined with the tax and depreciation parameters to determine the rental price of capital.

The firm has a financial plan F.

$$F = D_L + D_S + E, \qquad (3)$$

where D_L is long-term debt, D_S is short-term debt, and E is equity. Each source of financing has a cost per dollar, c_L, c_S, and c_E, where the cost varies with the amount of financing from each source already reflected on the balance sheet and the volumes currently being sought. The cost of equity capital is the dividend-price ratio plus expected growth in earnings per share. The total cost of the financial plan C_F is

$$C_F = c_L D_L + c_S D_S + c_E E,$$ (4)

which has the marginal conditions

$$dC_F/dD_L = c_L, \ dC_F/dD_S = c_S, \text{ and } dC_F/dE = c_E.$$ (5)

The incremental cost of financing a particular investment is

$$I = dC_F/dD_L \ \Delta \ D_L + dC_F/dD_S \ \Delta \ D_S + dC_F/dE \ \Delta \ E,$$ (6)

or

$$I = c_L \ \Delta \ D_L + c_S \ \Delta \ D_S + c_E \ \Delta \ E.$$ (7)

The unit cost of financing investment therefore is

$$c = c_L(D_L/I) + c_S(D_S/I) + c_E(E/I),$$ (8)

and this is the parameter which is combined with the tax and depreciation parameters to calculate the rental price of investment which, under the neoclassical Jorgensonian assumptions, is equal to the rental price of capital, c.[2] All debt and equity components in the cost of capital are generated endogenously through nonfinancial corporate flow-of-funds behavior.

The statutory need for pollution abatement expenditures is a further modification to the theory. It can be viewed as a modification of the desired capital stock. Thus, for any given expected output Q^e,

$$K^{*1} = (pQ^e/c)(1 + PABE),$$ (9)

where $PABE$ is the percentage which pollution abatement expenditures add to investment expenditures.

Actual investment, in the modern theory, is viewed as a partial adjustment of the capital stock toward the desired level, or

$$I = f(K^* - K_{-1}) + \alpha K_{-1},$$ (10)

[2]Previous attempts to incorporate the effects of finance on business fixed investment include W. H. L. Anderson, *Corporate Finance and Fixed Investment* (Cambridge, Mass.: Harvard University Press, 1964) and John Lintner, "Corporation Finance: Risk and Investment," in *Determinants of Investment Behavior*, ed. R. Ferber (New York: National Bureau of Economic Research, 1967), pp. 215-254. Tobin's "q" theory is a more recent approach to modelling the effects of finance on investment. See James Tobin and William C. Brainard, "Asset Markets and the Cost of Capital," in *Economic Progress, Private Values and Public Policy: Essays in Honor of William Fellner*, Richard Nelson and Bela Balassa, eds. (Amsterdam: North-Holland Publishing Co., 1977), pp. 235-262.

where K^* is the desired stock, K_{-1} the existing stock at the end of the previous period, and α is the replacement coefficient in the existing capital stock. The equation for investment can then be expressed as the basis for the empirical work,

$$I = g((pQ^e/c)(1 + PABE) - K_{-1}) + \alpha K_{-1}. \qquad (11)$$

3. Empirical Implementation

There are three principal sets of issues in the conversion of the theoretical eq. (11) into empirical form: How are output expectations formed and what is the reaction to surprises? How is the cost of capital measured and what is the adjustment for financial risk? How is the pollution abatement component modeled?

3.1 Output Expectations and Surprises

The typical firm has a long-term investment plan based on its assessment of the economy's prospects and its own market position and opportunities. Given the economic lives of large projects and the lengthy production process of capital projects, a long-term perspective is inevitable. However, a sizable fraction of all investment is not of this type, such as the purchase of automobiles and trucks, office equipment, and industrial, construction and farm equipment of a replacement or modernization character. Further, the large-scale projects can be postponed or stretched out. Short-term economic conditions therefore can modify investment decisions both by directly affecting the near-term profitability of the investments and by moderating the gradually formed long-term expectations.

Q_L^e is measured by an eight-quarter distributed lag on output, where output is real final sales minus government production and housing services. The average lag is 4.7 quarters. The equation is fitted in an autoregressive transformation to further reflect the lags of adjustment (table 7.1 and fig. 7.1).

Short-term expectations, Q_S^e, are measured in two forms in the equation: a "surprise" element in output, equal to the difference between actual current output and the long-term expectation, i.e.,

$$Q_S^e = Q - Q_L^e. \qquad (12)$$

The "surprise" element is measured by the difference between expected and actual output, where expected output is defined by the Pascal lag in the

Jorgenson variable for output. Because of the importance of manufacturing in the variation of total investment, the surprise concept is applied more

Table 7.1
Equation for Investment in Producers' Durable Equipment

Least Squares with First-Order Autocorrelation Correction

Quarterly (1959:1 to 1981:4): 92 Observations
Dependent Variable: IPDENR72

	Coefficient	Std. Error	t-Stat	Independent Variable
	-15.3512	4.206	-3.650	Constant
1)	-0.140029	0.07666	-1.827	KNPDENR72(-1)
2)	0.372099	0.1040	3.576	UCAPFRBMEXP* KNPDENR72(-1)
3)				PDL(LETIPDENR72PQC(-2),1, 6,FAR)
(-2)	0.00185888	0.001070		
(-3)	0.00154907	0.0008917		
(-4)	0.00123925	0.0007133		
(-5)	0.000929441	0.0005350		
(-6)	0.000619627	0.0003567		
(-7)	0.000309814	0.0001783		
Sum	0.00650609	0.003745	1.737	
Avg	1.66667	0.0		
4)				PDL(NFCDEBTSERVICE(-1),1, 6,FAR)
(-1)	-3.39060	2.715		
(-2)	-2.82550	2.263		
(-3)	-2.26040	1.810		
(-4)	-1.69530	1.358		
(-5)	-1.13020	0.9051		
(-6)	-0.565099	0.4526		
Sum	-11.8671	9.504	-1.249	
Avg	1.66667	0.0		
5)	-0.151391	0.01962	-7.716	QSTAR—LETOUTPUTPABE
6)	3.16685	1.152	2.749	DMYVIETWAR
	0.883087	0.05588	15.80	RHO

R-Bar squared: 0.9962
Durbin-Watson statistic: 1.6451
Standard error of the regression: 1.559   Normalized: 0.02139

IPDENR72 is real purchases of producers' durable equipment,
KNPDENR72 is the real stock of producers' real equipment,
UCAPFRBMEXP is the expected utilization rate,
LETIPDENR72PQC is the Jorgenson variable for the rental price of capital as described in the text,
NFCDEBTSERVICE is the ratio of interest payments to cash flow of nonfinancial corporations,
QSTAR is expected real output based on a Koyck distributed lag with a decay factor of 0.1,
DMYVIETWAR is a dummy for extra investment induced by military outlays during the Vietnam War.

Figure 7.1
Producers' Durable Equipment

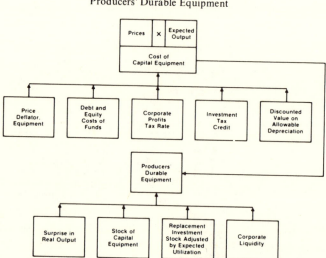

specifically to this sector. Surprise in the capacity utilization[3] in manufacturing is defined by the difference between the actual utilization rate and an expected rate defined by a Pascal lag with a decay factor of 0.1.

3.2 Measuring the Cost of Capital and Financial Risk

The variables of the flow-of-funds block for the nonfinancial corporate sector are the basis for the composite cost of capital. The sources of debt capital include long-term bonds, bank loans, commercial paper and mortgages, with interest rates applicable to each instrument. The cost of equity capital is the dividend yield on the S&P 500 index plus the expected growth in earnings per share expressed as a Koyck lag on historical values. The cost of financial capital is the sum of the weighted average cost of debt and equity.

The cost of capital is valued on an average rather than a marginal basis. While it would be desirable to identify the marginal cost, it is empirically impossible. The financing mix in any one quarter is too volatile, and some of the debt instruments with low nominal costs, such as short-term debt, are

---

[3]The role of utilization and capacity was highlighted in Frank DeLeeuw, "The Demand for Capital Goods by Manufacturers: A Study of Quarterly Time Series," *Econometrica* (July, 1962), pp. 407-423. Also see Robert Eisner, "A Distributed Lag Investment Function," *Econometrica* (January, 1970), pp. 1-29.

available in quantities limited by the liquidity condition of the balance sheet. In effect, the true optimal combination of financing has a greater fixity of proportion than the actual mix observed in a short period, and interest rates averaged over appropriate intervals are the effective interest costs pertinent to investment decisions.

To introduce a more sensitive measure of liquidity constraints and financial risk, a measure of debt service in relation to cash flow is employed.[4] This variable, defined as the ratio of interest charges to cash flow, reflects the drag of the existing debt burden on investment decisions: when high rates boost interest cost—as they do in periods of credit stringency—businesses become reluctant to borrow more and are faced by limits on borrowing. Diminished cash flow also makes interest payments more burdensome. The measure is also the inverse of the traditional "coverage" ratio, a measure of financial risk used by lenders to evaluate credit-worthiness. The debt service variable is able to reflect credit crunch conditions through lessened cash flow, rapidly rising outstanding debt and higher interest rates. This measure is empirically superior to balance sheet ratios which measure liquidity conditions more directly.

3.3 Modeling Pollution Abatement

The legally required modifications of the capital stock of processing industries add to investment requirements. Little is known of the true magnitudes of these requirements, with the principal information coming from an annual government survey of abatement expenditures. To use this information in the investment equation, the long-term output expectation variable is modified by the percentage of investment outlays devoted to abatement. This procedure assumes that these expenditures are fully incremental rather than substitutes for other investment in their initial, though not their later, impact.

4. Nonresidential Construction

The equation for nonresidential construction follows the same approach as equipment, with some modifications (table 7.2 and fig. 7.2). The "surprise" measures are less important because actual construction cannot respond quickly to the current situation. And the cost of capital has a different

---

[4]John R. Meyer and Edward Kuh, *The Investment Decision: An Empirical Study* (Cambridge: Harvard University Press, 1957) employed cash flow variables.

Table 7.2
Investment in Nonresidential Structures

Least Squares with First-Order Autocorrelation Correction

Quarterly (1964:1 to 1981:4): 72 Observations
Dependent Variable: ICNR72

	Coefficient	Std. Error	t-Stat	Independent Variable
	105.520	59.54	1.772	Constant
1)	-0.0953569	0.05657	-1.686	KNCNR72(-1)
2)	0.186295	0.06632	2.809	UCAPFRBMEXP*KNCNR72(-1)
3)				PDL(NFCDEBTSERVICE(-1),1, 6,FAR)
(-1)	-3.89109	2.029		
(-2)	-3.24258	1.691		
(-3)	-2.59406	1.353		
(-4)	-1.94555	1.015		
(-5)	-1.29703	0.6764		
(-6)	-0.648516	0.3382		
Sum	-13.6188	7.102	-1.918	
Avg	1.66667	0.0		
4)				PDL(LETICNR72PQC(-2),1,6, FAR)
(-2)	0.00190411	0.0007574		
(-3)	0.00158676	0.0006311		
(-4)	0.00126941	0.0005049		
(-5)	0.000952055	0.0003787		
(-6)	0.000634703	0.0002525		
(-7)	0.000317352	0.0001262		
Sum	0.00666439	0.002651	2.514	
Avg	1.66667	0.0		
5)	-283.913	147.8	-1.921	KNCNR72(-1)/GNP72FE(-1)
	0.917771	0.06981	13.15	RHO

R-Bar squared: 0.9320
Durbin-Watson statistic: 1.7286
Standard error of the regression: 1.063   Normalized: 0.02449

ICNR72 is real nonresidential construction,
KNCNR72 is the stock of structures,
UCAPFRBMEXP is the expected industrial utilization rate, based on the history of the actual rate with a decay coefficient of 0.1,
NFCDEBTSERVICE is the ratio of interest payments to cash-flow of nonfinancial corporations,
LETICNR72PQC is the Jorgenson measure of desired capital stock,
GNP72FE is potential GNP.

composition, of course, with more weight on long-term debt cost and less on equity financing.

While the distributed lag on output is the same for equipment as for structures, the speed of adjustment to the desired capital stock is shorter. The average lag of adjustment for equipment is 12.6 quarters as contrasted to 23.9 quarters for structures.

Figure 7.2
Nonresidential Construction

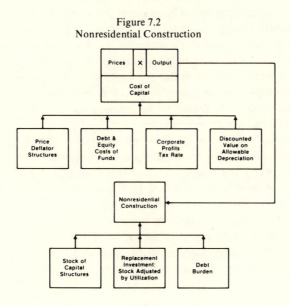

5. Other Equations

The detailed one- and two-digit industry-investment equations are discussed in the chapter on industry variables. Equations for various categories of construction are based on simple bridge equations driven by the determinants of total nonresidential construction and modified by the institutional characteristics affecting various types of construction.

The equations for small trucks embody both investment and consumption elements, and are partly driven by automobile sales, partly by equipment variables. Large-truck sales are determined by the variables which affect business investment in equipment.

6. Simulation Test: The Response of Investment to Higher Sales[5]

To illustrate the working of the investment sector, two simulations have been run. The first shows the response of investment to increased sales. Despite the neoclassical formulation of the investment equations, including the use of sophisticated measures of the rental price of capital and liquidity, it still remains true that movements of investment are heavily influenced by changes in sales expectations and the actual levels of sales and output. Traditionally, it was the accelerator-capital stock adjustment theories that emphasized these factors, and the arrival of the Jorgenson theory appeared to place investment on a different theoretical track. But even within the new framework, the data still point strongly toward a dominance of output effects over the various relative price effects. It seems to be impossible to have a high rate of investment in a slack market economy.

The solution showing the response of investment to stronger markets is summarized in table 7.3. The initial impulse to the simulation is a boost in government purchases designed to raise real final sales by 1%, assuming an accommodating monetary policy with nonborrowed reserves left unchanged. Multiplier effects boost consumer spending, though housing investment suffers small losses due to some crowding out.

The response of investment to output is strong. The boost in expected output raises the desired capital stock. The two "surprise" terms in the equation for equipment give a quick lift to spending. Cash flow is boosted

Table 7.3
Response of Investment to an Increase in Sales[1]
(Percent difference in levels)

	Year 1	Year 2	Year 3	Year 4	Year 5
Real GNP	1.3	1.5	1.4	1.0	0.6
Investment in Equipment	1.8	3.0	2.7	1.1	-1.2
Investment in Structures	1.4	2.4	2.2	0.9	-1.3
Stock of Equipment	0.4	0.9	1.2	1.2	0.8
Stock of Structures	0.1	0.4	0.5	0.6	0.4
		Elasticities			
Investment in Equipment	1.4	2.0	1.9	1.1	-2.0
Investment in Structures	1.1	1.6	1.6	0.9	-2.2
Stock of Equipment	0.3	0.6	0.9	1.2	1.3
Stock of Structures	0.1	0.3	0.4	0.6	0.7

[1]Test period: 1966-70.

[5]For the response of investment to tax changes, see Chapter 3, "The Supply Side in the DRI Model."

through higher profits and larger depreciation allowances, reducing the debt service burden. The elasticity of investment in equipment in response to output reaches a peak of 2.0 in the second year. The stock of equipment has a peak elasticity of 1.3. The corresponding elasticities for nonresidential structures are 1.6 and 0.7 respectively. After the fourth year, the overshoot on the stock adjustment is reversed and there is actually somewhat reduced investment. The multiplier then also reduces the gain in real GNP.

The results depend crucially on the monetary assumptions. If the money supply were left unchanged with increased federal purchases, real interest rates would be driven up, raising the rental price of capital and crowding out some private investment. The heaviest burden would fall on housing, however, and under normal economic conditions, the positive effect of increased sales would exceed the negative effect of crowding out, still leaving investment higher. Only under extreme financial stringency would this effect be lost.

The large size of the investment response is partly created by feedbacks between investment and the economy. A single equation estimate shows a peak elasticity of 1.2 for equipment which trails off to figures below 0.5 in five years. The elasticity for investment in structures peaks at 0.8 in a single-equation test, and then drops, though over a longer time span. Thus, about half of the investment stimulus originates in the direct impact of higher output; the rest in the repercussion effects.

7. Simulation Test: The Response of Investment to Lower Capital Costs

The second simulation lowers the composite rental price of capital by 1%, again leaving nonborrowed reserves unchanged. This decrease is achieved

Table 7.4
Response of Investment to a Higher Cost of Capital[1]
(Percent difference in levels)

	Year 1	Year 2	Year 3	Year 4	Year 5
			Elasticities		
Real GNP	0.0	0.1	0.1	0.1	0.1
Investment in Equipment	0.1	0.5	0.6	0.7	0.7
Investment in Structures	0.1	0.6	0.7	0.7	0.6
Stock of Equipment	0.0	0.1	0.2	0.3	0.4
Stock of Structures	0.0	0.1	0.1	0.2	0.2

[1]Test period: 1966-70.

through changes in tax rules, so that interest rates are left endogenous. The response is considerable, as the lower capital cost affects investment both directly and through repercussion effects. The elasticity of equipment demand peaks at 0.7, producing an elasticity for the stock of equipment of 0.4. The elasticity of demand for structures is also 0.7, but the implicit elasticity for the stock of structures is only 0.2 because of their longer economic lives.

8. Concluding Comments

This chapter has shown the investment equations and some of their implications for responses to changes in output and capital costs. Chapter 3 showed the responses to various tax changes.

Eisner and Chirinko[6] have recently published a critique of investment equations which questions the power of changes in taxation (and therefore capital costs) on the level of investment. They show that equations which abandon the full Jorgenson theoretical underpinning of profit maximization in favor of more flexible formulations produce smaller responses of investment to tax changes.

The Eisner-Chirinko critique can be rebutted in various ways. Economic theory argues against the "flexible" approaches which let output and price variables act independently of each other. The implementation lags relate to the investment decision as a whole, not to particular factors in it. Further full model simulation tests covering the historical record produce dramatically better results using DRI's extended version of the Jorgenson neoclassical theory than their more flexible formulas. Finally, ex-ante calculations of the impact of tax measures on present values of investment choices tend to produce results closer to the DRI equations than to the alternatives.

Nonetheless, it must be recognized that the specific parameters of the investment equations lack the robustness of remaining relatively constant under changes in the specifications of the equations. The enormous tax incentives to investment enacted in 1981 will provide a new historical record which should yield important new evidence on these important policy parameters. But as the simulations reported here show, the testing period will not be at hand until the devastating output effects of the 1981-82 recession are well behind us and resource utilization has returned to normal levels.

---

[6]Robert S. Chirinko and Robert Eisner. "Tax Policy and Investment in Major U.S. Macroeconomic Econometric Models," *Journal of Public Economics,* forthcoming. For a reply, see Allen Sinai and Otto Eckstein, "Tax Policy and Business Fixed Investment Revisited," Office of Tax Analysis, U.S. Treasury, Paper No. 52, April 1982.

CHAPTER 8

INVENTORIES

1. Introduction

Inventory investment in the DRI model is determined by the relationship between expected sales and the stock of inventories, and by conditions in the markets in which purchasing decisions are made. The main inventory equation goes beyond previous formulations principally in its explicit modeling of the market conditions under which purchasing, inventory and production policies are set. These conditions are represented by the well-established "leading indicator" measure, vendor performance, and by the change in the industrial utilization rate. The equation also includes the volume of defense contracts since the production of military equipment, such as airplanes, missiles and ships, is accompanied by an exceptionally large buildup of goods-in-process.

Unlike other topics, the theory of inventory investment has not seen an integration of the findings of micro- and macroeconomics. The microeconomic theory, as codified in the book by Arrow, Karlin and Scarf,[1] emphasizes the profit-maximizing decisions determining the optimal combination of production scheduling, ordering, and carrying costs, sometimes under conditions of particularly defined uncertainty. The macroeconomic theory of inventory investment, as developed by Metzler, Lovell, and Darling,[2] on the other hand, assumes that there is an optimal

[1] Kenneth J. Arrow, Samuel Karlin and Herbert Scarf, *Studies in the Mathematical Theory of Inventory and Production* (Stanford: Stanford University Press, 1958). A recent exception which is derivative from the micro theory is Alan S. Blinder, "Retail Inventory Behavior and Business Fluctuations," *Brookings Economic Papers*, 1981:2, pp. 443-505.

[2] Lloyd A. Metzler, "The Nature and Stability of Inventory Cycles," *Review of Economics and Statistics* (August 1941), pp. 113-129, reprinted in Metzler, *Collected Papers* (Cambridge, Mass.: Harvard University Press, 1973), ch. 15; Michael A. Lovell, "Manufacturers' Inventories, Sales Expectations, and the Acceleration Principle," *Econometrica* (July 1961), pp. 293-314; and Paul Darling, "Manufacturers' Inventory Investment, 1947-1958," *American Economic Review* (December 1959), pp. 950-962.

inventory-sales ratio, and that actual inventory investment is entirely determined by business decisions to adjust the inventory stock toward this ratio in the face of information lags and surprises in current sales. Attempts to find significant interest rate effects or speculative responses to inflation have found only very limited success.[3]

More recently, Feldstein and Auerbach[4] have shown that the accelerator-based stock adjustment theories are hardly sufficient to account for the extent of actual inventory fluctuations. Their econometric analyses of manufacturing and trade inventories show that the adjustment periods are extremely short, mostly within a single quarter in the case of trade and little more than a quarter for manufacturing. If inventories adjust so quickly to their proper level, the cause of their fluctuations must be found elsewhere. They do not advance a new theory, though citing the effect of the utilization rate on inventory behavior as the Brookings Model's inventory equations of Lovell and Darling had done earlier.[5]

2. Optimal Inventories and Macro Conditions

The theory of inventory investment in the DRI model assumes that profit maximization leads to a particular solution in static equilibrium. The macroeconomic situation sets certain parameters and signals particular risks, both expectational and financial, which affect the choice of target stock and the path to equilibrium. Adjustment dynamics are imposed to obtain the inventory accumulation process.

The optimal inventory stock depends upon:

(1) the cost of carrying inventory, including deterioration, interest, storage and obsolescence;

(2) the cost of ordering new supplies multiplied by the frequency of ordering in a given period;

(3) savings that can be realized from smoothing production through the existence of inventory buffer stocks, and

---

[3]Albert Ando, E. Cary Brown, Robert Solow, and John Kareken, "Lags in Fiscal and Monetary Policy," *Stabilization Policies* (Englewood Cliffs, N.J.: Prentice-Hall, Inc., 1961), pp. 11-163; and Lawrence R. Klein and Joel Popkin, "An Econometric Analysis of the Postwar Relationship Between Inventory Fluctuations and Changes in Aggregate Economic Activity," in *Inventory Fluctuations and Economic Stabilization* (Washington, D.C.: Joint Economic Committee, U.S. Congress, 1961), Part III, pp. 71-81.

[4]Martin S. Feldstein and Alan Auerbach, "Inventory Behavior in Durable Goods Manufacturing," *Brookings Papers on Economic Activity*, (2:1976), pp. 351-408.

[5]Michael A. Lovell and Paul Darling, "Factors Influencing Investment in Inventories," in *The Brookings Model of the U.S. Economy*, eds. James Duesenberry et al. (Chicago: Rand-McNally, 1965), ch. 4, pp. 131-161.

(4) the profit obtained from the avoidance of lost sales due to inventory stock-outs.

At the margin, the cost of ordering and carrying inventory just offsets the profit of smoother production and increased sales.

The empirical significance of these four factors varies greatly among industries and types of inventories. An electrical utility determining the desirable stock of coal will principally be concerned with the variability in electricity demand and with the dangers of supply interruptions due to strikes or transportation difficulties. The risk is primarily one of having to purchase emergency supplies in the spot market, of buying electricity from another utility, or of having to reduce the voltage provided to customers. The cost of carrying excess inventory is largely confined to the interest burden and whatever risk there may be in the price of coal.

At the other extreme, the decision to hold inventories in seasonal clothing is principally a gamble on the buyer's ability to discern the public's taste and on the near-term level of demand. If the choice is good and demand is high, the inventory will be sold at a high profit. If the quality of the buyer's judgment is low and total demand weak, a large percentage of the original purchase is sold at marked-down prices toward the end of the season or resold to discount outlets.

In a typical manufacturing industry, where the product cycle runs for several years or longer, the various benefits and costs of holding inventories can all be found with some significance. On the demand side, there is a risk of missing sales through insufficient availability of finished goods or longer-than-average delays in being able to produce for delivery. On the production side, the ready availability of materials and components allows the production process to proceed more smoothly and at lower cost. Finally, at the purchasing and supply end of the production chain, inventory-on-hand is a hedge against future price increases and insurance against disruptions of supply which may be created by strikes, oil embargoes, extremes of weather, or ordinary mismanagement.

Variations in the macroeconomic environment critically affect optimum inventory behavior. In a period of strong economic activity, benefits of large inventories are greater while the expected costs are likely to diminish. The probability of running out of stock becomes greater for two reasons. Demand is larger and likely to have a greater variance as customers undertake more discretionary spending and become more vulnerable to panic buying in fear of shortages. Second, when a firm places a new order, it is more likely to encounter stretched delivery periods, raising the risk of running out of stock before the shipment arrives.

The probability of successful sales is also greater in periods of high activity. Particularly where goods are seasonal and styles change rapidly, the probability of achieving a particular sales volume during the normal, full-price period is obviously greater in good times. As the economy weakens, the probability of holding inventories into the period of reduced-price liquidation becomes greater.

The cost of carrying inventory is also likely to be less in a period of high activity. While interest and warehousing costs may be higher, the probable loss from obsolescence is smaller. Overall, the biggest single cost of carrying inventories usually is the cost of being saddled with unneeded inventory for a prolonged period, a risk that is low in periods of high activity.

The benefit of inventories for the efficiency of production also becomes greater in periods of high activity. The risk of delivery delays of materials becomes greater, and imbalances in the provision of components and of goods-in-process also become more probable and more costly.

Finally, the speculative motive for holding inventories—betting on an increase in prices—also should induce larger increases in periods of high activity. However, compared to the other expected benefits in costs of inventories and the uncertainty of future price behavior, the potential benefit from correctly anticipating price movements is usually small.

Somewhat offsetting these extra benefits of inventories in periods of high activity are the increased costs and risks of finance. Interest charges are higher, and the risk of a sharp tightening in the availability of credit creates the danger of forced liquidation after the business cycle has passed its peak. This risk is greater if the firm's debt-service burden is high.

2.1 The Dynamics of Inventories

Because business cannot predict exactly the volume of sales in a given period, the stock of inventories will always include an unexpected component. When sales are surprisingly strong, inventories will be undesirably low. When sales weaken, inventories accumulate until ordering and production can be adjusted. Thus, while in the long run inventories show only a slight downtrend in relation to sales, in any particular period there may be a sizable difference between desired and actual inventories.

These considerations argue that a period's inventory investment will depend on the normal inventory-sales ratio, the expected volume of sales, actual sales which determine the stock disequilibrium, and general market conditions which reflect the strength of demand and the probability of supply and production delays.

Formally,[6] we can write

$$K^* = \alpha S^e + \beta UCAP, \tag{1}$$

where K^* is the desired stock of inventory determined by the expected level of sales (S^e) and α is the normal inventory-sales ratio. $UCAP$, the rate of capacity utilization, is a measure of the expected strength of demand. Utilization can be taken as representative of various measures of market conditions including delivery periods, order backlogs, as well as the utilization rate itself.

The expected level of sales is assumed to follow the expectations mechanism developed by Metzler, which defines the current sales expectation to be equal to the sales in the preceding period plus a repetition of the previous period's absolute sales increase as multiplied by an elasticity of expectations. Thus,

$$S^e = S_{-1} + \eta(S_{-1} - S_{-2}), \qquad -1 \leqslant \eta \leqslant 1, \tag{2}$$

where η is the elasticity of expectations.

The actual rate of inventory investment in the current period has two components: first, desired inventory investment is equal to a fraction of the gap between the desired inventory stock and the beginning-of-period inventory stock. Second, actual inventory investment contains a surprise element when actual sales differ from expected sales. Eq. (3) represents these hypotheses. Eq. (4) shows the explicit solution for inventory investment in terms of the sales of the current and the two previous periods, the utilization rate, and the previous stock of inventories. Eq. (5) restates the equation, combining constants.

$$I = \gamma(K^* - K_{-1}) + \delta(S^e - S), \qquad 1 \leqslant \gamma \leqslant 0, \delta > 0, \tag{3}$$

where γ is an adjustment coefficient and δ is the coefficient of "surprise."

$$I = (\alpha\gamma + \alpha\gamma\eta + \delta + \delta\eta)S_{-1} - (\alpha\gamma\eta + \delta\eta)S_{-2} - \delta S + \gamma\beta UCAP - \gamma K_{-1}, \tag{4}$$

or,

$$I = a_1 S_{-1} - a_2 S_{-2} - a_3 S + a_4 UCAP - a_5 K_{-1}. \tag{5}$$

It can be seen that the current level of inventory investment depends upon the volume of sales of the previous two periods through their impact on sales

[6]See David J. Ott, Attiat F. Ott, and Jang H. Yoo, *Macroeconomic Theory* (New York: McGraw-Hill, 1975), pp. 133-138, for an exposition of the traditional macrotheory of inventory behavior.

expectations, the current level of sales which embodies the surprise element, the utilization rate which helps to determine the desired stock of inventories, and the previous inventory stock.

2.2 Inventory–Production–Price Loop

The firm's production decision is similar to the inventory decision. The production plan is determined by sales expectations and the expected benefits and costs of producing too little or too much. In periods of high activity, the probable benefits of resolving production decisions on the high side are greater: the profit foregone from lost sales is larger and the risk of having to carry the finished product as unwanted inventory is less. The probability of fully executing a production plan and attaining the production goal is also smaller in periods of high activity, because of the increased probability of supply and production delays.

Unfortunately, production and inventory decisions at the various stages of the productive process can interact in a destabilizing manner. In "upstream" industries producing basic and processed materials and components, the volume of sales is measured by the orders received from finished goods industries. Thus, the decision to build inventory of finished goods appears as apparent final demand to the materials industries. Further, increased materials inventory desired by purchasing industries appears as increased demand to the materials producers, accentuating the upstream production swings. If information were complete and expectations rational, this would not be a significant source of instability. However, each firm at least partially reacts to its own demands as reported on its own order books. Inventory swings based on false expectations are readily observable in the historical record.

This process can be represented by an extension of the traditional inventory mechanism. Suppose that the first term in eq. (6) shows the effect of sales on utilization. The second term, however, more directly adds to the instability of the process. As inventories are accumulated by one group of firms, this accumulation appears as sales for others, stimulates production, and therefore adds to utilization and the perception of demand, i.e.,

$$UCAP = bS + cI. \tag{6}$$

Substituting eq. (6) in eq. (5) and solving for I gives eq. (7),

$$I = (a_1 S_{-1} - a_2 S_{-2} - (a_3 - a_4 b)S - a_5 K_{-1})/(1 - a_4 c). \tag{7}$$

The introduction of the loop between production and inventories does not change the apparent structure of the model at the conceptual level except to add some terms which make for instability. An examination of eq. (4) shows that if the findings of Feldstein and others are correct, the parameters in the equation are probably such as to produce quickly damped solutions of this difference equation system with two lags in sales. But the addition of the production loop moves the system away from the stability neighborhood. The addition of a positive term on current sales moves the system toward instability, and the addition of a denominator of less than 1, based on the feedback of inventory investment on itself, tends to move the system toward oscillation or explosion.

The behavior of prices accentuates this potential loop of economic instability. When demand is strong—whether because of inventory stocking or final demand—prices will increase, reinforcing the motivation to stock inventories. Eqs. (6) and (7) could readily be modified to add the loop between price and utilization, introducing a further destabilizing term into the denominator in (7). The price phenomenon seems of minor empirical significance, however, with the market assessment of expected delivery performance more important.

3. Empirical Implementation

Empirical implementation of the above inventory theory requires the following:

(1) How are sales expectations to be modeled and contrasted with actual sales to identify the "surprise" element for involuntary accumulation?

(2) How are the market conditions reflecting "high activity" to be measured and modeled?

(3) What are the inevitable "other" factors that have temporarily affected inventory behavior in the historical period of analysis, and which must be represented if the true behavioral specification is to emerge?

The DRI model equation for inventory investment deals with these matters in the following fashion. Actual sales are measured by economy-wide final sales (corrected for the sale of housing services and governmental production which do not give rise to measured inventories). Expected sales are assumed to be formed by a Koyck lag on previous sales. While this is a very simple mechanism, it is sufficient to show the major periods of errors-in-expectations, provides statistical qualities of fit equal to more elaborate equations and has better simulation properties.

The current market conditions which govern inventory policy are measured in two ways in the DRI model's inventory equation. The survey measure, "vendor performance," reflects the conditions actually encountered by purchasing executives, though only in a concentration of durable goods industries centered in the Midwest. This is a highly sensitive measure which is one of the short list of leading business-cycle indicators identified by the Bureau of the Census and which has considerable independent forecasting

Table 8.1
Equation for Real Nonfarm Inventory Accumulation

Ordinary Least Squares

Quarterly (1957:1 to 1978:3): 87 Observations
Dependent Variable: INVNF72CH

	Coefficient	Std. Error	t-Stat	Independent Variable
	-19.5809	2.495	-7.849	Constant
1)	9.76101	3.159	3.090	RDELYSLOW(-1)
2)	3.36237	0.7406	4.540	DMY331
3)	-8.42213	2.058	-4.092	DMY744
4)	3.97986	1.964	2.026	DPIANT
5)	88.5162	20.46	4.325	UCAPFRBM(-1)-UCAPFRBM (-2)
6)	0.0751466	0.01735	4.330	SALES72
7)	0.131916	0.03878	3.402	SALES72EXP-SALES72
8)	-0.247938	0.05849	-4.239	INV72$NF(-1)
9)				PDL(DODPCAUS72,2,4,FAR)
(-0)	0.0609210	0.07840		
(-1)	0.0911580	0.01951		
(-2)	0.0910835	0.03970		
(-3)	0.0606975	0.03794		
Sum	0.303860	0.06505	4.671	
Avg	1.49877	0.6261	2.394	

R-Bar squared: 0.8014
Durbin-Watson statistic: 2.0391
Standard error of the regression: 3.083   Normalized: 0.4602

RDELYSLOW is vendor performance,
DMY331 is a dummy for steel stocks,
DMY744 is a dummy for the fourth quarter of 1974, an observation that seems to contain extraordinary measurement error,
DPIANT is a dummy for the Nixon price controls,
UCAPFRBM is the industrial capacity utilization rate,
SALES72 is real sales excluding housing services and government production,
SALES72EXP is expected sales based on an extrapolative expectations process,
INV72$NF is the stock of nonfarm inventories,
DODPCAUS72 is the defense contracts.

value. Vendor performance is the response to a question on a monthly survey of purchasing executives in which they are asked whether delivery periods have become shorter or longer during the preceding month. In the DRI model, vendor performance is estimated from such variables as the level and change of utilization rates.

The change in utilization rate of manufacturing in the preceding quarter is another important indicator of market conditions. A high utilization rate in the preceding quarter makes purchasing executives increasingly concerned about their ability to obtain delivery. Consequently they add to their inventories beyond what the normal stock-flow relationships would indicate.

The special factors which must be included in the inventory equation are more extensive than for most equations because of the strong impact of a variety of shocks on this particular element of demand. The recent volume of defense contracts is highly significant, with a composite coefficient of 0.30. The severity of steel and automobile strikes has a major impact on inventories. The imposition of price controls in 1971 led to a brief, minor extra accumulation of inventories which cannot be explained in other terms. Finally, it is necessary to correct for measurement error in the extreme observation of the fourth quarter of 1974. The official government historical record reports that the bulk of the inventory accumulation of that year occurred in the final quarter. However, independent evidence from industries suggests that the accumulation actually occurred more generally all year long, and that the unwanted pile-up was not concentrated at that peak. If correction is not made for this measurement error, the equation's statistical properties are little affected but the coefficients appear to be biased.

In 1978, the Bureau of Economic Analysis made available inventory data for manufacturing, trade and "other," corrected for the inventory valuation adjustment made necessary by price changes. The DRI model uses the new data to model inventory behavior for these three components.

Table 8.2 shows the equation for manufacturing inventories. Its structure is generally similar to the aggregate equation, but superior in some regards. Current final sales appear with a negative sign, reflecting the unanticipated change in inventories created by sales surprises. Lagged sales have a positive sign and a larger coefficient. The previous stock of inventories has a negative impact on the current inventory investment rate, of course. Industrial production in relation to real final sales for the economy is a mix variable to reflect the changing relative importance of manufacturing in total activity over time and the business cycle. Finally, both vendor performance and defense contracts play important roles in this equation.

The equation for trade inventories has a similar structure, except that consumer sentiment plays a positive role. Apparently, retailers stock their

Table 8.2
Equation for Real Manufacturing Inventory Accumulation

Ordinary Least Squares

Quarterly (1961:1 to 1980:3): 79 Observations
Dependent Variable: INVM72CH

	Coefficient	Std. Error	t-Stat	Independent Variable
	-34.3082	9.695	-3.539	Constant
1)	-0.324531	0.08979	-3.614	INV72$M(-1)
2)	-0.0475093	0.02657	-1.788	SF72-CSHOUS72
3)	0.0787033	0.03068	2.565	SF72(-1)-CSHOUS72(-1)
4)	30.5816	14.92	2.050	JQINDM/SF72/782.425
5)				PDL(REALDODPCAUS,2,4, FAR)
(-0)	0.0501844	0.05877		
(-1)	0.0556876	0.01953		
(-2)	0.0491579	0.03837		
(-3)	0.0305954	0.03454		
Sum	0.185625	0.06511	2.851	
Avg	1.32412	0.9804	1.351	
6)	9.66390	3.794	2.547	RDELYSLOW(-1)

R-Bar squared: 0.6723
Durbin-Watson statistic: 1.4091
Standard error of the regression: 2.237   Normalized: 0.5814

INVM72CH is the change in real manufacturing inventories,
INV72$M is the stock of manufacturing inventories,
SF72 is real final sales,
CSHOUS72 is real consumption of housing services,
JQINDM is manufacturing production.
REALDODPCAUS is the real volume of defense prime contracts,
RDELYSLOW is vendor performance.

shelves more aggressively when consumer confidence is high. Finally, inventories for other sectors rely mainly on total sales of goods in the economy, the existing stock of inventories and the recent change in the utilization rate of industry.

CHAPTER 9

STATE AND LOCAL GOVERNMENT

1. The Framework

The formulation of the behavioral equations for state and local government activity reflects the high degree of interdependence of revenues and expenditures since this sector operates under a budget constraint. The specification also takes account of the interdependence of the various components of receipts resulting from the community's desire to maintain a relatively fixed long-term proportion between revenues from various tax sources. The use of long distributed lags reflects the slowness of adjustment by these units. The underlying theoretical model is one of utility maximization by the community, subject to a set of budget and tax constraints.

2. Theory[1]

Let the community's utility *(U)* depend positively on state and local government expenditures on goods and services, *(G)*, and negatively on two tax sources (personal taxes, T_1, and indirect taxes, T_2). Utility is also a negative function of the future interest burden caused by the local governments' operating deficit *(D)*. The community welfare function underlying this analysis thus can be specified as

$$U = U(G, T_1, T_2, D). \tag{1}$$

[1]The theoretical explanation of state and local government behavior in the form of constrained utility maximization was developed by James M. Henderson, "Local Government Expenditures: A Social Welfare Analysis," *Review of Economics and Statistics* (May 1968), pp. 156-163 and Edward M. Gramlich, "State and Local Governments and their Budget Constraint," *International Economic Review* (June 1969), pp. 163-182. The DRI model follows the approach of Otto Eckstein and Robert F. Halvorsen, "Behavioral Models of the Public Finances of the State and Local Sector," in *Public Finance and Stabilization Policy, Essays in Honor of Richard A. Musgrave*, Warren L. Smith and John M. Culbertson, eds. (Amsterdam: North Holland Publishing Co., 1974), pp. 309-331.

Underlying the utility of spending is the community's preference for public goods and services in the context of rising permanent income and the school-age population. The disutility of taxation is derived from the private spending and saving that is foregone.

The community maximizes its utility subject to three constraints. First, the state and local government sector must balance its operating accounts. Spending, therefore, must equal tax revenues plus the deficit:

$$G = T_1 + T_2 + D. \tag{2}$$

Second, there is a borrowing constraint, which provides an upper limit to the absolute size of the deficit that state and local governments can run. This upper limit could be imposed by law or by the ability to obtain credit from institutional lenders and is dependent on the size of the debt already in existence, so

$$D \leqslant D^*. \tag{3}$$

Third, the sector prefers to maintain an approximately fixed relationship between revenues from personal and indirect taxes.

$$T_1 = \alpha T_2. \tag{4}$$

The constrained maximization of the community's utility function can be expressed as

$$max \ \Phi = U - \lambda_1(T_1 + T_2 + D - G) - \lambda_2(T_1 - \alpha T_2) - \lambda_3(D - D^*), \tag{5}$$

which results in the first-order conditions,

$$\partial\Phi/\partial G = \partial U/\partial G + \lambda_1 = 0,$$
$$\partial\Phi/\partial T_1 = \partial U/\partial T_1 - \lambda_1 - \lambda_2 = 0,$$
$$\partial\Phi/\partial T_2 = \partial U/\partial T_2 - \lambda_1 + \lambda_2\alpha = 0, \ and$$
$$\partial\Phi/\partial D = \partial U/\partial D - \lambda_1 - \lambda_3 = 0. \tag{6}$$

This results in the following marginal conditions:

$$\partial G/\partial T_1 = (\lambda_1 + \lambda_2)/-\lambda_1;$$
$$\partial G/\partial T_2 = (\lambda_1 - \alpha\lambda_2)/-\lambda_1;$$
$$\partial G/\partial D = (\lambda_1 + \lambda_3)/-\lambda_1;$$
$$\partial T_1/\partial T_2 = (\lambda_1 - \alpha\lambda_2)/(\lambda_1 + \lambda_2);$$
$$\partial T_1/\partial D = (\lambda_1 + \lambda_3)/(\lambda_1 + \lambda_2);$$
$$\partial T_2/\partial D = (\lambda_1 + \lambda_3)/(\lambda_1 - \alpha\lambda_2).$$

In equilibrium, the marginal utility of an extra unit of expenditures should equal the disutility of the associated tax and borrowing package.

In balanced growth equilibrium, expenditures will grow at their equilibrium rate with the share of state and local spending in nominal GNP reflecting the income elasticity of the demand for public expenditures and of the various tax bases. The share of spending financed by borrowing will be small, determined by the disutility of borrowing and the severity of the deficit constraint. Since the economy is typically out of equilibrium, expenditures and taxes contain an adjustment component, and the difference between equilibrium and actual magnitudes depends on various cyclical variables, such as inflation, growth, interest rates, and the debt position inherited at the beginning of the period.

3. Empirical Implementation: Expenditures

The volume of state and local government expenditures on goods and services is determined by the community's need or desire for additional public goods and by the availability of funds. On the demand side, permanent income, approximated by a five-year history of real gross national product, captures the desire for public goods and services as part of a real increase in the standard of living. The ratio of school-age to total population is an indicator of the importance of education services and school construction in the outlays of this sector (Figure 9.1 and Table 9.1).

Depending on their nature, federal grants-in-aid can be substitutes or complements to state and local financing.[2] Open-end matching grants, where the federal government pays a certain portion of the cost of specific expenditures, encourage state and local governments to expand service levels by reducing the incremental cost from own revenue sources. Lump sum transfers with no restriction on use lead to lesser incentives to raise spending; the general revenue-sharing program was the first major federal aid policy of this type. Closed-end categorical grants are transfers of specific sums from the federal to the state and local levels to be used for specific programs. They represent a hybrid of the two other types of grants in that the cost from own sources is lowered for a specific project but the size of the grant is limited. The current pattern of grants produces a marginal spending coefficient of 0.57, with short lags. The remaining funds are used to reduce taxes or are added to the surplus.

---

[2]See Edward W. Gramlich and Harvey Galper, "State and Local Fiscal Behavior and Federal Grant Policy," *Brookings Papers on Economic Activity,* (1:1973), pp. 17-19.

Figure 9.1
State and Local Government Receipts and Expenditures

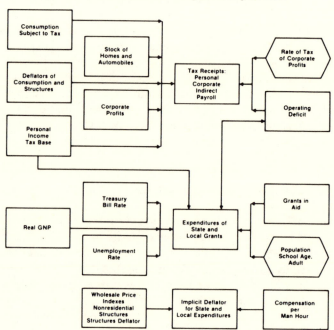

Since state and local governments are required to hold the deficits in their operating budgets to low levels, the recent experience of this variable plays an important role in determining current expenditures. Expenditures respond to the real surplus in the previous two years with a coefficient of 0.34. Finally, the relation between the Treasury bill rate and the yield on AAA state and local government bonds, an indicator of credit crunches, affects the cost and availability of borrowing, and therefore of spending.

State and local government transfers to persons are determined primarily by the unemployment rate and by the lagged percentage change in nominal per capita income. The unemployment rate reflects the cyclical outlays for unemployment insurance and other transfers. Per capita income affects average benefit levels, with an elasticity of 0.56. A dummy variable for the "Great Society" program of the Johnson Administration, which affected both the extent and the administration of welfare programs, equals a time trend initialized in 1964:1, rising quarterly until 1971:3, and remaining constant thereafter. A dummy to reflect the impact of the partial federalization of welfare is set at -1.0 in 1974, -1.3 in 1975, and -1.0 thereafter.

Table 9.1
Equation for Real State and Local Government Purchases

Ordinary Least Squares

Quarterly (1960:1 to 1977:4): 72 Observations
Dependent Variable: GSL72

	Coefficient	Std. Error	t-Stat	Independent Variable
	-252.816	19.23	-13.15	Constant
1)				PDL(VAIDGF72,1,4,FAR)
(-0)	0.227318	0.04689		
(-1)	0.170489	0.3517		
(-2)	0.113659	0.02345		
(-3)	0.568296	0.01172		
Sum	0.568296	0.1172	4.848	
Average	1.00000	0.0		
2)	1.14145	0.09092	12.55	N+N-N22&
3)	0.0466718	0.01025	4.552	YPERM
4)	0.341403	0.1029	3.319	((DEFGSLO(-4)/PGSL(-4))+
				(DEFGSLO(-5)/PGSL(-5))+
				(DEFGSLO(-6)/PGSL(-6))+
				(DEFGSLO(-7)/PGSL(-7))+
				(DEFGSLO(-8)/PGSL(-8))+
				(DEFGSLO(-9)/PGSL(-9))+
				(DEFGSLO(-10)/PGSL(-10))+
				(DEFGSLO(-11)/PGSL(-11)))/
				8.0)

R-Bar squared: 0.9956
Durbin-Watson statistic: 1.7415
Standard error of the regression: 2.061   Normalized: 0.01475

GSL72 is real purchases of state and local governments,
VAIDGF72 is real federal grants-in-aid,
N is population,
N22& is population aged 22 or older,
YPERM is a five-year average of real GNP,
DEFGSLO is the deficit in state and local government sector, excluding social insurance funds.
(+) means surplus,
PGSL is the deflator for state and local government.

3.1 State and Local Purchases Over the Business Cycle

The pro- rather than counter-cyclical nature of state and local government expenditures is illustrated by the positive, significant coefficients for permanent income and for the average of past surpluses. The variables are lagged over several quarters, indicating that expenditures will be highest when surpluses have been positive for a while and income has been growing rapidly. The lagged response of expenditures to grants-in-aid is one of the implementation lags of federal fiscal policy, and may contribute to the pro-cyclical nature of expenditures. In recession, state and local purchases fall below their long-run trend. Revenues are surprisingly small, enlarging the deficit and putting downward pressure on spending.

Fortunately, there are a few equilibrating forces. As the economy reaches a peak, prices as well as interest rates will begin to rise. Credit conditions will limit borrowing and depress expenditures. Moreover, as the price of state and local purchases increases, the real value of grants-in-aid is lowered. Inflation also makes the budget constraint effective at lower real outlay levels since receipts do not respond fully to higher prices while the high labor and construction components of outlays tend to worsen the relative price position of these governments.

4. Receipts

Indirect taxes, which are the main source of state and local revenues, are modeled as five elements: property taxes, gasoline taxes, sales taxes, motor vehicle licenses and other indirect taxes. Property taxes are modeled in quarterly first-difference form, dependent on the spending level and the percentage of the population that is of school age. The equations for the remaining taxes are developed on annual data, aggregated, and entered in the model converted into quarterly form. Gasoline taxes are mainly determined by gasoline consumption and an exogenous tax rate. Sales taxes are determined by consumer spending on durable goods and nondurables, with lower weights on clothing and a still lower weight on food. Motor vehicle licenses rest on the number of registered cars and a time trend to reflect rising fees. The "other" category depends on the spending level and the operating deficit in earlier years.

The personal income tax rate is determined by the tax base, by the desire of state and local governments to balance receipts and expenditures, and by past operating deficits. The relevant tax base is personal income net of government transfer payments to persons and other labor income, augmented by personal contributions for social insurance.

Because the postwar period saw a one-time move of personal taxes to an equilibrium level, the growth rate is very high and has already proved unsustainable. Therefore the equation is fitted in the logit form, which asymptotically limits the average effective rate to 4.5% (table 9.2).

State and local governments levy employment taxes principally on their own employees in the form of withheld pension contributions. The tax base is estimated from nominal expenditures, corrected for new public construction

Table 9.2
Equation for Personal Taxes of State and Local Governments

Least Squares with First-Order Autocorrelation Correction

Quarterly (1966:1 to 1978:2): 50 Observations
Dependent Variable: log(((TPGSL/TAXBASE)/(0.045-TPGSL/TAXBASE)))

	Coefficient	Std. Error	t-Stat	Independent Variable
	-18.9200	2.106	-8.986	Constant
1)	3.88782	0.3219	12.08	log(TAXBASE)
2)	-4.81279	2.109	-2.282	log(((TGSL(-4)-TWGSL(-4))/ (GEXPSL(-4)-GSIFSL(-4)))+ ((TGSL(-5)-TWGSL(-5))/ (GEXPSL(-5)-GSIFSL(-5)))+ ((TGSL(-6)-TWGSL(-6))/ (GEXPSL(-6)-GSIFSL(-6)))+ ((TGSL(-7)-TWGSL(-7))/ (GEXPSL(-7)-GSIFSL(-7)))/ 4.0)
	0.792757	0.09229	8.590	RHO

R-Bar squared: 0.9837
Durbin-Watson statistic: 1.6274
Standard error of the regression: 0.1357   Normalized: 0.08742

TPGSL is personal taxes of state and local governments,
TAXBASE is personal income minus other labor income minus transfer payments plus personal contributions to social insurance,
TGSL is state and local taxes,
TWGSL is state and local payroll taxes,
GEXPSL is state and local outlays,
GSIFSL is state and local outlays for social insurance,
RHO is the autocorrelation coefficient.

put-in-place, yielding a proxy for wages and salaries paid by state and local governments. Corporate tax receipts are defined by the same base, with corporate profits before tax multiplied by an exogenously determined tax rate.

5. Simulation Results

The state and local government sector equations can be used to test the impact of various factors on the behavior and the finances of these governments. The following scenarios were considered:

(1) Increased (reduced) federal aid, induced by a $5 billion sustained increase (reduction) in federal grants-in-aid, valued at 1972 prices.

(2) High growth induced by a $5 billion sustained increase in federal government military spending through the solution interval.

(3) Higher inflation induced by a 1% sustained increase in the index of average hourly earnings.

5.1 Effect of Grants

The effect of a change in federal grants-in-aid is summarized in table 9.3. A $5 billion sustained increase in the real level of grants results in a $3.2 billion rise in real state and local expenditures on goods and services in the third year. Expenditures rise not only due to the increased aid, but also due to the improvement in deficits. Furthermore, tax revenues are pulled up slightly by the increase in expenditures and by the induced rise in domestic activity. The change in revenues other than grants derives largely from increased indirect

Table 9.3
Effect of a Real $5 Billion Increase in Grants-in-Aid
on State and Local Governments
(Billions of 1972 dollars)

	1966	1967	1968	1970	1973	1977
—State and Local Budget						
Surplus or Deficit Except Social Insurance	2.4	1.4	1.3	1.3	2.1	2.7
—Expenditures	1.2	2.1	2.8	3.7	4.5	7.7
Purchases of Goods and Services—1972 dollars	1.7	2.7	3.2	3.1	2.7	3.0
Purchases of Goods and Services	1.2	2.1	2.8	3.6	4.3	7.4
Transfer Payments to Persons	0	0	0	0.1	0.2	0.3
—Revenues	3.7	3.6	4.3	5.3	6.9	10.9
Federal Grants-in-Aid	3.4	3.6	3.9	4.6	5.7	8.1
Federal Grants-in-Aid—1972 dollars	5.0	5.0	5.0	5.0	5.0	5.0
Personal Tax and Nontax Receipts	0.1	-0.5	-0.4	0.1	0.2	0.9
Indirect Business Tax and Nontax Accruals	0.1	0.3	0.5	0.4	0.8	1.3
Contributions for Social Insurance	0.1	0.2	0.2	0.3	0.3	0.5
—Surplus or Deficit (-)	2.5	1.6	1.5	1.6	2.4	3.3
—Other Variables						
Gross National Product—1972 dollars	2.7	5.3	6.7	2.7	-0.6	1.8
Gross National Product	2.1	5.0	7.9	7.7	8.2	21.7
Yield on AAA State and Local Government Bonds	-0.04	-0.01	0.07	0.14	0	0.08
Average Market Yield on 3-Month U.S. Government Bills	0.06	0.10	0.15	0.14	0.10	0.28

taxes and, to a lesser extent, from personal income taxes. The multiplier on grants peaks at 1.34 in the third year, but then falls to zero as crowding out takes over.

5.2 Effect of Economic Growth on the State and Local Government Sector

State and local government behavior under a situation of initially higher growth in the domestic economy is summarized in table 9.4. A 1% rise in real GNP induces an equal percentage increase in real state and local purchases of goods and services. Higher real incomes raise the demand for public services, and also aid revenue growth. The surplus of state and local governments initially will be aided by higher growth, but this gain is partially lost as extra inflation raises outlays. The stronger economy, originally achieved by federal stimulus, is gradually crowded out, bringing the effects on state and local governments to an end.

Table 9.4
Effect of Higher Growth on State and Local Government Activity,
Changes From Base Solution
(Billions of dollars)

	1966	1967	1968	1970	1973	1977
—State and Local Budget						
Surplus or Deficit Except Social Insurance	0.7	0.4	-0.3	-1.0	0	-1.6
—Expenditures	0.3	1.3	2.7	4.4	4.8	11.1
Purchases of Goods and—1972 dollars	0.3	0.9	1.4	1.0	-0.2	0.3
Purchases of Goods and Services	0.4	1.4	2.6	4.0	4.3	10.1
Transfer Payments to Persons	-0.1	0	0	0.4	0.5	0.9
—Revenues	1.0	1.8	2.6	3.7	5.1	10.1
Personal Tax and Nontax Receipts	0.6	0.9	1.2	1.7	1.6	3.0
Indirect Business Tax and Nontax Accruals	0.2	0.5	0.8	1.1	2.1	3.6
Contributions for Social Insurance	0	0.1	0.2	0.3	0.3	0.7
—Surplus or Deficit (-)	0.7	0.4	-0.1	-0.7	0.3	-0.9
—Other Variables						
Gross National Product—1972 dollars	16.3	19.9	18.6	5.6	-0.4	1.5
Gross National Product	13.1	20.1	24.7	22.7	27.7	64.5
Yield on AAA State and Local Government Bonds	0.07	0.29	0.48	0.55	0.09	0.32
Average Market Yield on 3-Month U.S. Government Bills	0.24	0.41	0.50	0.42	0.26	0.87

5.3 Effect of Inflation

Table 9.5 summarizes state and local government behavior in a more inflationary environment. A 1% sustained rise in average hourly earnings leads to an initial rise in overall inflation in wholesale prices by 0.4%, gradually increasing to 0.9%. The percent increase in nominal state and local

Table 9.5
Effect of More Inflation on State and Local Government Activity,
Changes From Base Solution
(Billions of dollars)

	1966	1967	1968	1970	1973	1977
—State and Local Budget						
Surplus or Deficit Except Social Insurance	-0.1	-0.3	0	-0.2	0.2	-0.2
—Expenditures	0.6	0.9	0.9	0.9	0.7	1.5
Purchases of Goods and Services—1972 dollars	-0.1	0	-0.1	-0.3	-0.5	-0.3
Purchases of Goods and Services	0.6	0.8	0.8	0.7	0.5	1.2
Transfer Payments to Persons	0.1	0.1	0.1	0.2	0.2	0.3
—Revenues	0.6	0.7	0.9	0.7	0.9	1.5
Personal Tax and Nontax Receipts	0.3	0.3	0.4	0.2	0.3	0.5
Indirect Business Tax and Nontax Accruals	0.2	0.2	0.3	0.3	0.3	0.5
Contributions for Social Insurance	0	0.1	0.1	0.1	0	0.1
—Surplus or Deficit (-)	-0.1	-0.2	0	-0.2	0.2	-0.1
—Other Variables						
Gross National Product—1972 dollars	-1.1	-2.5	-2.8	-5.3	-4.5	-4.4
Implicit Price Deflator—GNP (%)	0.6	0.8	0.8	0.8	0.8	0.9
Wholesale Price Index (%)	0.4	0.6	0.7	0.6	0.7	0.9
Implicit Price Deflator—						
Purchases of Goods and Services (%)	0.8	0.9	0.9	0.8	0.6	0.7
Yield on AAA State and Local Government Bonds	0.07	0.20	0.20	0.09	-0.05	0.01
Average Market Yield on						
3-Month U.S. Government Bills	0.18	0.06	0.07	0.06	0.02	0.18

government purchases is less than the rise in inflation (0.7% in 1976), thereby lowering the level of real purchases by 0.3%. The fall in real expenditures is due to the reduction in the real value of grants-in-aid, the fall in permanent income and the lessened real value of tax revenues.

6. Concluding Comments

The state and local sector has strong behavioral characteristics for responses to external factors such as federal grants, growth and inflation. The closed loop of revenues and expenditures leads to self-correcting responses to surpluses or deficits. Thus, over the cycle, the sector operates under a budget constraint.

The results of this chapter are based on the 1978 edition of the DRI model. Later editions have retained the same structure, with generally small changes in the coefficients. There are some changes created by the three additional years of data and the data revisions: the response of expenditures to surpluses or deficits has risen from 0.12 to 0.19. Also, the elasticity of transfer payments with respect to permanent income is up from 0.56 to 0.71, but this elasticity may diminish with reduced federal grant support and changed political attitudes.

The statistical quality of the equations for this sector is strong, and the forecasting record, both in ex-post dynamic simulations and in genuine ex-ante forecasting, is particularly good. To a degree, these qualities may be due to the paucity of data on which the national income accounts are based, resulting in smooth, well-behaved series. But—at least in part—the results are due to the theory used in the model which seems to come close to reflecting the actual behavior of this sector.

CHAPTER 10

FEDERAL GOVERNMENT

1. Introduction

Federal government policies, both fiscal and monetary, are considered exogenous variables in the DRI model. Indeed, one of the purposes of the model is to permit the simulation studies which reveal some of the impacts of policies at the macroeconomic level. While it is certainly tempting to treat the federal government as a behavioral unit, perhaps responding to unemployment and inflation rates, election dates, political philosophies of the ruling party and the particular economic theories governing the Washington intellectual scene, such an approach would sharply limit the usefulness of the model. In any event, the study of the behavioral theories of central governments is still in its infancy.

The fiscal impact of the federal government on the economy is treated at length in various other chapters. Some of the multipliers of the federal budget are discussed in Part I of this volume. This chapter, therefore, is confined to the more mechanical aspects of the treatment of the federal government in the model and to a fuller account of multipliers.

Although fiscal policy is treated as exogenous, it does not set actual revenue or expenditure levels; it can only define such policy parameters as tax rates and high employment expenditure rates. The economy determines the growth of the tax bases and effective rates, and therefore revenues. The economy also determines the cyclical components of expenditures. Inflation rates also affect revenues and expenditures, although there is some ambiguity to what extent expenditures are determined in real or nominal terms. Interest rates have become particularly important determinants of budget outlays. These feedbacks from the economy to revenues and expenditures are represented by behavioral equations, with the policy parameters set as exogenous variables.

2. Policy Levers

Some of the more general policy options are built into the model as policy levers. Table 10.1 lists the exogenous variables representing federal fiscal policy levers and the methods for introducing specific values. The reader intent on actually using the model for policy simulations should also turn to the full technical documentation from which the table is reproduced.

The policy levers follow the definitions of the federal budget in the national income accounts. The four principal spending categories, military spending, civilian spending on goods and services, grants-in-aid and transfers to persons can be specified exogenously either in real or in nominal terms. For short-run forecasting, the nominal form is usually preferred because surprises in the behavior of prices initially tend to be absorbed in given nominal budget totals; the Congress usually votes spending in nominal terms. In longer-run analyses, however, the spending figures must be specified in real terms because there is an adjustment process to higher prices, partly through supplementary appropriations, partly through higher program requests in succeeding years.

In the case of transfers to persons, the widespread introduction of price escalation has meant that it is the real rather than the nominal totals which are

Table 10.1
Policy Levers for the Federal Government Sector

Concept	Variable	What to do	Notes
Military Spending (Goods and Services)	GFML GFML72	If GFLEVER=1, enter new values for GFMLEXO (current-dollar military spending) If GFLEVER=0, enter new values for GFML72EXO (constant-dollar military spending)	Only one of current- and constant-dollar expenditures can be exogenous; GFLEVER determines whether current or constant-dollar spending is exogenous. Real purchases are determined by deflating nominal expenditures by the federal price deflator (PGE).
Civilian Spending (Goods and Services)	GFO GFO72	If GFLEVER=1, enter new values for GFOLEXO (current dollar nondefense spending If GFLEVER=0, enter new values for GFO72EXO (constant-dollar nondefense spending)	
Grants-in-Aid	VAIDGF@SL VAIDGF@SL72	If GFLEVER=1, enter new values for VAIDGF@SLEXO (current-dollar grants-in-aid) IF GFLEVER=0, enter new values for VAIDGF@SL72EXO (constant-dollar grants-in-aid)	

Transfers to Persons	VGF@PER	Change VGF@PERHI72 or &VGF@PER	Normally, change real high-employment transfers (VGF@PERHI72).
Personal Tax Receipts	RTPGF	Effective rate on tax base.	
Corporate Tax Receipts	TCGF	Enter new values for RTCGFS, RTCGFRESID, RITC, or RITCR&D	RTCGFS is the statutory corporate tax rate. RTCGFRESID is the difference between the statutory and effective rates. RITC is the effective rate on the investment tax credit, RITCR&D, for research and development expenditures.
Federal Pay Increases	PAYGF	Set rate of pay increase in percent.	
Government Production	PERG72	Fraction of government purchases versus government production. Exogenous variable.	
Defense Contracts	DODPCAUS	Change values endogenously. Derived from GFML72 for simulations. Affects inventories.	
Military Personnel	EDODML	Set values through add factor. Affects unemployment.	
Personal Tax Receipts	TPGF	Enter new values for &RTPGF, &TPGF, or REBSUR.	Use REBSUR for temporary rebate or surtax.
Social Insurance Tax Receipts	TWGF	Enter new values for RTWGF.	RTWGF is the tax rate which is applied to wage and salary disbursements (WSD).
Indirect Business Tax Receipts	TXGF	Change add-factor (&TXGF), the federal gasoline tax (GASTAXF), or "windfall profits" tax (TXGFWF).	

legislated. Further, policy relates to the normal, high employment level of expenditure. Since transfers respond to the business cycle, it is high employment transfers which are exogenous and a behavioral equation adjusts actual transfers for unemployment.

On the tax side, the average effective tax rate is the normal exogenous policy variable. For corporate tax receipts, various corrections must be specified. The difference between the statutory tax rate and the average effective tax rate is set exogenously and derived from recent evidence. Receipts are corrected for the investment tax credit endogenously, whose average effective rate is an exogenous variable. The tax base is the book value of profits as estimated in the national income accounts, which is conceptually equivalent to the Internal Revenue Service definitions of taxable income. Personal tax receipts are calculated from a behaviorally determined average effective tax rate (see below) and a national income account approximation of the tax base.

3. Personal Taxes

Personal taxes are estimated by a behavioral equation for the average effective tax rate and from the size of the tax base. The base is calculated as an identity, subtracting the nontaxable components from personal income and adding the taxable portion of payroll taxes.

The equation for the effective tax rate is intended to meet the following goals:

(1) To accurately reflect the impact of a progressive income tax system during periods of inflation;

(2) To discriminate among past changes in personal taxes due to tax law changes, family income increases and population growth;

(3) To permit easy manipulation of the policy lever for forecasts.

The average effective tax rate, the ratio of revenues to the estimated tax base, is the dependent variable. Independent variables were introduced into the equation to reflect progressivity, the enactment of new tax laws and the growth of household income (Table 10.2).

The approach follows that of Brown and Kruizenga.[1] The average effective tax rate is principally a function of average income and of the various changes in the tax law. The increase of incomes can be due to real gains or to an increase of the price level, the latter phenomenon representing "bracket-creep."

The consensus of the public finance literature indicates that the elasticity of the personal income tax with respect to income growth falls between 1.2 and 1.6. The equation, at 1981 parameters, suggests an elasticity of 1.47, though a full model simulation boosts the elasticity to 1.60 through indirect feedbacks. The tax legislation of 1981, with its reduction of rates to be followed by inflation-indexing, will lower that elasticity toward unity. This will reduce the degree of automatic stabilization provided by the tax system.

[1] E. Cary Brown and R.J. Kruizenga, "Income Sensitivity of a Simple Personal Income Tax," *Review of Economics and Statistics*, August 1959, pp. 260-269.

Table 10.2
Equation for Federal Personal Income Tax

Ordinary Least Squares

Quarterly (1963:1 to 1980:3):—71 Observations
Dependent Variable: 100*RTPGF/(1+REBSUR)

	Coefficient	Std. Error	t-Stat	Independent
	0.89148	0.6912	1.29	Constant
1)	1.50728	0.3606	4.18	100*YSURNW/TAXBASE
2)	5.95853	0.3693	16.14	log(TAXBASE/EHH)
3)	0.59625	0.0862	6.92	DMYRTPGF1
4)	-1.62406	0.1402	-11.59	DMYRTPGF2
5)	-0.91920	0.1736	-5.30	DMYRTPGF3
6)	0.12564	0.1426	0.88	DMYRTPGF4
7)	-1.35702	0.1433	-9.47	DMYRTPGF5
8)	-0.25385	0.1512	-1.68	DMYRTPGF6

R-Bar squared: 0.9345
Durbin-Watson statistic: 1.0886
Standard error of the regression: 0.2400   Normalized: 0.01956

RTPGF is the average effective federal personal income tax rate on the NIPA approximation of the tax base.
REBSUR is the policy lever for surcharges and rebates,
SURNW is the Vietnam surcharge rate,
DUMMIES are for statutory changes of the tax code of 1964, 1968, 1969, 1971 and 1975

4. Indirect Business Taxes

Federal indirect business taxes are divided into three categories: the gasoline tax, the windfall profits tax on crude oil, and all other. The gasoline tax rate is exogenous and is multiplied by the volume of gasoline consumption. Windfall profits tax revenues are treated as exogenous and are obtained from DRI's Energy model.

The remaining indirect business taxes include tariffs, excise taxes on liquor and tobacco, and miscellaneous other revenues. Table 10.3 shows the behavioral equation. The volume of imports determines tariff revenues. Liquor and tobacco revenues are approximated from aggregate real food consumption, since the model does not contain separate consumer categories for these items and the taxes are levied on a unit basis. The dummy variable represents the federal excise taxes on luxuries that have gradually been terminated. The final term in the equation includes telephone service and other items.

Table 10.3
Equation for Federal Excise Taxes

Ordinary Least Squares

Quarterly (1962:1 to 1979:4): 72 Observations
Dependent Variable: TXGF-TXGFWF-DMYTXGF-(.01*GASTAXF*QGAS)

	Coefficient	Std. Error	t-Stat	Independent Variable
	-2.84527	1.205	-2.362	Constant
1)	0.03599	0.0071	5.072	MENDT
2)	0.06834	0.0116	5.895	CNFOOD72
3)	0.1076	0.0253	4.250	.45*CSHHOP+.3*CSTRANS +.25*CDMV&P

R-Bar squared: 0.9927
Durbin-Watson statistic: 0.9520
Standard error of the regression: 0.4433   Normalized: 0.03162

TXGF is federal indirect taxes and accruals,
TXGFWF is the windfall profits tax,
DMYTXGF is the dummy for cumulative effects of statutory changes,
GASTAXF is the federal gasoline tax,
QGAS is the demand for gasoline,
MENDT is total imports of goods,
CNFOOD72 is real consumer expenditure on food and beverages,
CSHHOP72 is real consumer expenditures for household operations,
CSTRANS is consumer expenditures for transportation services,
CDMV&P is consumer expenditures for motor vehicles and parts.

5. Other Revenue and Expenditure Items

There are various other items in the national income account statement of the federal government, some of which are represented by behavioral equations, others calculated from identities. Interest paid by the federal government, a very large budget item, is calculated from the pertinent rates and the volume of debt of different maturities outstanding. Contributions for social insurance are derived directly from total wage and salary disbursements and an average effective tax rate which reflects both the statutory rate and the taxed earnings ceiling. Other minor categories, including transfers to foreigners, wage accruals, and subsidies to government enterprises, are treated as exogenous variables in nominal terms.

6. Supplementary Workspaces

Policy interests change over time, so it is impossible to build all of the potential desired policy changes into the model's permanent structure. On the other hand, certain kinds of simulations must be carried out in considerable detail when they are the center of policy concerns. In response to this need, DRI has developed a series of supplementary workspaces which allow for the studies to be carried out in full detail.

The Depreciation Workspace: Prior to the adoption of the massive depreciation reform of 1981, numerous proposals were under discussion. A special workspace allows economic lives to be varied by type of equipment and buildings, and the implications of such lives to be traced into the rental price of capital for different forms of investment, and therefore into investment levels, cash flows of business and revenues to be yielded by the corporate income tax. This workspace was developed because the distribution of depreciation lives made a significant difference to their economic effects beyond the sheer quantity of depreciation to be taken or the overall average depreciation life.

Defense Budget Workspace: The large increase in defense spending projected for the 1980s requires a particularly careful analysis of its impact on the economy. The DRI model distinguishes between defense purchases of goods and services and actual production in the defense sector, and also treats military prime contracts and military manpower as explicit variables. But this is not a sufficient breakdown to trace the industrial impact or to estimate the inflationary impacts with sufficient precision.

To solve this problem, a special workspace has been developed which uses a breakdown of defense spending into 53 categories, and traces their impact through the input-output table built into the model. The direct effects are based on special input-output studies which yielded the pertinent input-output coefficients. The indirect effects are estimated principally from the changed industrial composition of output and the subsequent effects on prices, employment, productivity and other variables.

The two workspaces discussed here are examples of policy analyses of particularly broad interest. Other policy studies require similar detailed analysis of the direct inputs into the model simulations. The levers discussed in Table 10.1 are built permanently into the model. Thus, across-the-board changes in personal income taxes, changes in the investment tax credit, payroll tax rates and other taxes and spending categories can be analyzed by the model directly. But most other kinds of fiscal policy changes require an initial microanalysis to derive adequate estimates of the inputs for the particular policy levers included in the model.

7. The Multipliers

The fiscal policy instruments have been evaluated traditionally by the standard multiplier which shows the ratio of real GNP to the real change in the value of the policy instrument. As Part I of this volume discussed, the concept of the multiplier becomes quite ambiguous as the associated monetary policy assumptions change and as the extent of financial and real crowding out changes. Various economic conditions, including the rate of inflation, affect the multiplier.

However, it is still useful to analyze the traditional multiplier, if only to bring out the relative impacts of the various fiscal tools. Table 10.4 summarizes a series of simulation studies for major tax and expenditure policies. These simulations were conducted under conditions of relatively

Table 10.4
Fiscal Policy Multipliers Under Various Monetary Assumptions
(Test period: 1966-1971)

	Quarters After Policy Change						
	1	4	8	12	16	20	24
Multipliers for a Sustained $10 Billion Increase in Real Government Spending							
Unchanged Nominal Interest Rates	1.181	1.932	2.009	1.448	0.949	0.641	0.441
Unchanged Real Interest Rates	1.169	1.799	1.539	0.805	0.297	0.340	0.453
Unchanged Nonborrowed Reserves	1.065	1.451	1.548	0.983	0.519	0.593	0.208
Unchanged Money Supply	0.756	0.597	0.440	0.321	-0.038	-0.098	-0.261
Multipliers for a $5 Billion Cut in Personal Taxes							
Unchanged Nominal Interest Rates	0.176	1.189	1.432	1.096	0.793	0.528	0.548
Unchanged Real Interest Rates	0.174	1.132	1.142	0.687	0.327	0.290	0.475
Unchanged Nonborrowed Reserves	0.146	0.921	1.102	0.731	0.450	0.504	0.449
Unchanged Money Supply	0.146	0.258	0.093	0.159	-0.072	-0.030	-0.052
Multipliers for a $10 Billion Cut in Corporate Taxes							
Unchanged Nominal Interest Rates	0.123	0.380	0.444	0.472	0.648	0.795	0.530
Unchanged Real Interest Rates	0.124	0.358	0.402	0.372	0.480	0.659	0.513
Unchanged Nonborrowed Reserves	0.187	0.407	0.463	0.546	0.832	0.996	1.046
Unchanged Money Supply	0.089	0.131	0.124	0.098	0.125	0.242	0.272
Multipliers for an Increase in Investment Tax Credits							
Unchanged Nominal Interest Rates	0.163	1.271	1.591	1.522	1.036	1.602	2.326
Unchanged Real Interest Rates	0.164	1.210	1.475	1.162	0.711	1.356	2.233
Unchanged Nonborrowed Reserves	0.191	1.074	1.217	0.933	0.689	1.320	1.615
Unchanged Money Supply	0.105	0.475	0.505	0.285	0.244	0.523	0.843

high employment with moderate and rising inflation, using the period 1966 to 1971 as the test period.

Various conclusions can be seen from these multiplier exercises. Under conditions of unchanged nominal interest rates, an over-accommodative monetary policy which has, in the past, been considered an adequate baseline for fiscal policy analysis, the multipliers are large and typical of the results found in the earlier literature. For an increase in real government spending on goods and services, the multiplier reaches a maximum of 2.0 after eight quarters but is crowded out to a value of 0.44 at the end of 24 quarters. A permanent reduction in the effective personal tax rate has a peak multiplier of 1.43 after eight quarters, but is also crowded out to a value of 0.55 by the end of 24 quarters. The cut in corporate tax rates has a very different multiplier pattern. It reaches a peak of only 0.80, mainly because its effect on the rental price of capital is quite modest, so that the bulk of the effect originates in improved cash flow. The effect is also much more drawn out because the stimulus comes through the channel of boosted business investment, a final demand which responds to economic conditions after a considerable lag. The multiplier for an increase in the investment tax credit, a powerful boost to the rental price of capital, shows a more favorable pattern. The multiplier is at a peak of 2.33 at the end of the 24 quarters, largely because it has a very significant supply effect. The extra investment adds to potential GNP in cumulative fashion, raising potential GNP by 1.1 times the stimulus by the end of the period. As a result, inflation experience is somewhat more favorable after an initial demand-induced price level boost. Increased real activity acts as a further stimulus to investment; higher real incomes boost consumption as well.

The other polar assumption about monetary policy holds the money supply unchanged. In actual practice, the Federal Reserve would find this quite difficult to accomplish and would have to act on forecasts of the impacts of fiscal policy on the economy including the demand for money. This approach requires that the Federal Reserve tighten up immediately upon announcement of a fiscal stimulus; indeed to achieve perfect results it would have to engage in anticipatory tightening before the fiscal move takes effect. Under this assumption, multipliers are small and temporary. For government purchases, the peak multiplier is 0.76, reached in the first quarter, indicating that there is crowding out even in the very first period. After four quarters, the crowding out has grown, lowering the multiplier to 0.60, and after 16 quarters the multiplier has turned negative, as the higher price level, at a given money supply, allows room for less real activity.

The results for personal tax cuts with an unchanged money supply are also quite unfavorable. The peak multiplier of 0.26 is reached after four quarters, indicating that there is crowding out of the benefits of the personal tax cuts from the very beginning. After 16 quarters, the results turn slightly negative. The corporate rate reduction, on the other hand, has more permanent benefits. The multiplier is small, 0.13 during its initial peak in the second year, but it stays positive and in years five and six moves toward 0.30. The result is steadily positive because the cash flow created by the corporate tax reduction is particularly helpful when the money supply is kept unchanged, permitting some increase in investment which ultimately also has some beneficial supply effects.

The multiplier for investment tax credits under a condition of unchanged money supply is the most favorable because of its power as a supply-side stimulus. The multiplier reaches an initial peak of 0.51 in the second year and a value of 0.84 at the end of the test period in the 24th quarter.

The other monetary assumptions are intermediate in nature between the two polar cases. Unchanged real interest rates produce results only slightly lower than unchanged nominal interest rates because the amount of inflation created by these limited fiscal moves is quite small and delayed. The peak values tend to be about three-fourths of the magnitudes reached under unchanged nominal interest rates and to come slightly earlier. The interest rate chosen for real constancy in the exercise was the Federal funds rate, the rate at the very short end of the interest rate yield curve. The other rates were allowed to move freely.

The traditional simulation assumption of unchanged nonborrowed reserves turns out to be closer to the polar case of unchanged nominal interest rates than it is to the unchanged money supply results. According to the DRI model, the movements of the economy have a powerful effect on the demand for money, and somewhat higher interest rates produce a larger supply of money through adjustments in the bank reserve market. The stronger economy created by the fiscal stimulus induces considerable borrowing of bank reserves, an element of financial behavior that is modeled by a portfolio equation for the commercial banking system. This potential variation in the reserve multiplier linking nonborrowed reserves to the money supply gives a monetary policy of predetermined nonborrowed reserves an accommodative characteristic.

Table 10.5 shows the supply multipliers of the fiscal policies, defined as the ratio of the change in potential GNP to the change in the fiscal instrument. The comparison shows that policies to boost consumer spending are necessary to achieve quick results, because in the short run, aggregate supply can only be boosted by creating a tighter economy which draws more people into the labor force and boosts the productivity trend. But these gains are short lived and in the case of government spending are ultimately nearly

Table 10.5
Supply Multipliers of Fiscal Policies
(Test period: 1966-1971)

	Unchanged Real Interest Rates		Unchanged Money Supply	
	Qtr. 8	Qtr. 24	Qtr. 8	Qtr. 24
Government Spending	0.247	0.079	0.092	0.178
Personal Tax Cut	0.216	0.281	0.132	0.061
Corporate Rate Cut	0.037	0.474	0.033	0.356
Investment Tax Credit	0.095	1.372	0.082	1.109

totally lost. The personal tax cut does retain some permanent supply benefits because higher aggregate demand keeps the labor force bigger and the lower taxes induce some extra labor supply and some improved productivity.

The corporate tax changes have bigger supply effects in the long run. Corporate rate reduction boosts aggregate supply by 0.47 per unit of real revenue reduction, and the investment tax credit actually shows a supply multiplier in excess of unity. The effects are not visible for eight quarters because the investment process takes considerable time, first to reach decisions and then to convert the decisions into investment put in place. Ultimately the supply effects are significant and gradually outweigh the demand effects.

A policy of unchanged money supply largely neutralizes the demand effect of fiscal moves. Supply multipliers for government spending or personal tax cuts are also very small, some negative, because the induced supply of labor and capital created by a tighter economy is nullified. On the other hand, the supply effects of corporate tax cuts and investment credits largely survive the monetary offset because they mainly originate in a reduced rental price of capital and improved cash flow. Other demands are crowded out, of course, and it is housing which mainly relinquishes the resources flowing into enhanced business fixed investment.

CHAPTER 11

EXPORTS AND IMPORTS

1. Introduction

The modeling of international trade has become increasingly important because of its very rapid growth and its strategic role in determining industrial development. The behavior of the exchange rate has been a significant influence on the behavior of the price level. Monetary policy has frequently been constrained by exchange rate changes. The DRI Model of the U.S. Economy limits its treatment of foreign trade to those dimensions which directly impact domestic GNP and the price level. Because the model as a whole is very detailed, including a disaggregated industrial sector, the treatment of foreign trade also has to be disaggregated. On the other hand, the model does not contain a treatment of international capital flows, nor is the model a mechanical component of a fully linked set of national models. DRI's inas a whole impacts the domestic economy mainly through the balance on goods udes a set of linked models of the major inand services, which affects the , but they are considerably more aggregated.

The foreign sector of the DRI model comprises groups of behavioral equations for merchandise trade, services trade, circular flow of demands and incomes. ports and exports, implicit Various production equations are affected nd exports of services, the current by specific exports and imports, and dollar exchange rate. The sector pass some additional effects into the macro economy.

The major problem faced in the estimations is the well-known asymmetry in the development of equations for imports and exports. Since many variables relating to the foreign economies are not available, export functions tend to be underdetermined. Import equations, on the other hand, make use of a broad selection of domestic variables. For the price equations, the problem is reversed. While export prices are largely determined by domestic prices, import prices are a function of prices abroad which have to be approximated by an imperfect weighted average of price indexes for industrial countries.

2. Merchandise Trade

Real exports of merchandise, disaggregated into six end-use categories, are related to a weighted average of foreign activity variables and relative prices. The categories are listed in Table 11.1. The ratio of the unit value index of each end-use export category to a weighted average of foreign prices measures relative price. The typical export equation for commodity i takes the form:

$$X_i/p_{xi} = a + b\Sigma^n_{j=1}w_j Y_j - cp_{xi}/\Sigma^n_{j=1}v_j(p_{wj}/exch) \tag{1}$$

where i is a commodity index, j a country index, Y_j a foreign activity variable valued at constant prices, and the final term the exchange rate correction.

Similarly, real imports of merchandise are determined by domestic activity variables and by relative prices, defined as the unit value index of each import category relative to a weighted average of wholesale prices of the domestic commodities. The typical import demand equation for commodity i can be written as:

$$M_i/p_i = d + eX_i + p_{mi}/p_i \tag{2}$$

where X_i is a real domestic final demand variable, p_{mi} is the price of the import and p_i is the wholesale price of the competing domestic product.

To produce meaningful statistical relationships, trade flows must be disaggregated. When the analysis is confined to aggregate imports, the domestic activity variable is assumed to be the same for each underlying category, with the import content of the various final demand components assumed to be equal. In other models, this problem has been circumvented at least partly by weighting the expenditures components by their import content as derived from input-output analysis.[1] A high degree of aggregation also poses difficulties for the construction of adequate time series on trade prices and on prices for domestically produced close substitutes.[2] To allow each category to be modelled with appropriate demand and price variables and differentiated functional forms and parameters, the DRI model explains six separate categories of exports and seven of imports.

The data for the trade flows are on a census end-use basis rather than the Standard International Trade Classification (SITC). Income elasticities as

---

[1] An example of this approach is provided by N.K. Choudry, Y. Katowitz, J.A. Sawyer and John L. Winder, *The TRACE Model of the Canadian Economy*, Toronto, 1972. The same approach was applied in the RDX2 model of the Canadian economy. John F. Helliwell et.al., *The Structure of RDX2*, Bank of Canada Staff Research Studies, 7, 1971.

[2] See Hendrik S. Houthakker and Stephen P. Magee, "Income and Price Elasticities in World Trade," *Review of Economics and Statistics* (February 1969), pp. 111-125. Edward E. Leamer and Robert M. Stern, *Quantitative International Economics*, Boston, 1970, p. 15.

well as relative price elasticities tend to be higher when end-use categories are the dependent variables. Export and import prices are unit value indexes, computed as weighted averages of unit values of individual commodities. The use of unit values constructed from aggregate exports and imports should be avoided because, besides price effects, they also reflect changes in commodity composition and income.[3] Appropriately constructed unit value indexes derived from individual commodity prices, however, help to yield the correct sign and size of relative price elasticities in the structural equations.

2.1 Exports

Exports of merchandise are determined on the basis of relative prices and indexes of industrial production of our major trading partners (Canada, OECD-Europe, and Japan), weighted by the share of exports of each end-use category shipped to these countries. For example, exports of automotive vehicles and parts have been traditionally destined largely for Canada, which explains its weight of 0.91 in the pertinent index of foreign industrial production.

A trade-weighted average of wholesale prices in the same countries is used as a relative price variable. The choice of wholesale prices places emphasis on the foreign counterpart of our export prices. The trade weights are an average of imports and exports rather than exports alone. This permits use of the index of foreign wholesale prices as an explanatory variable in the import price equations as well. The structural equation for exports of foods, feeds, and beverages differs from the other categories in that relative prices do not play a significant role. However, the presence of the exchange rate captures at least an aggregate relative price effect.

Other explanatory variables are sparse in the export equations. In the equation for exports of foods, feeds, and beverages, the world grain supply outside the United States, divided by the non-U.S. population of grain-consuming nations, explains the wide swings in the U.S. exports of foods due to crop failures in Russia and elsewhere. The elasticity of exports with respect to this variable is very high (2.18 in absolute terms) and substantially overshadows the long-run elasticity with respect to foreign demand (1.15). A dummy variable was included in each export equation to assess the effect of the major dock strikes that occurred in 1965:1, 1969:1, and 1971:4.

[3]See Uwe Westphal, *A Disaggregated Analysis of German Merchandise Imports,* Research Memo 7, University of Hamburg (December 1976).

Table 11.1
Estimated Elasticities of Merchandise Exports and Imports
With Respect to Activity Variables and Relative Prices

	Real Activity		Relative Price	
	Short-Run	Long-Run	Short-Run	Long-Run
Exports				
Food	0.125	1.312		
Raw Materials	0.868	0.868	-0.078	-0.259
Capital Goods	0.246	1.232	-0.167	-0.836
Automotive	0.537	1.611	-0.056	-0.395
Consumer Goods	0.498	0.997	-0.210	-1.472
Other	0.375	0.936	—	—
Weighted Sum	0.470	1.137	-0.097	-0.487
Imports				
Food	0.697	1.743	-0.334	-0.808
Raw Materials	0.393	1.178	-0.098	-0.685
Fuels and Lubricants	0.600	1.400	-0.080	-0.798
Capital Goods	1.269	2.341	-0.498	-0.996
Automotive	0.379	1.137	-0.202	-0.404
Consumer Goods	0.818	2.453	-0.423	-1.057
Other	0.432	1.513	-0.277	-1.937
Weighted Sum	0.616	1.624	-0.245	-0.816

A comparison of the income and relative price elasticities of merchandise exports in the current period and in the long run is presented in table 11.1. It shows that the results of standard demand theory carry over to international transactions. For example, the long-run income elasticity is higher and the lag is longer for exports of capital goods than for industrial materials. The same applies to relative price elasticities. This is not surprising, since most capital goods have domestic substitutes in the industrialized importing countries, while many supplies and materials do not. For automobiles—a luxury good—the price elasticity is quite low, only -0.09 in the short run and -0.64 after four quarters. The long-run income elasticity is relatively high and reaches 1.24 after five quarters.

2.2 Imports

The structural equations for imports by end-use category allow a much richer specification than do the corresponding export equations because proper measures of domestic activity and prices are available.

For imports of food, feeds, and beverages, the domestic demand variable is the lagged wages and salaries component of personal income, deflated by the consumer price index for food. In the raw materials imports equation, industrial production in the materials-producing sector and in the manufacturing sector as a whole are the relevant variables, with weights of 0.3 and 0.7, respectively. Imports of capital goods are driven by a polynomial distributed lag on nonresidential investment in producers' durable equipment. Total employment in the previous two quarters is a further indicator of the domestic business cycle and of the need for incremental foreign supplies of capital goods. The deviation of the index of capacity output in manufacturing from its own long-run trend captures increased domestic potential for production of capital goods and thus affects imports negatively.

Although a wide variety of automotive products is contained in imports of automobiles and parts, imported new automobiles account for approximately 60% of this category, and the lagged values of imported retail car sales proved to be the best explanatory variable for this component. To account for the less important parts component (largely the result of the auto pact with Canada), domestic production in the automobile sector was included.

Figure 11.1
Imports and Exports

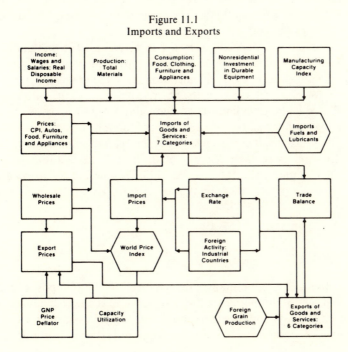

Consumer goods imports are explained by the corresponding elements in consumer expenditures. The ratio of the unit value of the specific end-use category, divided by the price(s) of its domestic counterpart, enters with the proper negative sign and with an elasticity ranging from a low of 0.4 for raw materials to a high of 1.755 for goods not elsewhere classified.

3. Imports and Exports of Services

The export of travel, transportation, and fees is explained by the growth of industrial production of our major trading partners, which serves as a proxy for growing real foreign income. The exchange rate captures the relative price effect. Transportation services are determined by both exports and imports of merchandise.

Income on U.S. investments abroad includes revenues from direct investment (branch profits), other private assets, and government assets. It is determined by the growth of foreign industrial production and by the exchange rate. This simple equation captures only the trend in foreign investment income, because relevant determinants such as interest differentials and capital flows are not taken into account. The swings resulting from the large capital flows between the U.S. and OPEC during the oil crisis have to be captured by a dummy variable.

Imports of services include payments to foreigners for military services rendered and income payments on foreign investment in the U.S. These components are exogenous. Transportation services are positively related to imports of goods, which explains the positive elasticity of 0.8 with respect to the distributed lag of total imports of merchandise. The exchange rate serves both as a relative price and as a determinant of foreign income, much of which is designated in foreign currencies. A dummy variable was included in the imports of services to take account of the strong fluctuations in foreign investment income in the U.S. in the 1973-1974 period as a result of the payments by American oil companies to their OPEC affiliates after the oil price hike.

4. Trade Prices

Import prices are predominantly determined by the composite index of wholesale prices of our major trading partners and the exchange rate. Prices of imported capital goods are further influenced by pressures on capacity in the exporting countries and in the domestic manufacturing sector. In the case of automobile import prices, pressures on capacity in the Japanese industrial sector, approximated by a distributed lag of changes in her industrial production index, as well as the domestic wholesale price index in the automobile sector, play important roles in addition to world prices. The implicit deflator for imports of services is explained on the basis of the same theoretical specification as the other import prices.

Unit values of exports are related to domestic wholesale prices and, hence, will be better explained than import prices. Table 11.2 summarizes the price elasticities of the unit values of imports and exports by end-use category, both in the first quarter and in the long run.

Table 11.2
Price Elasticities of Unit Value Indexes of Imports and Exports

Unit Value Index	Short-Run Elasticity	Long-Run Elasticity	Lag in Quarters
Unit Values of Imports, by End-Use Category			
Food	0.467	0.933	2
Fuels and Lubricants	0.250	1.000	4
Raw Materials	0.441	0.883	4
Capital Goods	0.082	0.763	6
Automotive	0.219	0.631	4
Consumer Goods	0.084	1.001	4
Implicit Price Deflator for Imports	0.355	1.065	5
Unit Values of Exports, by End-Use Category			
Food	0.379	1.196	2
Raw Materials	0.912	0.912	1
Capital Goods	0.455	1.137	4
Automotive	0.485	0.970	3
Consumer Goods	0.454	1.136	4
Implicit Price Deflator for Exports	0.127	1.021	4

5. Simulation Results

The size of the foreign trade multiplier is approximately 1.5 at its peak, defined as the ratio of the change in real GNP to the change in net exports, and is reached after five quarters. More than half of the effect is found in the first quarter.

Table 11.3
Summary of the Effects of Alternative Scenarios on the
U.S. Goods and Services Balance
(Billions of dollars)

	1966	1967	1968	1970	1973	1977
5% Appreciation of the Dollar	-0.3	-1.4	-1.6	-2.0	-3.5	-6.5
5% Depreciation of the Dollar	0.4	1.7	1.9	2.4	4.1	7.8
Higher Domestic Growth	-0.3	-0.6	-0.9	-0.7	-0.2	-0.3
Lower Domestic Growth	0.4	0.6	0.9	0.8	0.3	0.6
Tight Money	0	0.4	0.3	0.3	0.1	0.3
Easy Money	0	-0.4	-0.3	-0.2	0.1	-0.1
More Domestic Inflation	-0.1	-0.2	-0.1	0.2	0.6	1.0
Less Domestic Inflation	0.1	0.2	0.1	-0.2	-0.6	-1.1

Table 11.3 summarizes the effect of alternative scenarios on the goods and services balance and shows fairly symmetric responses to positive and negative shocks. Even for relatively large shocks, the behavioral responses within the foreign sector remain quite linear in the model. Accordingly, only the effect of one-directional disturbance will be explained in detail.

Table 11.4
Effects of Higher Domestic Growth on Selected Variables
in the Foreign Trade Sector
(Billions of dollars)

	1966	1967	1968	1970	1973	1977
Real Exports	0.1	0.5	0.7	0.3	-0.3	0.2
Real Imports	0.6	1.5	2.2	1.4	0.1	1.1
Export Prices*	0.1	0.6	1.0	1.4	1.5	2.8
Import Prices*	0	0.2	0.5	1.1	1.3	1.6
Real Balance	-0.5	-1.0	-1.5	-1.1	-0.4	-0.9
Nominal Balance	-0.3	-0.6	-0.9	-0.7	-0.2	-0.3
Wholesale Prices*	0.1	0.5	0.8	1.3	1.6	2.6
Change in Policy Variable:						
Real Other Government Spending	1.0	1.0	1.0	1.0	1.0	1.0

*Percent change from baseline

Conforming to *a priori* expectations, higher growth in the domestic economy created by a $5 billion sustained increase in Federal government military spending leads to increased imports by intermediate and final goods industries, totalling $1.1 billion at the peak of the multiplier. Wholesale price inflation is fed by the increased pace of the economy and spills over into higher export prices. After four years, the implicit deflator of total exports lies 1.9% above its control value. The international trade mechanism then transmits some of this rise to world prices and, hence, our own import prices. This worsening of the U.S. competitive position on world markets and the increased real demand for imports results in a deterioration of the balance on goods and services by $0.9 billion.

Table 11.4 shows the effect of higher domestic growth on selected variables. The increase of exports is due to the simulation rule which makes foreign production respond to U.S. activity. Imports are up a lot more, of course. Similarly, import prices respond to a simulation rule.

5.1 Effect of Higher Inflation

The effect of higher inflation in the domestic economy is presented in table 11.5. Average hourly earnings were raised by 1% throughout the solution interval. This 1% sustained rise in the level of average hourly earnings affects wholesale prices in the domestic economy with a lag. As a result, export prices exceed their baseline solution value by 1% in 1971 and by 1.5% in 1975. Import prices are also affected because of the interdependence of world

Table 11.5
Effects of Higher Domestic Inflation on Selected Variables
in the Foreign Trade Sector
(Billions of 1972 dollars)

	1966	1967	1968	1970	1973	1977
Real Exports	0	-0.1	-0.1	-0.2	-0.3	-0.2
Real Imports	0.3	0.3	0.1	-0.4	-0.6	-0.4
Export Prices*	0.3	0.6	0.7	0.6	0.6	0.9
Import Prices*	0.1	0.4	0.5	0.6	0.5	0.6
Real Balance	-0.3	-0.4	-0.2	0.2	0.3	0.2
Nominal Balance	-0.1	-0.2	-0.1	0.2	0.6	1.0
Wholesale Prices*	0.4	0.6	0.7	0.6	0.7	0.9
Change in Policy Variable:						
Average Hourly Earnings*	1.0	1.0	1.0	1.0	1.0	1.0

*Percent change from baseline

economies, but to a lesser extent than export prices, thus leading to a small increase in relative prices. While the relative price of U.S. products on world markets also increases in the high growth scenario, the effect of high inflation is different because the demand for imports does not rise. On the contrary, real imports fall owing to the reduction in domestic activity that is induced by the consistently higher inflation. After the first two years of the solution interval, the income effect overshadows the relative price effect, so that the merchandise balance and the services balance improve, both in constant and in current prices. This solution holds the exchange rate constant, and monetary policy is not accommodating. These assumptions largely create the long-term result.

5.2 Effect of Easier Monetary Policy

Easier monetary policy, achieved by a $1 billion sustained rise in nonborrowed free reserves, affects the foreign sector primarily through its effect on domestic real growth and inflation. Real GNP surpasses its base value by 1.7% in 1967 and by 0.8% in 1968, and thereafter falls gradually below the Control solution path. The strong cyclical response in the real sector, together with a gradual increase in inflationary pressures, affects the foreign sector through a cyclical response in import demand coupled with a small change in relative prices in favor of the outside world. The pattern in real imports reflects the change in domestic growth and the reduced relative price of imports. The real trade balance deteriorates, of course. The nominal trade

Table 11.6
Effects of Increase in Nonborrowed Free Reserves on
Selected Variables in the Foreign Sector
(Change, billions of dollars)

	1966	1967	1968	1970	1973	1977
Real Exports	0.1	0.5	0.6	-0.1	-0.1	0.1
Real Imports	0.1	1.2	1.2	0.2	0	0.2
Export Prices*	0.1	0.6	0.9	0.8	0.8	0.6
Import Prices*	0	0.3	0.7	0.7	0.8	0.4
Real Balance	-0.1	-0.7	-0.6	-0.3	0	-0.2
Nominal Balance	0	-0.4	-0.3	-0.2	0.1	-0.1
Wholesale Prices*	0.2	0.7	0.8	0.8	0.8	0.5
Change in Policy Variable:						
Nonborrowed Free Reserves	1.0	1.0	1.0	1.0	1.0	1.0

*Percent change from baseline

balance deteriorates less than its real counterpart, since exports are now valued at higher prices relative to total imports (table 11.6). This solution again assumes a fixed exchange rate.

5.3 Effect of Changing Exchange Rate: The J-Curve

Viewed as a group, the relative price elasticities of weighted aggregate long-run imports and exports are -0.816 and -0.487, respectively (table 11.1). According to the familiar Marshall-Lerner conditions, a depreciation of the home currency in a two-country world leads to an improvement of the balance of payments provided that the sum of the import and export elasticities exceeds unity. While the two-country assumption does not apply precisely to the real world, the specification of the foreign sector outlined above treats the rest of the world like one foreign country. Since the sum of the price elasticities equals 1.303, a depreciation of the exchange rate should lead to an improvement of the trade balance. This was tested in a dynamic simulation. The exchange rate was depreciated by 5% throughout the solution interval. The results (table 11.7) show an improvement in the real goods and services balance of about $5 billion in the long run. Table 11.7 also shows near symmetry in the results of an appreciation or depreciation of the dollar by equal amounts. This is due to both the high degree of linearity of the model and to the smallness of the shock.

Table 11.7
Effects of 5% Changes in the Trade-Weighted U.S. Dollar Exchange Rate
on the Balance of Goods and Services

	Balance at Current Prices ($ billions)	Balance at 1972 Prices ($ billions)	Exports Deflator (% change)	Imports Deflator (% change)
Exchange Rate +5%				
1968	-1.6	-3.6	-1.6	-4.2
1971	-2.2	-4.1	-2.0	-4.4
1973	-3.5	-5.1	-1.8	-4.4
1975	-5.3	-4.9	-2.1	-4.6
1977	-6.5	-5.5	-2.5	-4.6
Exchange Rate -5%				
1968	1.9	3.8	1.7	4.6
1971	2.7	4.4	2.1	4.9
1973	4.1	5.5	2.0	4.8
1975	6.3	5.2	2.3	5.2
1977	7.8	5.8	2.8	5.2

CHAPTER 12

THE INCOME SIDE

1. Introduction

The income side of large-scale macroeconometric models has traditionally received less attention than the equations for final demands. The equations tend to be fairly routine, with the determination of taxes and capital consumption allowances usually containing a passive, less behavioral structure. The wage share of income has most commonly been determined as a by-product of the labor market analysis, with final demand and productivity determining man-hours and the wage-price sector providing the wage rates.

To a degree, a less behavioral approach is justified. Decisions are rarely made about incomes but rather about output, spending, work, price and wage. Incomes are a goal of decisions, but the behavioral initiative lies elsewhere.

Income distributions of gross national income play a pivotal role in the behavior of the macro economy. It has been recognized since the earliest days of economics that the division between households, business, and governments has important effects on the division of output between consumption and investment and on the dynamic characteristics of the economy. In addition, the tax share of the gross national income has important short- and long-term implications for the economy's development.

In a national income accounting sense, gross national product must equal gross national income since all of the economy's value added accrues to some sector. There are four possible methods in models to assure consistency of the income and output sides. The simplest approach leaves the reconciliation to the statistical discrepancy. This method does not face up to the reconciliation problem. The most commonly used approach has been to let the model equations calculate all income shares except profit, which is treated as a residual. This method has the fault that it accumulates the errors in the profit estimate, which then is a particularly error-prone variable. But profit should be estimated with a high degree of precision, both because of its intrinsic significance and because it plays an important role in determining business spending and financing decisions. A third approach, used in the DRI model until 1978, treats the wage bill and personal income as residuals. This method focusses attention on the critical division between household and profit incomes. The residual wage bill and personal income are assessed independently by calculating the wage bill implicit in the wage and man-hour results and comparing the two estimates for consistency. The fourth method of reconciling the output and income sides is to let the system be initially overdetermined, with all income shares determined even if they do not add up to gross national income. An algorithm then allocates the difference between the income and output estimates among the components of income. As a result, a consistency of the income and output estimates of GNP is assured, and no single income share becomes a residual with its inevitably large errors. This method is now used.

The DRI model's income sector follows the organization of the national income accounts very closely. Table 12.1 summarizes the standard NIA table which reconciles the gross national product (gross national income) with household disposable income, and also shows how the gross national income is divided among the three receiving sectors—businesses, households, and governments.

Table 12.1
Relation of GNP to Disposable Income

Relation of GNP to Disposable Income		Income-Receiving Sector
	Gross National Product *(GNP)*	
	(= Gross National Income)	
less:	Capital consumption allowances *(CCA)*	Business
equals:	Net national product *(NNP)*	
less:	Indirect business taxes *(TX)*	Government
	Business transfer payments *(VBUS)*	Business
	Statistical discrepancy *(STAT)*	
plus:	Subsidies less current surplus of govt. enterp. *(SUB@SRPG)*	Government
equals:	National income *(YN)*	
less:	Corporate profits and inventory valuation adjustment *(ZBADJ)*	Business
	Contributions for social insurance *(TW)*	Government
plus:	Government transfer payments to persons *(VG)*	Households
	Interest paid by govt. and consumers *(INTC+INTNETGF)*	Households
	Dividends *(DIV)*	Households
	Business transfer payments *(VBUS)*	Business
equals:	Personal income *(YP)*	
less:	Personal taxes *(TP)*	Government
equals:	Disposable income *(YD)*	Households

2. The Income Equations

2.1 Corporate Profits—National Income Account Basis

The corporate profits equation is one of the most important in the model. It is also one of the most difficult. Specifications drawn from the literature,[1] emphasizing utilization rates and the relationship between price and unit labor costs as determinants of an economy-wide profit margin, have good statistical properties. However, small changes in specifications substantially alter the extent of cyclicality of the equation as well as the trend properties of the profit share in GNP. The particular equation was chosen for its good performance in complete model simulations. The equation's cyclicality is not among the most extreme. In the first year, the elasticity of profits with regard to GNP increments may be as high as four, depending on the composition of the GNP change. But after a few more quarters the elasticity settles down near unity. The elasticities found for publicly reported company profits are higher.

The national income accounts define profits on the Internal Revenue Service book basis. This concept is less cyclical for reasons that are little understood; in the 1975 recession, this concept of profit showed no decline, even though publicly reported profits were down 2.7% (as measured by the 600 companies in the DRI Industry Financial Service).

The model equation shows a very gradual drop in the pretax profit share of GNP if the economy is on its balanced growth path. During the postwar period there was a substantial decline in the profit ratio, and much of this decline was due to the worsening cyclicality of the last few years. Whether there is a long-term downdrift of profits remains a subject of controversy.[2]

The dependent variable in the main equation is book profits plus capital consumption allowances. This comprehensive concept was used because there have been several large changes in depreciation practices in the postwar period which substantially affected pre-tax profits on the Internal Revenue Service basis. This form of the variable does imply, however, that changes in corporate profit taxation are not shifted and that changes in the tax treatment

---

[1] Earlier studies include Edwin Kuh, "Profits, Profit Markups, and Productivity," Study Paper No. 15, *Employment, Growth and Price Levels* (U.S. Congress, 1960); James S. Duesenberry, Otto Eckstein and Gary Fromm, "A Simulation: The United States Economy in Recession," *Econometrica* (October 1960), pp. 749-809; and Charles L. Schultze, "Short-Run Movements of Income Shares" (NBER Conference on Income and Wealth, 1961).

[2] See William D. Nordhaus, "The Falling Share of Profits," in *Brookings Paper on Economic Activity* (1974:1), pp. 169-208; and Martin Feldstein and Lawrence Summers, "Is the Rate of Profit Falling?" in *Brookings Papers on Economic Activity* (1977:1), pp. 211-227, for contrasting views.

of depreciation or investment credits do not affect the total of this measure of gross "cash flow."

The profit concept is the pretax concept before the corrections for inventory profits and underdepreciation. This concept is chosen because the corrections are quite synthetic and based on very limited information. The corrections are estimated in separate equations and applied to the book profit concept in order to preserve the accounting identities of the national income accounts.

The major variables in the profit equation (Table 12.2) are (1) the manufacturing utilization rate, which reflects the degree to which overhead capital costs are spread over the volume of production, and (2) GNP adjusted for government purchases of services. These variables have been prime ingredients of profit equations for the last two decades. The ratio of an appropriately weighted price index to economy-wide unit labor cost reflects the price-labor cost relationship as affected by productivity swings and the numerous forces which determine prices.

Table 12.2
Equation for Profits,
National Income Accounts Basis

Ordinary Least Squares

Quarterly (1960:1 to 1980:3): 83 Observations
Dependent Variable: ZB—EXSFI+MSFI+CCACORPBOOK+TXGFWF

	Coefficient	Std. Error	t-Stat	Independent Variable
	-324.110	26.36	-12.29	Constant
1)	0.173447	0.001988	87.25	GNP-(1-PERG72)*G
2)	-0.109742	0.008935	-12.28	(1-UCAPFRBM)*(GNP-(1-PERG72)*G)
3)	187.377	15.32	12.23	TEMP@ZBIN

R-Bar Squared: 0.9978
Durbin-Watson Statistic: 1.2827
Standard Error of the Regression: 4.101   Normalized: 0.02445

ZB is corporate profits before tax, excluding adjustments for inventory valuation and historical depreciation,
EXSFI and MSFI are exports and imports of factor income,
CCACORPBOOK is corporate capital consumption allowances—book value,
TXGFWF is the windfall profits tax,
PERG72 is government purchases except compensation as a fraction of total purchases,
G is government purchases of goods and services,
UCAPFRBM is the utilization rate of manufacturing (FRB),
TEMP@ZBIN is the ratio of a reweighted industrial price index to unit labor costs.

2.2 Publicly Reported Profits

All the profit concepts estimated in the national income accounts take the measure of profits reported on corporate income tax returns as their point of departure. ZB, called "profits before tax" in the national income accounts, is the measure of book profits as shown on the tax returns. The official profit measures correct for inventory profits and economic depreciation, applying the corrections to ZB.

None of these concepts correspond closely to the profit measures used by the financial community. These measures are based on the public reports of corporations, and are governed by the elaborate professional rules and practices of the public accounting profession. The Security and Exchange

Table 12.3
Equation for Publicly Reported Profits of
600 Large Corporations

Ordinary Least Squares

Quarterly (1960:1 to 1980:3): 83 Observations
Dependent Variable: ZADRI+(1-RTCGFS)*TXGFWF

	Coefficient	Std. Error	t-Stat	Independent Variable
	-123.709	22.08	-5.603	Constant
1)	0.0536006	0.001721	31.15	GNP-CSHOUS-(1-PERG72)*G
2)	-0.0350470	0.006166	-5.684	(1-UCAPFRBM)*(GNP-CSHOUS-(1-PERG72)*G)
3)	36.6258	8.758	4.182	WPI05/WPI05(-1)
4)	47.6555	10.78	4.420	ZADRIIN
5)	0.150081	0.01524	9.849	DMYZADRI*(1/EXCH)*EXSFI

R-Bar Squared: 0.9923
Durbin-Watson Statistic: 2.5578
Standard Error of the Regression: 2.392   Normalized: 0.05549

ZADRI is the total publicly reported profit of 600 companies,
RTCGFS is the statutory tax rate,
TXGFWF is the windfall profits tax,
UCAPFRBM is the utilization rate in manufacturing (FRB),
CSHOUS is housing services,
PERG72 is government purchases except compensation as a percentage of total government purchases,
G is government purchases of goods and services,
WPI05 is the wholesale price of fuels and related products and power,
ZADRIIN is the weighted price term divided by unit labor costs,
DMYZADRI is a dummy for the change in accounting standards which required companies to report profits earned overseas,
EXCH is the U.S. trade-weighted exchange rate,
EXSFI is the export-factor incomes.

Commission enforces these rules, though they are largely developed by the Accounting Principles Board, a professional group of the accounting profession.

While there may have been a desirable solidity to the tax basis for profits 30 years ago, the tax system has absorbed numerous special incentive provisions which are designed to change the taxable income of corporations. As a result, the tax basis differs greatly from the public reporting basis of profits. Since the accounting profession must aim to report profits in as meaningful a form as is feasible to the stockholders and to the financial community through its methods, it provides a better estimate than the tax basis. At least that is the assessment of the financial community which has a considerable stake in the best possible profit reporting.

The DRI model therefore includes estimates of a profit total compiled from the publicly reported profits of about 600 large corporations. These companies, which account for over two-thirds of the economy's profits, are covered in the DRI Industry Financial Service. The data bank developed for this service contains historical records for these companies which are restated for acquisitions and spinoffs. The SEC requires such a record in the annual reports of these companies.

The equation for *ZADRI* (Table 12.3), the time series of total aftertax profits for the 600 companies, follows the general pattern of the profit equation for before-tax profits in the national income accounts. The tax revenues implied by applying the statutory rate of corporate taxation to windfall profits taxes is part of the dependent variable. Because there is a greater continuity to the aftertax profits on the publicly reported basis, *ZADRI* can be used as the dependent variable without broadening the variable to include the other components of "cash flow." Profits are determined by the level of GNP, the utilization rate, the change in energy prices and, since the adoption of a new financial accounting convention, the foreign exchange earnings associated with changing exchange rates.

2.3 Capital Consumption Allowances

The methodology employed by BEA for estimation of capital consumption allowances underwent a major revision in 1976. The old method used data from IRS tabulations of tax returns. BEA gave two reasons for changing its procedure: (1) tax return depreciation is based on asset service lives and depreciation formulae that do not reflect the using up of fixed capital; (2) tax return depreciation is valued in terms of the historical costs of assets whereas capital consumption allowances should be evaluated in current period prices.

The new estimates of depreciation are derived from stocks of fixed capital calculated by the perpetual inventory method. While the information content is diminished, the conceptual basis is stronger. Estimates of gross investment and service lives are derived from

$$K_{g,t} = \Sigma^N_{i=1} I_{g,t-i} - DISC, \tag{1}$$

where $K_{g,t}$ is gross capital stock, $I_{g,t}$ is gross investment, and $DISC$ is discards.

Corporate capital consumption allowances, $CCACORP$ and CCA, are calculated by the Bureau of Economic Analysis as follows:

$$CCACORP_t = PIPDENR_t \, \Sigma^N_{i=1} \, w_i \, IPDENR72_{-i}$$
$$+ PICNR \, \Sigma^M_{j=1} \, w_j \, ICNR72_{-j}, \tag{2}$$

where $PIPDENR$ is the price deflator for producers' durable equipment *(IPDENR72)* and $PICNR$ is the deflator for investment in nonresidential structures *(ICNR72)*.

Noncorporate depreciation is largely attributed to the residential housing stock, so

$$CCA_t = CCACORP_t + PICR_t \, \Sigma^Q_{k=1} \, w_k \, ICR72_{-k}, \tag{3}$$

where $PICR$ is the deflator for investment in residential structures *(ICR72)*. N, M, and Q represent the lifetimes of *IPDENR72, ICNR72,* and *ICR72,* the three forms of fixed investment, respectively.

The final item to be estimated is the capital consumption adjustment to corporate profits *(CCADJZB)*. This synthetic construct is designed to measure the differences between the new and the old definitions of economic and historical depreciation, $CCACORP$. Historical cost depreciation allowances are calculated from historical investment figures and service life estimates. To calculate depreciation rates, the adjustment is calculated as an identity, as the difference between the two depreciation estimates.

2.4 Inventory Valuation Adjustment

The corporate inventory-valuation adjustment *(IVACORP)* is a necessary part of the income side to bring the pretax profit estimates into consistency with the national income account concepts. *IVACORP* measures the difference between the change in the physical volume of corporate business inventories valued at average prices during the period and the change in book value of these same inventories. This adjustment is made to remove the inventory profits that occur in business accounting when the book cost of goods sold or materials used from inventories differs from the current replacement cost. The equation for *IVACORP* multiplies the stocks of farm and nonfarm inventories by the change in the applicable wholesale prices, or

$$IVACORP = d_0 - d_1 \, (\Delta WPIIND) \, (INV72\$NF(-1)) -$$
$$d_2 \Delta((WPI01 + WPI02)/2) \, (INV72\$AF(-1)), \qquad (4)$$

approximating the BEA procedure for estimating this adjustment, where *WPIIND* is the wholesale price index for industrial commodities, *INV72\$NF* is the stock of nonfarm real inventories, *WPI01* is the wholesale price index for farm products, *WPI02* for processed foods and *INV72\$AF* is the stock of farm product inventories.

2.5 Dividends

The DRI model follows the formulation of dividend equations developed by John Lintner.[3] His theory represents dividend policy as an adjustment process which gradually moves actual dividends toward a target dividend-payout ratio. Because of the adjustment process, dividends lag behind earnings and show a smoother pattern. The dividend equation is

$$DIV = -.161178 + .0211506(ZA) + .015863(ZA_{-1}) +$$
$$.0105753(ZA_{-2}) + .00528766(ZA_{-3}) + .911596(DIV_{-1}), \qquad (5)$$

making for a long-run payout ratio of 59.7%.

2.6 Interest Payments of Consumers, Governments, and Businesses

The underlying theory used for interest payments by consumers *(INTC)*, businesses *(INTBUS)* and net interest payments by the Federal Government *(INTNETGF)* is as follows.

D^* represents the desired amount of debt, which is assumed to be related to an interest rate *(R)* and a measure of income *(Y)*, and is written as:

$$D^* = a - bR + cY. \qquad (6)$$

[3]John Lintner, "Distributing of Incomes of Corporations Among Dividends, Retained Earnings, and Taxes" *American Economic Review* (May 1956), pp. 97-113. A more elaborate, portfolio-based theory of dividends is used in the model's dividend equation for the nonfinancial sector's flow-of-funds data.

Portfolio adjustment is gradual, so

$$D = g(D^* - D_{-1}). \tag{7}$$

Upon substitution, the following relationship between observables is obtained:

$$D = ag - bgR + cgRY - gD_{-1}. \tag{8}$$

Assuming that interest payments are the product of D and R, i.e.:

$$INT = DR, \tag{9}$$

the equation to be estimated becomes:

$$INT = b_0 + b_1 R - b_2 R^2 + b_3 RY + b_4(R)(INT(-1))/R(-1). \tag{10}$$

In the case of government, this formulation represents the gradual turnover of debt and the resultant adjustment process of interest costs to interest rates. Business interest payments are divided into the payments of nonfinancial corporations and all others. The payments of nonfinancial corporations are determined as part of the flow-of-funds model for the nonfinancial corporate sector; an equation multiplying the sector's outstanding credit by appropriate interest rates produces that estimate. The remaining business interest payments are principally by the financial sector and are calculated from interest rates and debt outstanding.

2.7 Taxes

The various equations for taxes are treated in detail in the discussions of the government sectors (Chapters 9 and 10). The bases for all federal taxes are determined by the model. The base of federal indirect business taxes is principally determined by the sales volumes of taxed items, defined in real terms where the tax is on the unit basis, in nominal terms where the taxes are ad valorem. For the personal income tax, the average effective tax rate is determined behaviorally from the tax base per capita and the changes in the tax laws that have occurred since the mid-1950s. For corporate and employment taxes, the average effective rate is an exogenous variable.

Taxes of state and local governments are treated behaviorally. While the various tax bases are important variables in the equations, the sector's financial situation also matters. In the long run, revenues must match expenditures, so deficits are entered in the tax equations. In the case of personal income taxes, the share of indirect taxes in total revenue is an additional explanatory variable to reflect the long-run tendency of this sector to keep a normal relationship among the tax sources.

2.8 Personal Income

Personal income is derived by identity from its components:

$$YP = WSD + YOL + V + YINTPER + DIV + YRENTADJ + YENTNFADJ + YENTAFADJ - TWPER. \tag{11}$$

where WSD is wage and salary disbursements, YOL is other labor income, V is transfer payments, $YINTPER$ is personal interest income, DIV is dividends, $YRENTADJ$ is rental income of persons with capital consumption adjustment, $YENTNFADJ$ is nonfarm proprietors' income, $YENTAFADJ$ is the same concept for farm income and $TWPER$ is personal contributions for social insurance.

Wages are modeled as the product of the wage rate and man-hours for the private sector, and as an exogenously determined proportion for the public sector. Transfer payments, personal interest income and dividends were discussed earlier. The determination of personal contributions for social insurance is facilitated by an exogenous share variable and total contributions. The other personal income components are primarily passive in nature. "Other labor income," the national income account estimate of fringe benefits, is estimated as a share of total labor compensation, with a negative sign on the real wage rate allowing for a shift between wage and nonwage labor income. Farm proprietors income is explained by the wholesale prices for farm products and processed foods, as well as several prices which represent the main costs of farming including interest rates. Nonfarm proprietors income, which includes both professional income and income of unincorporated enterprises, is largely modeled from the behavior of profits, a negative time trend and the ratio of consumer to economy-wide prices. Rental income of persons is calculated from the final demand category, consumer housing services, and several cost variables reflecting mortgage and tax payments.

3. Reconciliation of the Income and Product Accounts

The initial estimates of income aggregates, based on the solution of stochastic equations, may result in a GNP total which is different from that determined on the product side of the accounts. This is reconciled in the DRI model by an allocation algorithm. The following simplified example, based on a system in which the only types of income are profits and wages, illustrates the methodology of the algorithm.

First, GNP is estimated from the product side of the accounts, using the demand equations:

$$GNP \equiv C + I + G + EX - M, \tag{12}$$

Then, initial income estimates are derived from the behavioral equations for the income side. The estimate for profits is

$$TEMP_{at}ZB = f(UCAPFRBM, GNP, WPIIND, JULCNF), \tag{13}$$

where $UCAPFRBM$ is the utilization rate, $WPIIND$ is the industrial wholesale price index, and $JULCNF$ is unit labor costs. The estimate for wages and salaries is

$$TEMP_{at}WSD = f(MHEAP, JAHEADJEA), \tag{14}$$

where $MHEAP$ is manhours paid and $JAHEADJEA$ is the wage rate.

Next, a discrepancy is calculated as the difference between GNP from eq. (12) and the income-side total:

$$NIARESID = GNP - (TEMP_{at}ZB + TEMP_{at}WSD). \tag{15}$$

This discrepancy, finally, is allocated to the income components to derive final estimates:

$$ZB = TEMP_{at}ZB + \alpha NIARESID \tag{16}$$

and

$$WSD = TEMP_{at}WSD + (1-\alpha)NIARESID. \tag{17}$$

In the complete modeling of the income accounts in the DRI model, allocation is made to five different income components rather than just to the two shown in this example. The weights are determined subjectively, since single-equation estimation errors give little clue as to the accuracy of the equations in full dynamic model solution. Sixty percent of the discrepancy is allocated to various personal income components, with the remaining 40% allocated to profits. The discrepancy is prevented from feeding back on itself in simultaneous solution—which could cause an unstable solution and greatly increase the number of iterations of a solution—by using estimated interim results before allocation for income variables which affect current-period spending decisions.

4. The Disposition of Personal Income and Personal Saving

The disposition of personal income requires the estimation of only two minor, additional components. Besides personal taxes and consumer spending, personal income is also absorbed by personal transfer payments to foreigners and by consumer interest payments. Transfers to foreigners are exogenous. Interest payments of consumers are discussed earlier in this chapter.

Personal saving is defined as a residual after subtracting personal outlays from disposable income, where personal outlays include consumer spending, interest paid by consumers and personal transfer payments to foreigners. The estimate of personal saving obtained by this method is dependent upon the accuracy of estimates of disposable income and of the several components of consumer outlays. It therefore contains exceptionally great measurement error. In previous historical data revisions, the saving rate has been changed by more than a full percentage point, and consequently the DRI model does not rely on the personal saving rate except to calculate it recursively to correspond to the government estimation method. The flow-of-funds equations for household savings in various financial media are independent of the personal savings estimates and relate directly to income and other variables.

5. Simulation Results: The Automatic Stabilizers

To illustrate the effects of automatic stabilizers, table 12.4 shows the effect of a sustained $10 billion reduction in real nondefense federal spending on consumer purchasing power. The automatic stabilizers cushion the decline, limiting the value of the "multiplier." The single biggest stabilizer is the highly cyclical nature of corporate profits. Because the response of profits to the real GNP decline has an elasticity of about 3 and because profits represent about 13% of the total income share, the profit downswing absorbs about 40% of the initial decline and acts as a major buffer to household incomes. Second in importance is the personal income tax, both federal and state and local, which absorbs 11.8% of the decline. Altogether, the stabilizers offset 60% of the initial effect of lower real GNP on the consumer. The reduced incomes of businesses, governments and the outside world have negative spending effects of their own, of course.

The Income Side

Table 12.4
Effect of Automatic Stabilizers on Consumer Purchasing Power
(Percent of autonomous decline offset by various stabilizers)

	1966:1	1966:2	1966:3	1966:4	1967:1	1967:2	1967:3	1967:4
Autonomous Disturbance[1] (level)	-100.0	-100.0	-100.0	-100.0	-100.0	-100.0	-100.0	-100.0
Less Depreciation *(CCA)*	0	0.8	0.8	1.4	1.7	2.1	2.8	3.4
Profits *(ZBADJ)*	37.6	50.8	42.9	37.5	38.5	33.2	29.4	26.7
Indirect Business Taxes *(TX)*	4.7	4.9	4.5	5.6	5.6	6.2	7.1	6.9
Employment Taxes *(TW)*	3.5	2.5	3.0	3.5	3.4	3.6	4.3	4.3
Plus Transfer Payments *(VG)*	2.4	4.1	4.5	4.9	3.9	4.1	3.8	3.0
Dividends *(DIV)*	0	-0.8	-1.5	-2.1	-2.2	-2.6	-2.8	-3.0
Interest *(INTC+INTNETGF)*	0	-0.8	-1.5	-2.1	-1.7	-2.1	-2.4	-2.6
Equals Offset to								
Personal Income Decline	48.2	61.5	52.7	48.7	49.2	44.5	42.2	38.7
Less Personal Taxes *(TP)*	11.8	9.0	11.3	12.5	11.7	13.0	13.3	13.8
Equals Offset to								
Disposable Income Decline	60.0	70.5	64.0	61.2	60.9	57.5	55.5	52.5
Equals Decline of Disposable Income	40.0	29.5	36.0	38.8	39.1	42.5	44.5	47.5

[1]Disturbance is a maintained $10 billion decline in real federal nondefense purchases.

CHAPTER 13

PRICES AND WAGES

1. Introduction

The wage-price sector in the DRI model embodies four principal ideas not available in its predecessors:

(1) A wage equation in which the total long-run effect of price inflation is reflected with a coefficient near unity, but the price expectations factor has separate long- and short-run components;

(2) A stage-of-processing approach which traces the cost effects of prices through the several stages of production from raw materials, to semi-finished goods, to wholesale finished goods, to retail prices, to GNP deflators;

(3) A set of market measures which more sensitively reflect various supply constraints for industrial commodities than those used in previous studies. Vendor performance, as seen by purchasing executives, is one of these measures. Utilization rates for materials industries, manufacturing capacity and energy availability are direct supply indicators;

(4) A decomposition of inflation into its core, demand and shock components.

In other regards, the wage-price sector follows previous results.[1] Labor costs are measured in the standard unit labor cost form, where the effect of short-run swings in productivity is excluded, approximating labor cost at normal rates of operation. Labor, materials and tax costs affect prices, along with the demand variations. The wage equation uses the inverse of the unemployment rate as the labor market measure. Productivity is estimated

---

[1] Otto Eckstein and Gary Fromm, "The Price Equation," *American Economic Review* (December 1968), pp. 1159-1183. William D. Nordhaus, "Recent Developments in Price Dynamics," in Otto Eckstein, ed., *The Econometrics of Price Determination* (Washington, D.C.: Federal Reserve Board, 1972), pp. 28-30. Otto Eckstein and Thomas A. Wilson, "The Determination of Money Wages in American Industry," *Quarterly Journal of Economics* (May 1962), pp. 379-414; and George I. Perry, "The Determinants of Wage Rate Changes and the Inflation-Unemployment Tradeoff for the United States," *Review of Economic Studies* (August 1964), pp. 287-303.

from the aggregate production function of the model and a cyclical adjustment.

The wage-price sector contains eleven behavioral equations for wholesale prices, a behavioral equation for wages and one for productivity, twenty-two equations for implicit GNP deflators, plus three equations for components of the consumer price index.

Numerous other price equations are scattered through the model, particularly in the foreign trade and energy sectors. This chapter is limited to the main wage-price relations.

The equations for some of the GNP deflators, such as the deflator for producers' durable equipment, are rather mechanical conversions of the wholesale prices from which these deflators are calculated. In other cases, such as the deflator for other consumer services, the deflator is mainly moved by wages. In a third category of cases, such as the deflator for clothing and shoes, the pertinent wholesale price indexes represent only a fraction of retail value added, and so additional variables are included to reflect distribution costs and retail demand conditions. There are also some dummy variables for the periods of price controls in the early 1970s.

All the price equations are estimated in log difference (percent change) form. Wholesale prices are determined by their factor input costs and demand. Wages, adjusted for productivity gains, enter each of the wholesale price equations along with a term giving the input-quantity weighted average of other wholesale prices. The implicit price deflators are, in turn, driven by the input-quantity weighted averages of wholesale prices. The price level feeds into wages and final demands, which, in turn, feed back into prices. Figure 13.1 summarizes these interrelationships.

Figure 13.1
Overview: Prices and Wages

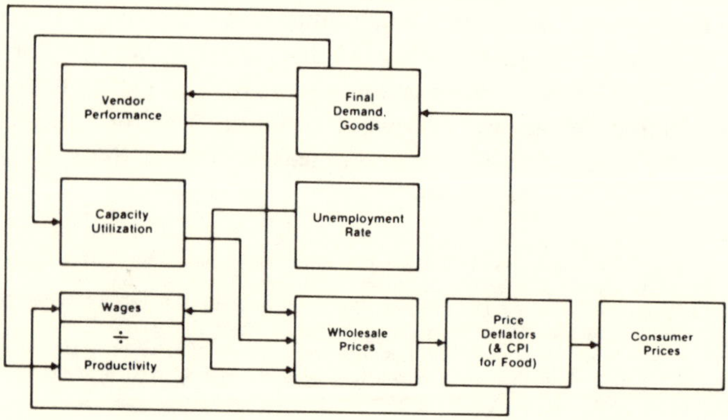

2. Theoretical Summary

The model's wage-price sector can be illustrated with the following few equations, which apply to a static case where leads and lags do not matter.

$$\dot{w} = \alpha_1 \dot{p}^e - \alpha_2 u, \tag{1}$$

where $\dot{w}$ is the current period's rate of wage increase, $\dot{p}^e$ is the rate of expected price inflation, and u is the unemployment rate.

The typical price equation is represented by

$$\dot{p}_i = \beta_{1i}\dot{m}_i + \beta_{2i}\dot{w}_i + \beta_{3i}\dot{d}_i - \beta_{4i}, \tag{2}$$

where $\dot{p}_i$ is the price index of a particular sector, $\dot{m}_i$ is unit material and tax cost, $\dot{d}_i$ is the measure of market disequilibrium and β_{4i} is the trend in factor productivity. $\dot{m}_i$ is defined by the input-output weights of the materials used by the particular industry.

Consumer prices are derived from stage-of-processing price equations summarized in eq. (2), and thus,

$$\dot{p} = \Sigma^n_{i=1} \gamma_i \dot{p}_i. \tag{3}$$

Eq. (4) defines price expectations for the static case to be equal to the observed price changes, so

$$\dot{p}^e = \dot{p}. \tag{4}$$

In the static case, the input-output relations among prices can be solved out of the system, so that

$$\dot{p} = \delta_1 m + \alpha_1 \delta_2 \dot{p} - \alpha_2 \delta_2 u + \delta_3 d - \delta_4, \tag{5}$$

where m represents an index of those material costs which are exogenous to the system (such as world oil and agricultural prices), d is the aggregate index of product market disequilibrium, and δ_4 is the productivity trend. Eq. (5) can be solved for the tradeoff between inflation and the strength of demand in product and labor markets,

$$\dot{p} = (\delta_1 \dot{m} - \delta_2 \alpha_2 u + \delta_3 d - \delta_4)/(1 - \alpha_1 \delta_2). \tag{6}$$

If $\alpha_1 \delta_2 = 1$, eq. (6) is indeterminate. This is the pure, static accelerationist case. More realistic short-run dynamics may make the system determinate even in that case, however.

This static representation of the wage-price process is quite conventional. The novelty lies in the empirical implementation, which takes the static model, injects some (short-lived) dynamics within the industrial price structure through the stage-of-processing equations, decomposes the critical price expectations term of the wage equation into short-and long-term effects, and increases the sensitivity of prices to supply and demand conditions by the introduction of new disequilibrium measures. The model also is quite elaborate in its treatment of various energy prices.

3. Core, Demand and Shock Inflation

The inflation rate in the DRI model is produced by the disaggregated equations for prices, costs and wages, the aggregate production function which determines long-run productivity, the level and composition of aggregate demand, and the various measures of supply. While it is necessary to represent the inflation process in this elaborate way, the sheer complexity hides the fundamentals that are driving this complicated structure.

An aggregated satellite model of the inflation process run recursively aims to reveal the essentials. This model decomposes the inflation rate into three components: the core inflation rate of factor costs which is largely inherited from the past, the shock inflation rate which is the contribution from exogenous factors and micro public policies, and the demand inflation rate which is the contribution of the current state of excess or deficient aggregate demand.

3.1 The Core Inflation Rate[2]

The core rate of inflation can be viewed as the rate that would occur on the economy's long-term growth path, provided the growth path were free of shocks, and the state of demand were neutral in the sense that markets were in long-run equilibrium. The core rate reflects those price increases made necessary by increases in the trend costs of the inputs to production. The cost increases, in turn, are largely a function of underlying price expectations. The core rate is the increase in the aggregate supply price.

In a competitive Cobb-Douglas economy with Hicks-neutral technological change, the long-term equilibrium price, P_c, can be written as,[3]

$$P_c = A q^a w^{1-a} e^{-ht}, \qquad (7)$$

---

[2]The following discussion is drawn from Otto Eckstein, *Core Inflation* (Prentice-Hall, 1981), ch. 2, pp. 7-10.
[3]For a fuller theoretical treatment of equilibrium price, see William D. Nordhaus, op. cit.

where q is the rental price of the capital required per unit of output in a base period, w is the wage rate of the unit labor requirement, h is the aggregate factor-productivity rate of technological progress, and a and $1-a$ are the Cobb-Douglas factor-share weights which, under the assumption of constant returns to scale, must sum to unity.

The core inflation rate is the change in the long-term equilibrium price along the balanced growth path. It can be written

$$\dot{p}_c = a_1\dot{q} + a_2\dot{w} - h, \tag{8}$$

where $a_1 + a_2 = 1$.

The rental price of capital depends on the supply price of capital goods, depreciation and tax parameters, interest rates and equity rates of return. In particular, let

$$\dot{q} = \alpha(\dot{r}, \dot{J}_q), \tag{9}$$

where r is the composite cost of capital and J_q is the composite tax variable on capital and its income. The cost of capital is determined by the long-term inflation expectation embodied in nominal interest rates and equity yields, so that

$$\dot{q} = \alpha(\dot{p}^e_q, \dot{J}_q). \tag{10}$$

Similarly, wages embody the price expectations underlying wage claims, or

$$\dot{w} = \beta(\dot{p}^e_w, \dot{J}_w), \tag{11}$$

where J_w is the tax variable on wages. Therefore, the core rate of inflation depends on long-term price expectations in labor and capital markets, productivity and tax provisions,

$$\dot{p}_c = a_1\alpha(\dot{p}^e_q, \dot{J}_q) + a_2\beta(\dot{p}^e_w, \dot{J}_w) - h. \tag{12}$$

Price expectations are formed on the basis of inflation experience, as measured by distributed lags on actual prices. They need not be the same for bond buyers as for workers. Thus,

$$\dot{p}_c = a_1\alpha((\Sigma^{-\infty}_{t=0} \lambda_t\dot{p}_t), \dot{J}_q) + a_2\beta((\Sigma^{-\infty}_{t=0} \mu_t\dot{p}_t), \dot{J}_w) - h. \tag{13}$$

The actual price record, p, includes the effects of shocks p_s and disequilibrium demand conditions p_d, or

$$\dot{p} = \dot{p}_c + \dot{p}_s + \dot{p}_d. \tag{14}$$

The price expectations of any period therefore are created by shocks, demand conditions and previous core inflation. Productivity performance enters the present core rate through its past effects in holding down the core rate and its current offset to rising factor prices.

This analysis can be given empirical quantification through functions and variables derived from the DRI model. The core inflation rate is the trend rate of increase of average hourly earnings, weighted by the Cobb-Douglas coefficient of 0.65, plus the trend rate of increase of the rental price of capital as used in the investment equations weighted by 0.35, minus the trend rate of increase of aggregate factor productivity. The price expectation in the long-term interest rate reflects a second-degree Pascal lag on the deflator for consumer spending with speed of adjustment of 0.79, an average lag of almost two years. The wage-determining price expectations include a long-term element, based on a second-degree Pascal lag on the consumption deflator with speed of adjustment of 0.85 for an average lag of two-and-a-half years, as well as a short-term factor based on the four-quarter change of this index, lagged once. Aggregate factor productivity is calculated as the residual of the growth of potential real GNP corrected for increases in aggregate factor inputs. Fig. 13.2 shows the historical movement of the core inflation rate.

Figure 13.2
The Core Inflation Rate
(Percent)

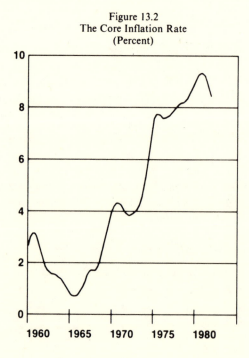

3.2 The Shock Inflation Rate

Exogenous factors such as oil, agricultural prices and exchange rate changes produce an independent inflationary effect. Through full-model simulation it is possible to identify the short-run impact of movements in these exogenous variables on the price level. The relationship identified through the model yields a time series which is combined with the historical values for the exogenous variables to derive the total shock effects from these three sources. The actual relationships linking the energy, agriculture and exchange rate changes to the consumer price index are

$$\dot{p}_{sWPI05} = .008(\Delta WPI05) + .013(\Delta WPI05_{-1}) + \\ .014(\Delta WPI05_{-2}) + .015(\Delta WPI05_{-3}) \tag{15}$$

$$\dot{p}_{sWPI01} = .007(\Delta WPI01) + .012(\Delta WPI01_{-1}) + \\ .014(\Delta WPI01_{-2}) + .014(\Delta WPI01_{-3}) \tag{16}$$

$$\dot{p}_{sEXCH} = -.001(\Delta EXCH) - .003(\Delta EXCH_{-1}) - \\ .005(\Delta EXCH_{-2}) - .008(\Delta EXCH_{-3}) \tag{17}$$

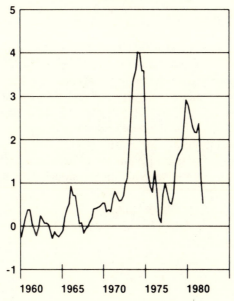

Figure 13.3
Total Shock Contribution to Inflation
(Percent)

where *WPI05* is the wholesale price index for fuels, *WPI01* is the wholesale price index for food, and *EXCH* is the Morgan Guaranty Trust index of the trade-weighted exchange rate for the U.S. dollar.

In addition to the food, energy and exchange rate shocks, the federal government creates exogenous or shock inflation through increases in tax rates, minimum wages, agricultural price-support policies, regulatory policies, and in numerous other ways. Two of these factors, payroll taxes and minimum wages, are built into the DRI model and it is therefore possible to derive a function for the inflation shocks created from these sources.

$$p_{sRTWGF} = 15.4(\Delta RTWGF) + 16.8(\Delta RTWGF_{-1}) + \\ 9.5(\Delta RTWGF_{-2}) + 1.0(\Delta RTWGF_{-3}), \tag{18}$$

$$p_{sMINWAGE} = .00039(\Delta MINWAGE) + .001(\Delta MINWAGE_{-1}) \\ + .002(\Delta MINWAGE_{-2}) + .003(\Delta MINWAGE_{-3}), \tag{19}$$

where *RTWGF* is the tax rate for federal Social Security contributions and *MINWAGE* is the federal minimum wage.

Combining food, energy and the exchange rate with these additional shock inflation sources, the composite shock rate of inflation is calculated and is shown in fig. 13.3.

3.3 Demand Inflation

The demand factor in the short-term inflation rate is measured by a function which relates current demand indicators to the price level. Since the actual inflation rate is largely determined by the core rate and shocks, direct correlations between demand measures and inflation would misspecify the effects. It is necessary to first identify the inflation that remains after allowance has been made for the core and shock elements. The procedure identifies the residual inflation rate by subtracting the core and shock rates from the actual record, and uses an equation which relates this residual to the more powerful of the demand variables in the model. This equation is

$$p_d = -7.7 + \Sigma^{t-1}_{t-7}(\alpha_t/(RU-RUADJ)) + \\ \Sigma^{t-1}_{t-7}(\beta_t/(1.1-UCAPFRBM)) + 0.20(DMYPRICE) - \\ 0.05(DMYPRICECUM)$$

$$\Sigma\alpha_t = 13.8, \ \Sigma\beta_t = 1.1,$$

R-Bar squared: 0.91; Durbin-Watson statistic: 0.75 $\qquad$ (20)

where *UCAPFRBM* is capacity utilization for manufacturing, *RU* is the unemployment rate, *RUADJ* is the adjustment for demographic changes and *DMYPRICE* and *DMYPRICECUM* are dummy variables to capture the effects of the price controls of the early 1970s. The results are shown in fig. 13.4.

Figure 13.4
The Demand Contribution to Inflation
(Percent)

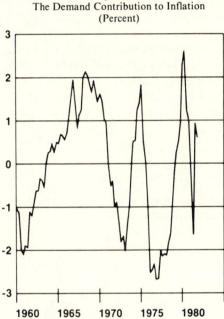

3.4 Historical View

The above analysis can be applied to the historical record. The core inflation rate was approximately 3% in 1959, even though aggregate demand was somewhat below equilibrium. The Korean War and the inflationary episode of the mid-1950s had left a residue of inflationary expectations. The years of balanced growth and moderate resource utilization, as well as the absence of shocks, brought the core inflation rate down to 1% by 1964. The introduction of tax incentives for investment also lowered the rental price of capital to help wipe out the core inflation rate.

The period of over-full employment during the early years of the Vietnam War created a significant demand inflation. Because expectations were still good and the core rate low, the effects of excess demand were largely hidden at that time. But the core rate was rising sharply, to near 4%, and the 1970 recession brought little relief. The period of price controls from 1971 to 1973 had a retarding benefit, but in the subsequent years, the energy and food shocks raised the core inflation rate. The worldwide boom worsened the situation further. The Great Recession of 1974-75 did not halt the core inflation rate because price expectations were still rising. Recovery began to make things worse once more. The shock inflation rate remained positive after 1974; as energy prices advanced, the dollar began a sharp downhill slide in 1977 and food prices went through a major surge in 1978-79. As the boom continued, demand ultimately became excessive and pushed the core rate up further still, reaching 9% in 1980. Thereafter it improved because of tax incentives to lower the rental price of capital, world oil and food price declines, and weak demand.

Figure 13.5
Year-Over-Year Changes in the
Consumer Price Index Compared to the
Sum of Core, Shock and Demand Inflation Rates

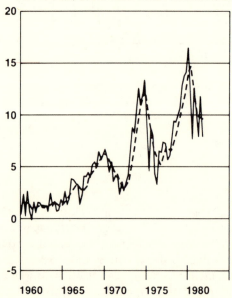

Solid line is actual movement of the Consumer Price Index,
Dotted line is the sum of core, shock and demand inflation estimates.

Table 13.1
Three Estimated Components of Inflation
Compared to the Consumer Price Index
(Average annual percent change)

	1960-69	1970-78	1979-81
Core Rate	1.5	5.4	9.0
Labor Costs	3.9	6.0	7.9
Capital Costs	1.4	6.1	11.1
Productivity	1.5	0.7	0.0
Shock Rate	0.2	1.4	1.4
Food	0.1	0.5	0.3
Energy	0.0	0.8	1.1
The Dollar	0.0	0.1	-0.1
Government	0.1	0.1	0.1
Demand Rate	0.7	-0.1	-0.5
Total	2.4	6.6	9.9
Consumer Price Index	2.3	6.6	9.8

The above analysis shows that the demand element was a major factor in ultimately creating the high core inflation rate. Demand was much above equilibrium in the Vietnam War period and in two briefer bouts in 1971-73 and 1978-79. The shock rate of inflation was at its worst in 1974-75 and 1979-80, mainly due to energy. The net impact was to episodically worsen the core inflation after its low point in 1965, with no real spells of improvement until 1981.

4. Wages and Productivity

The fundamental wage equation is for average hourly earnings adjusted to exclude the impact of changing overtime payments and interindustry shifts between high and low paying industries. The equation relies heavily on the four-quarter change in consumer prices to show the short-run adjustment process of wages to inflation, including the cost of escalator clauses. The long-run adjustment is geared to a Koyck lag variable which represents the gradual learning process that determines long-term inflation expectations. The inverse of the unemployment rate for married males captures the upward pressure placed on wages in a tight labor market and the opposite impact for slack labor market conditions. A fuller and updated account of this equation is presented in Chapter 2.

Compensation per hour differs from the corrected average hourly earnings index primarily through the addition of employer contributions to social insurance, fringe benefits, industrial mix, and premium overtime payments. Thus, the equation for compensation relies on social insurance contributions as a ratio to wage and salary supplements. The level of capacity utilization captures overtime payments and industrial mix effects. The constant includes the trend growth in fringe benefits.

Productivity is determined as a near-identity from the model's estimate of output for the nonfarm business economy and the equation for manhours. The latter embodies the effects of improving technology, changing labor-

Table 13.2
Equation for Average Hourly Earnings

Ordinary Least Squares

Quarterly (1955:1 to 1978:3): 95 Observations
Dependent Variable: 400*log(JAHEADJEA/JAHEADJEA(-1))

	Coefficient	Std. Error	t-Stat	Independent Variable
	4.77445	0.3061	15.60	Constant
1)	0.273990	0.06055	4.525	100*log(PC(-1)/PC(-5))
2)	0.533834	0.08487	6.290	PCEXP85(-1)
3)	-1.99952	0.2528	-7.910	log(RUMM)
4)				PDL(MINWAGEAVG,1,4,FAR)
(-0)	0.00980448	0.003856		
(-1)	0.00735336	0.002892		
(-2)	0.00490224	0.001928		
(-3)	0.00245112	0.0009639		
Sum	0.0245112	0.009639	2.543	
Avg	1.00000	0.0		
5)	-2.36081	0.7843	-3.010	DMY641
6)	0.786482	0.2158	3.644	DGPOST
7)	2.15475	0.6842	3.149	ALTPl

R-Bar squared: 0.8427
Durbin-Watson statistic: 1.7394
Standard error of the regression: 0.7624   Normalized: 0.1464

JAHEADJEA is the BLS earnings index corrected for mix and overtime,
PC is the implicit price deflator for consumption,
PCEXP85 is the corresponding price expectation based on a Koyck lag with a decay factor of 0.15,
RUMM is the unemployment rate for married males,
MINWAGEAVG is the increase in the minimum wage,
DMY64 is a dummy for data discontinuity in 1964:1,
DGPOST is a guidepost dummy, value of -1 during 1964-67,
ALTPI is a price control dummy, sums to zero over period of controls and decontrol, 1971:4 to 1974:4.

Figure 13.6
Wages and Productivity

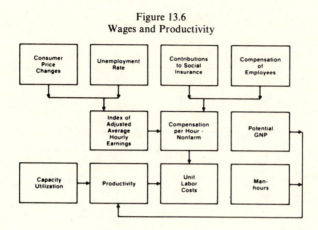

capital ratios and adjustment processes associated with hiring and firing and with the overhead character of much of today's labor. Unit labor costs are derived by dividing compensation by productivity.

5. Wholesale Price Block

The fundamental determinants of each wholesale price equation are materials and wage cost indexes, entering with a lag structure based on stage-of-processing relationships, as well as demand variables. Specific characteristics of the wholesale price block are detailed below. Table 13.4 shows a typical equation.

5.1 Materials and Wage Cost Indexes

Each wholesale price equation has variables representing material and labor input costs. The input weights used are from the 1967 input-output matrix prepared by the Bureau of Economic Analysis. Table 13.3 shows the input weights applied to each wholesale price index, the excise tax term, and the unit labor cost term. While constraining the coefficients to their 1967 input weights excludes the introduction of shifting weights over time into the equations, it helps overcome the problem of multicollinearity. The relations among energy prices are discussed in Chapter 16 describing the energy sector. Fig. 13.7 summarizes the relations among wholesale prices.

Figure 13.7
Wholesale Price Block

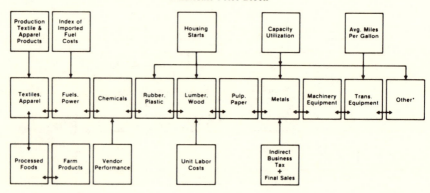

Table 13.3
Material and Wage Quantity Weights
in Wholesale Price Equations

	Farm Products[3]	Processed Foods	Textiles, Apparel	Fuels, Power	Chemicals
Employee Compensation[1]	.247	.248	.631	.481	.461
Indirect Taxes[2]	.125	.083	.012	.341	.021
Farm Products[3]	--	.502	.076	.000	.006
Processed Foods	.270	--	.002	.002	.035
Textiles, Apparel	.007	.003	--	.002	.006
Fuels, Power	.101	.017	.021	--	.173
Chemicals	.178	.013	.030	.057	--
Rubber, Plastics	.015	.014	.158	.008	.093
Lumber, Wood Products	.008	.002	.001	.001	.004
Pulp, Paper	.002	.048	.020	.011	.049
Metals	.009	.046	.004	.033	.099
Machinery, Equipment	.024	.005	.010	.045	.025
Transportation Equipment	.002	0	.001	.000	.001
Other Industrial Products	.012	.019	.033	.016	.026

[1]Unit Labor Costs = Compensation per hour *(JRWSSNF)* divided by productivity *(JQ%MHNF*—smoothed by nine-quarter average) indexed to 1967=100.
[2]Indirect Taxes = Ratio of Indirect Taxes *(TX)* to Final Sales *(SF)* indexed to 1967=100.
[3]The index of wholesale farm product prices *(WPI01)* is exogenous in the DRI Model. In simulations, the index *(WPI01EXO)* moves according to the overall inflation generated in the model.

(Table 13.3, cont'd.)

Rubber, Plastics	Lumber, Wood Products	Pulp, Paper	Metals	Machinery, Equipment	Transportation Equipment	Other Industrial Products
.398	.685	.557	.677	.568	.441	.488
.042	.024	.022	.025	.012	.052	.050
0	.026	0	0	0	0	.026
.004	0	.007	0	0	0	.006
.058	.008	.024	.003	.002	.019	.024
.150	.051	.060	.073	.018	.012	.024
.238	.047	.083	.033	.010	.006	.026
--	.016	.056	.016	.016	.027	.036
.003	--	.121	.009	.003	.008	.023
.043	.020	--	.013	.011	.003	.031
.026	.063	.034	--	.271	.252	.116
.014	.018	.018	.105	--	.121	.117
.004	.003	.002	.019	.027	--	.032
.018	.037	.016	.026	.062	.057	--

Source: "The Input-Output Structure of the U.S. Economy: 1967," *Survey of Current Business,* February 1974, Table 1. The coefficients have been reestimated with a more recent I-O table.

Input weights are found by reading down each column. For example, wages comprise 63.1% of textile input costs, indirect taxes 1.2%, farm products 7.6%, etc. Columns sum to unity.

5.2 Stage-of-Processing Lag Structure

Each materials and wage cost index enters the individual wholesale price equation with a lag structure dependent on the adjustment timing of each wholesale price index to its input costs. The changes in the materials and wage cost indexes over one to three periods were found to be significant, with the impact beginning either in the current or the immediately following period. Thus, the lag structure among prices is short, and the slow adjustment process of the price level originates mainly in wage and capital costs.

5.3 Vendor Performance

Vendor performance measures the percentage of purchasing executives reporting slower deliveries in a monthly survey of the National Association of Purchasing Executives. It is an expectational variable which captures the presence of a build-up in demand pressing against supplies. Vendor performance itself is explained by world production levels, the two-quarter change in nonfarm goods sales with a distributed lag for six periods, the four-quarter change in the ratio of inventory stocks to goods sales, and the industrial utilization rate.

Vendor performance enters eight of the wholesale price equations. Response of the WPIs to changes in vendor performance is nonlinear, with dramatic impacts occurring when vendor performance approaches the boom levels where 70% of purchasing executives report slowing deliveries.

5.4 Capacity Utilization

The impact of capacity pressures in bidding up prices is captured to a large extent by the vendor performance variable. But capacity utilization also enters independently into three of the wholesale price equations. For metals and rubber and plastics prices, the change in the utilization rate of materials industries is pertinent. For other industrials, the inverse of utilization is used in nonlinear form.

5.5 Other Indicators

Four of the wholesale price equations have additional explanatory variables. The production of textiles is a demand measure in the equation for textile prices. Housing starts, with a seven-period distributed lag, affect lumber prices.

On the cost side, the index of imported fuel costs affects fuel with a four-period distributed lag. The legislated standard for average miles per gallon enters into the equation for transportation equipment with a positive sign to capture the impact of efficiency standards on production costs.

The dummy variable for price controls is negative for the quarters when price controls were in effect and is positive to capture the bulge in prices when they were eliminated. It was constrained to have a mean of zero, to assure restoration of normal price-cost relations after the controls were over. It was significant in nine of the eleven wholesale price equations. The exceptions are fuels and lumber and wood products.

6. Price Deflators

Most price deflator equations include labor compensation per hour and input-quantity weighted wholesale prices. Both terms enter with a lag structure reflecting timing adjustments. Table 13.5 shows a typical equation.

Table 13.4
Sample Equation for Wholesale Price Index for Chemicals

Ordinary Least Squares

Quarterly (1962:1 to 1977:4): 64 Observations
Dependent Variable: log(WPI06/WPI06(-1))

	Coefficient	Std. Error	t-Stat	Independent Variable
	-0.00856534	0.002783	-3.078	Constant
1)				PDL (%WPI06INPUT,2,5,FAR)
(-0)	0.227465	0.1077		
(-1)	0.217320	0.04287		
(-2)	0.189501	0.02367		
(-3)	0.144008	0.03502		
(-4)	0.0808411	0.02911		
Sum	0.859135	0.1203	7.142	
Avg	1.57334	0.3322	4.735	
2)	0.00290255	0.001443	2.011	1/(1.1-RDELYSLOW(-1))
3)	0.00471227	0.002011	2.343	DMYPRICE
4)	0.0528427	0.006811	7.758	DMY74

R-Bar squared: 0.9397
Durbin-Watson statistic: 1.7185
Standard error of the regression: 0.006357   Normalized: 0.6124

%WPI06INPUT = log(WPI06INPUT/WPI06INPUT(-1))
WPI06INPUT = 0.07226*JMEND1A+0.92774*TEMP@WPI06
JMEND1A is the unit value index of U.S. imports of supplies and materials except fuels,
TEMP@WPI06 + 0.461*TEMP@ULC+0.021*TX/SF/0.0893393582+0.006*WPI01+
0.035*WPI02+0.006*WPI03 +0.173*WPI05+0.093*WPI07+0.004*WPI08
+0.049*WPI09 +0.099*WPI10+0.025*WPI11+0.001*WPI14+0.026*WPIIND0

Several other variables are important in some of the deflators. The link between wholesale prices and the deflators is not direct in certain instances. Wholesale farm prices are translated first into the CPI for food and then into the food consumption deflator. Similarly, wholesale prices of household equipment are first translated into the deflator for furniture and appliances and then into the deflator for investment in housing equipment. The deflator for housing services is affected by the deflator for residential construction in conjunction with the mortgage rate, and demand as measured by the vacancy rate. Finally, the import and export deflators are derived indirectly from the deflators for the individual end-use categories. These, however, are partly driven by the wholesale prices.

Table 13.5
Equation for Price Deflator for Other Nondurables

Ordinary Least Squares

Quarterly (1962:1 to 1977:4): 64 Observations
Dependent Variable: log (PCNO/PCNO(-1))

	Coefficient	Std. Error	t-Stat	Independent Variable
	0.000159099	0.001263	0.1260	Constant
1)	0.194092	0.05562	3.490	log (PCNOINPUT/ PCNOINPUT(-1))
2)	0.228170	0.05293	4.311	log (PCNOINPUT(-1)/ PCNOINPUT(-2))
3)	0.197761	0.05215	3.792	log (JAHEADJEA(-1)/(0.4+ JAHEADJEA(-2)+0.3* JAHEADJEA(-3)+0.2* JAHEADHEA(-4)+0.1* JAHEADJEA(-5)))
4)	0.00322528	0.0008223	3.922	DMYPRICE

R-Bar squared: 0.8967
Durbin-Watson statistic: 1.4823
Standard error of the regression: 0.002704   Normalized: 0.2763

PCNO is the deflator for other consumer nondurable expenditures,
PCNOINPUT = 0.05156*JMEND4+0.94844*(0.64*WPIINDO+0.36*(0.72830*WPI06+0.27170 *WPI07))
JMEND4 is the unit value index of U.S. imports of consumer goods except food and autos,
WPIINDO is the wholesale price index for other nondurable industrial products,
WPI06 is the WPI for chemicals,
WPI07 is the WPI for rubber and plastic products,
JAHEADJEA is the index of hourly earnings corrected for mix and overtime of private nonfarm production workers,
DMYPRICE is a price control dummy.

7. Consumer Price Index

The final pieces of the wage-price block are two remaining components of the CPI. The index for commodities other than food is a weighted average of the price deflators for commodities. The CPI for services is a similar weighted average of the service deflators, modified by the overweighting of mortgage interest costs that is built into the CPI. Because costs to consumers are more adequately captured by the economy-wide market basket of households, the price deflator rather than the CPI is generally used in other equations. The only major exception to this is the equation for the consumer sentiment index, which relies on the highly publicized CPI.

8. Concluding Comment

Simulation results for the wage-price sector are scattered through this book, particularly in the opening chapters and in the chapter on energy. In building the model, it is particularly important to attach weights to cost factors which correspond to their role in value-added and finished goods prices. The use of input-output weights in the stage-of-processing approach helps assure this property, along with a careful monitoring of the coefficients on labor costs in the equations. The other challenge in modeling is to represent demand effects fully, both in their importance and timing. The demand variable in the core inflation submodel provides a useful check on this property.

CHAPTER 14

UNEMPLOYMENT AND ITS STRUCTURE

1. Introduction

The modeling of the labor market in the DRI model contains considerable detail, but the basic structure is quite plain. Labor supply is determined by the working age population and its age composition, real wages, the personal tax burden and the unemployment rate. Labor supply helps determine potential GNP and productivity, and together with the unemployment rate determines the level of employment as measured by the household survey. Unemployment follows a modified version of "Okun's Law." Thus, employment as measured by the household survey is derived from aggregate supply considerations and the unemployment rate.

Payroll employment, on the other hand, is derived from the production process. It is calculated for two-digit industries in manufacturing and for the other sectors of the economy from the recent history of production. Total nonfarm payroll employment is derived by adding the individual industry estimates, and is used as a check on the estimates of household employment. The model also contains an optional constraint which forces payroll employment and its composition to be consistent with the household employment estimate.

Another check on the estimates of employment is provided by the analysis of total manhours worked. Total manhours depend upon aggregate economic activity and productivity. The average workweek depends upon cyclical conditions. These two estimates imply another figure for total employment, which must reconcile with the other calculations.

The model also contains a breakdown of the composition of unemployment by age, sex and race. This "social indicator" block of equations shows the implications of any given macroeconomic environment on the work opportunities of various groups, including such disadvantaged groups as teenagers and nonwhites. At the time the model was first designed in 1969, it appeared that the unemployment rates of disadvantaged groups would be important determinants of economic policy and so these equations promised to have an importance beyond the value of the specific estimates themselves. It must be acknowledged that economic policy has not reflected much influence from the unemployment rates of disadvantaged groups. The equations are useful, however, for introducing the effects of manpower policies which directly operate on the structure of unemployment.

Some of the key equations for the labor market are discussed in Chapter 3 on supply economics. That chapter discusses the equation for the supply of labor as well as the determination of potential GNP and productivity. The industry employment equations are treated in Chapter 15 on the industrial sector. The remaining equations are discussed here.

2. The National Unemployment Rate

While it is possible to calculate unemployment as a residual from estimates of labor force and employment, experience has suggested that more reliable estimates are produced through the direct estimation method using "Okun's Law."[1] This theory explains unemployment in terms of the gap between potential GNP and actual GNP. It is a reduced-form equation which implicitly embodies within it the four elements that determine cyclical unemployment, including the level of aggregate demand in relation to supply, the reductions of productivity, the workweek and labor supply. The response of unemployment to changes in the gap between actual and potential GNP (the demand-supply gap) is less than one-half, since much of the adjustment is provided by the other three factors.

The equation expressing Okun's Law is shown in Table 14.1.

The critical parameters in the Okun equation have changed since he did his work 20 years ago. Where he found that the coefficient on the gap was 0.32, which required a three-percentage-point reduction in the gap to lower unemployment by one percent, the sum of the coefficients in the DRI equation is 0.38, implying a reduction of 2.6% in the gap to cut unemployment by one percentage point. The later data also argue for a lag structure to reflect adjustment processes, with a mean lag of 1.3 quarters.

[1] Arthur Okun, "Potential GNP: Its Measurement and Significance," *Proceedings of the American Statistical Association*, Washington, D.C., 1962.

3. Unemployment by Sex, Race, and Age

The equations for the structure of unemployment in the DRI model can be summarized as follows.

3.1 Females

Because adult women are employed more heavily in nondurable goods industries, the equation for their unemployment rate relies on the ratio of nondurable goods consumption to GNP as a modifying variable on the national unemployment rate. Nondurable goods consumption, which helps determine retail sales as well as apparel and textile manufacturing, probably also serves as a proxy for labor-intensive services.

3.2 Males, Married Males, Whites, and Heads of Households

The equations for males, married males, whites and heads of households follow the same form, with a shift toward nondurable consumption raising

Table 14.1
Equation for the Unemployment Rate

Ordinary Least Squares

Quarterly (1961:1 to 1980:3): 79 Observations
Dependent Variable: RU-RUFE

	Coefficient	Std. Error	t-Stat	Independent Variable
1)	-37.3638	1.227	-30.45	Constant
(-0)	12.5243	1.486		PDL(GAPRATIO,2,5,FAR)
(-1)	10.0074	0.4162		
(-2)	7.49655	0.5179		
(-3)	4.99170	0.7623		
(-4)	2.49285	0.5977		
Sum	37.5127	1.203	31.19	
Avg	1.33147	1.553	0.8572	

R-Bar squared: 0.9261
Durbin-Watson statistic: 0.3395
Standard error of the regression: 0.3289   Normalized: 0.3668

RU is the national unemployment rate,
RUFE is the full employment unemployment rate using the official Council of Economic Advisers estimates,
GAPRATIO is the ratio of potential GNP to actual real GNP.

these prime unemployment rates. This indicates that the split between female and male unemployment can largely be explained by the composition of demand rather than the composition of labor supply.

3.3 Blacks

Because blacks are employed particularly in services, the black unemployment rate depends upon the share of service consumption in GNP. The equation for this variable combines the measure of the composition of demand with the national unemployment rate. The elasticity of black unemployment on national unemployment is near unity.

3.4 Teenagers 16-19 Years Old

The response of teenage unemployment to changes in national unemployment has an elasticity of only 0.65, indicating that this group suffers from exceptional structural difficulties. In addition, the teenage unemployment rate is affected by the number of teenagers in relation to the total working age population. The large increase in the number of teenagers explains the relative deterioration of their unemployment situation beginning in the mid-1960s. Their number falls in the 1980s, holding out the promise of a small decline in the unemployment of this category.

3.5 Adults 20 and Over

This equation is also modified by the supply side. The share of adults in the total labor force has a small positive effect on this unemployment rate. Thus, adult unemployment is relatively lower today because more of the total burden is born by teenagers.

CHAPTER 15

INDUSTRIAL SECTOR

1. Industrial Production

1.1 Introduction

The industry sector in the DRI model consists of equations for production in seventy-five industries, equations for real and nominal plant and equipment investment plus real capital stocks in thirty-three industries, and equations for employment in thirty-one industries. Four capacity utilization rates are also calculated. The production equations form the heart of the sector, serving as explanatory variables for both investment and employment. The production block is fully simultaneous with the rest of the model.

1.2 The Framework

The production equations represent an evolution of the "flexible-coefficient" bridge model that was used in earlier versions of the DRI model. Input-output (I-O) relationships between supplying and using industries are used to construct "generated output" (GO) series.

These variables show the level of production that would prevail if the constraint coefficient assumptions of classical input-output analysis were precisely correct. Standard regression techniques permit trend and cycle correction variables to model the changes in I-O coefficients which are implied by the changing relationship between actual and "generated" output. The new equations depart from earlier embodiments[1] of this approach in several respects.

[1]The basic approach was developed by Kenneth J. Arrow and Marvin Hoffenberg, *A Time Series Analysis of Interindustry Demands* (Amsterdam: North-Holland Publishing Co., 1959).

(1) Considerable attention was devoted to the construction of each generated output series. Because of differences in the industry definitions employed by the BEA in its 87-level I-O table and those employed by the Federal Reserve Board, in many cases the more detailed 367-level table replaced the 87-level table as the starting point in the construction of the GO. In all cases, the weights derived from the I-O tables were carefully monitored, and in those cases where 1967 proved an atypical year or where structural changes since 1967 have profoundly altered interindustry relationships, the I-O results were overwritten with information from other sources. The equations have been refitted with a more recent input-output table, which covers the year 1972, but these reestimates caused only small changes in the parameters.

(2) Generated outputs for materials industries are expressed directly in terms of output levels in the industries which they supply. In earlier models, these generated outputs were constructed from sets of final demand expenditures, using weights which represented the indirect requirements generated by each final demand category for the particular material in question.

For example, the generated output for primary ferrous metals had included the variable for consumption of automobiles and parts, with the weight which represented the translation of a dollar of expenditure first into production of automobiles and then into derived demand for steel for use by the automobile industry. In the current model, only the GO for the automobile industry contains the consumption variable; the GO for steel is driven directly by the output index for the automobile industry (as well as the indexes for all other steel-using industries).

This advance permits more precise specification of the supply relationships existing within the industrial sector. It also makes it possible to trace the implications of different production assumptions in a particular industry through the entire sector to that industry's direct and indirect suppliers.

(3) Widespread use has been made of mix variables to capture the effects of changes in the composition of spending within final demand categories. For example, the mix of single- and multi-unit housing starts in the equation for lumber production (whose generated output includes the real residential construction variable) models the effect of changes in the mix of construction.

1.3 The Empirical Implementation

The estimated form of a typical production equation is

$$log(X_i / GO_i) = a + b \, log \, u + cm + d \, log \, time, \tag{1}$$

where X_i is the production index for industry i, GO_i is the generated output for industry i, u is the relevant cyclical variable (e.g., capacity utilization or vendor performance) and m is the relevant mix variable.
A typical equation is shown in Table 15.1.

Table 15.1
Sample Industrial Production Equation:
Industrial Production Index—Rubber Products Except Tires

Ordinary Least Squares

Quarterly (1960:1 to 1980:4): 84 Observations
Dependent Variable: log(JQIND302@6/GO302@6)

	Coefficient	Std. Error	t-Stat	Independent Variable
	2.17665	0.7776	2.799	Constant
1)	0.403297	0.02412	16.72	log(TIME)
2)	0.186733	0.02187	8.537	log(RDELYSLOW(-1))
3)	2.13274	0.3986	5.351	log(CNO72+CSO72)/(GNP72)

R-Bar squared: 0.8756
Durbin-Watson statistic: 0.7283
Standard error of the regression: 0.05245   Normalized: 0.9504

JQIND302@6 is the industrial production index for rubber products except tires,
GO302@6 is the corresponding generated output calculated from the input-output bridge table relating output to final demands,
RDELYSLOW is vendor performance,
CNO72 is real other nondurable consumption,
CSO72 is real other services.

1.4 Simulation Properties

Fig. 15.1 shows the results of solving the industry sub-model in isolation from the rest of the model (i.e., using actual values for the final demand categories, but allowing any errors from one production equation to feed through to its suppliers). The errors for the total of production are small. Fig. 15.2 shows the linkages between the industry sector and the rest of the model. Thirty-two final-demand categories of the GNP are the ultimate drivers of the production equations. Even though the GO for a material industry may be expressed only in terms of output levels in other industries to which it sells, the outputs of these industries in turn are ultimately derived from final demand expenditures. Table 15.3 summarizes these relationships, showing the elasticities of output in each industry with respect to changes in final demand expenditures. This table was produced by successively boosting each final demand category,

Figure 15.1
Ex-Post Dynamic Solution of the
Industry Model in Isolation, Industrial Production
(1967=1)

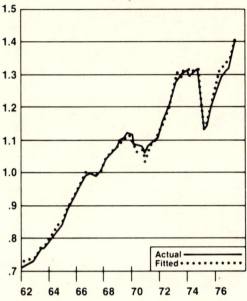

Figure 15.2
Industry Sector

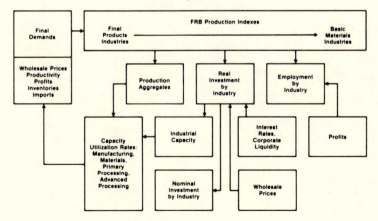

Table 15.2
Relative Importance of Intermediate and Final Demands in the Generated Outputs
(SIC code definitions)

	MI	49&G	19&G	20	21	22	23	24	251	252&4&9	26	27	281	282	283	284	285
JQIND	.056	.083	.022	.119	.006	.037	.052	.017	.017	.007	.041	.057	.044	.038	.025	.070	.005
JQINDPF&I	-	.050	.032	.152	.011	.001	.058	.047	.028	.008	.009	.001	.006	.001	.038	.027	.008
JQINDPF	-	.065	.041	.191	.014	-	.075	-	.022	.009	.001	-	.008		.049	.034	-
JQINDC	-	.104	-	.307	.022	-	.120	-	.036	-	.002	.001	.012	-	.079	.055	-
JQINDEQPBUS	-	-	-	-	-	-	-	-	.033	-	-	-	-	-	-	-	-
JQINDEQPD&S	-	.436	-	-	-	-	-	-	-	-	-	-	-	-	-	-	-
JQINDPI	-	-	.001	.019	-	.002	.002	.205	.049	.005	.035	.003	.002	.002	.002	.001	.035
JQINDMATL	.149	.036	.006	.061	-	.089	.045	.002	.011	.004	.091	.030	.105	.110	.007	.015	.009
JQINDMI	1.000	.244	-	-	-	-	-	-	-	-	-	-	.065	-	-	-	-
JQIND49&G	-	1.00	-	.032	-	-	-	-	-	-	.017	-	.041	-	-	-	-
JQINDM	.001	.002	.025	.133	.007	.043	.059	.020	.020	.008	.046	.065	.042	.043	.029	.023	.006
JQINDMD	-	-	.043	.014	-	-	-	.035	.029	.012	.006	.001	.001	-	-	.001	-
JQINDMN	.002	.004	.002	.280	.015	.094	.131	.001	.008	.003	.094	.143	.094	.096	.064	.051	.013
JQINDMPP	-	.001	.005	.070	-	.113	.063	.053	.025	.005	.122	.038	.106	.108	.007	.015	.004
JQIND19&G	-	-	1.000	-	-	-	-	-	-	-	-	-	-	-	-	-	-
JQIND20	-	-	-	1.000	-	-	-	-	-	-	-	-	-	-	-	-	-
JQIND21	-	-	-	-	1.000	-	-	-	-	-	-	-	-	-	-	-	-
JQIND22	-	-	-	-	-	1.000	7.44	-	.052	.008	-	-	-	-	-	-	-
JQIND23	-	-	-	-	-	-	1.000	-	-	-	-	-	-	-	-	-	-
JQIND24	-	-	-	-	-	-	-	1.000	.235	.023	.158	-	-	-	-	-	-
JQIND25	-	-	-	-	-	-	-	-	.644	.356	-	-	-	-	-	-	-
JQIND251	-	-	-	-	-	-	-	-	1.000	-	-	-	-	-	-	-	-
JQIND252&4&9	-	-	-	-	-	-	-	-	-	1.000	-	-	-	-	-	-	-
JQIND26	-	-	.007	.320	.002	.009	.011	.006	.003	.002	1.011	.373	.011	.008	.008	.005	.001
JQIND27	.020	.025	.007	.086	.002	.010	.011	.006	.003	.002	.012	1.016	.012	.009	.008	.006	.001
JQIND28	-	-	.003	.011	-	.094	.001	-	-	-	.018	.001	.317	.356	.224	.168	.047
JQIND281	-	-	.009	.029	-	.032	-	-	-	-	.054	-	1.000	.378	.033	.065	.035
JQIND282	-	-	-	-	-	.355	-	-	-	-	-	-	-	1.000	-	-	-
JQIND283	-	-	-	-	-	-	-	-	-	-	-	-	-	-	1.000	-	-
JQIND284	-	-	-	-	-	-	-	-	-	-	-	-	-	-	-	1.000	-
JQIND285	-	-	.009	.041	.003	.012	.014	.007	.004	.002	.015	.020	.015	.011	.010	.007	1.002
JQIND287	-	-	-	-	-	-	-	-	-	-	-	-	-	-	-	-	-
JQIND29	-	.024	-	-	-	-	-	-	-	-	-	.159	-	-	-	-	-
JQIND30	-	-	.001	.139	-	.001	.001	.001	.041	.020	.058	.002	.001	.001	.030	.060	-
JQIND301	-	-	-	-	-	-	-	-	-	-	-	-	-	-	-	-	-
JQIND302å6	-	-	.003	.016	.001	.005	.005	.003	.002	.001	.050	.008	.006	.004	.004	.003	.001
JQIND307	-	-	-	.227	-	-	-	-	.067	.032	.081	-	-	-	.049	.099	-
JQIND31	-	-	-	-	-	-	-	-	-	-	-	-	-	-	-	-	-
JQIND32	-	-	-	.052	-	-	-	-	-	-	-	-	-	-	-	-	-
JQIND33	-	-	.013	-	-	-	-	-	.009	.005	-	-	-	-	-	-	-
JQIND331VR	-	-	.012	-	-	-	-	-	.015	.008	-	-	-	-	-	-	-
JQIND331	-	-	.008	-	-	-	-	-	.019	.010	-	-	-	-	-	-	-
JQIND332	-	-	.027	-	-	-	-	-	-	-	-	-	-	-	-	-	-
JQIND333VR	-	-	.014	-	-	-	-	-	-	-	-	-	-	-	-	-	-
JQIND34	-	-	.005	.079	-	-	-	.009	.012	-	-	-	-	-	-	.005	.003
JQIND341	-	-	-	.083	-	-	-	-	-	-	-	-	-	-	-	.072	.045
JQIND342å4	-	-	-	-	-	-	-	-	-	-	-	-	-	-	-	-	-
JQIND345å9	-	-	.012	.036	-	-	-	.019	.027	-	-	-	-	-	-	-	-
JQIND35	-	-	-	-	-	-	-	-	-	-	-	-	-	-	-	-	-
JQIND351	-	-	-	-	-	-	-	-	-	-	-	-	-	-	-	-	-
JQINDEQPAF	-	-	-	-	-	-	-	-	-	-	-	-	-	-	-	-	-
JQIND353	-	-	-	-	-	-	-	-	-	-	-	-	-	-	-	-	-
JQIND354	-	-	-	-	-	-	-	-	-	-	-	-	-	-	-	-	-
JQIND355&6	-	-	-	-	-	-	-	-	-	-	-	-	-	-	-	-	-
JQIND357å9	-	-	-	-	-	-	-	-	-	-	-	-	-	-	-	-	-
JQIND36	-	-	.008	-	-	-	-	-	-	-	-	-	-	-	-	-	-
JQIND361&2	-	-	-	-	-	-	-	-	-	-	-	-	-	-	-	-	-
JQIND363	-	-	-	-	-	-	-	-	-	-	-	-	-	-	-	-	-
JQIND365	-	-	-	-	-	-	-	-	-	-	-	-	-	-	-	-	-
JQIND366	-	-	-	-	-	-	-	-	-	-	-	-	-	-	-	-	-
JQIND367	-	-	.029	-	-	-	-	-	-	-	-	-	-	-	-	-	-
JQIND369	-	-	-	-	-	-	-	-	-	-	-	-	-	-	-	-	-
JQIND37	-	-	-	-	-	-	-	-	-	-	-	-	-	-	-	-	-
JQIND371	-	-	-	-	-	-	-	-	-	-	-	-	-	-	-	-	-
JQIND371A	-	-	-	-	-	-	-	-	-	-	-	-	-	-	-	-	-
JQIND371T&B&TT	-	-	-	-	-	-	-	-	-	-	-	-	-	-	-	-	-
JQIND371MVP	-	-	-	-	-	-	-	-	-	-	-	-	-	-	-	-	-
JQIND372	-	-	-	-	-	-	-	-	-	-	-	-	-	-	-	-	-
JQIND373	-	-	-	-	-	-	-	-	-	-	-	-	-	-	-	-	-
JQIND374	-	-	-	-	-	-	-	-	-	-	-	-	-	-	-	-	-
JQIND379	-	-	-	-	-	-	-	-	-	-	-	-	-	-	-	-	-
JQIND38	-	-	-	-	-	-	-	-	-	-	-	-	-	-	-	-	-
JQIND381å4	-	-	-	-	-	-	-	-	-	-	-	-	-	-	-	-	-
JQIND385å7	-	-	-	-	-	-	-	-	-	-	-	-	-	-	-	-	-
JQIND39	-	-	.009	.042	.003	.012	.014	.008	.004	.002	.015	.020	.015	.011	.010	.007	.002

287	29	301	302@6	307	31	32	331	332	333VR	341	342@4	345@9	351	EQPAF	353	354	355&6	357@9	361&2	363	365	366
.008	.065	.011	.009	.035	.006	.035	.033	.007	.027	.007	.032	.031	.009	.008	.016	.015	.022	.046	.021	.014	.009	.031
.025	.024	-	-	.001	.008	.054	.002	-	.001	-	.059	.001	.012	.012	.025	.021	.033	.061	.013	.016	.007	.033
-	.031	-	-	-	.010	.001	.002	-	.001	-	-	-	.016	.015	.032	.027	.041	.076	.016	.021	.009	.042
-	.050	-	-	-	.016	.002	.003	-	.002	-	-	-	-	-	-	-	-	.001	-	.034	.014	-
-	-	-	-	-	-	-	-	-	-	-	-	-	.055	.063	.112	.096	.145	.269	.057	-	-	.032
-	-	-	-	-	-	-	-	-	-	-	-	-	-	-	-	-	-	-	-	-	-	.345
.108	.001	.001	.001	.002	-	.231	.002	-	.002	.002	.257	.003	.001	.001	.001	.001	.004	.0088	.001	.001	-	.002
.008	.117	.009	.025	.109	.003	.059	.086	.021	.080	.021	.016	.089	.019	.003	.003	.005	.008	.027	.038	.013	.015	.026
-	.753	-	-	-	-	.059	.082	-	.054	-	-	-	-	-	-	-	-	-	-	-	-	-
-	.024	-	-	-	-	.018	.027	-	.019	-	-	-	-	-	-	-	-	-	-	-	-	-
.010	.025	.012	.020	.040	.007	.035	.030	.008	.026	.008	.037	.035	.010	.010	.019	.017	.026	.052	.024	.016	.011	.035
-	-	-	-	-	-	.060	.052	.014	.046	.014	.065	.062	.018	.016	.032	.030	.045	.093	.043	.025	.019	.062
.021	.054	.027	.023	.089	.015	.004	.003	.001	.002	.001	.002	.002	.001	.001	.002	.001	.001	.003	.001	.005	.001	.002
.009	.065	.033	.027	.106	.003	.093	.081	.021	.069	.021	.098	.094	.003	.004	.004	.006	.009	.015	.008	.013	.001	.004
-	-	-	-	-	-	-	-	-	-	-	-	-	-	-	-	-	-	-	-	-	-	-
-	-	.034	-	-	.020	-	-	-	-	-	-	-	-	-	-	-	-	-	-	-	-	-
-	-	-	-	-	-	-	-	-	-	-	-	-	-	-	-	-	-	-	-	-	-	-
.002	.007	.003	.003	.008	.002	.010	.008	.002	.007	.001	.009	.009	.002	.002	.005	.004	.006	.012	.006	.003	.001	.007
.002	.007	.003	.003	.008	.002	.011	.008	.002	.008	.001	.010	.010	.003	.003	.005	.005	.007	.013	.006	.003	.001	.008
.078	.015	.020	.014	.119	-	.005	.006	-	-	.001	.002	.001	-	-	-	-	-	.001	-	-	-	-
.089	.047	-	-	-	-	.015	.019	-	-	-	-	-	-	-	-	-	-	-	-	-	-	-
-	-	.086	.057	.503	-	-	-	-	-	-	-	-	-	-	-	-	-	-	-	-	-	-
-	-	-	-	-	-	-	-	-	-	-	-	-	-	-	-	-	-	-	-	-	-	-
.002	.009	.003	.003	.010	.002	.013	.011	.003	.010	.040	.053	.037	.003	.003	.007	.006	.009	.016	.008	.004	.002	.010
1.000	-	-	-	-	-	-	-	-	-	-	-	-	-	-	-	-	-	-	-	-	-	-
-	1.000	-	-	-	-	-	-	-	-	-	-	-	-	-	-	-	-	-	-	-	-	-
-	.001	.203	.200	.598	.013	.006	.001	-	.001	-	.001	.001	-	.008	.006	-	.001	.001	.001	.042	.007	.001
-	-	1.000	-	-	-	-	-	-	-	-	-	-	-	.039	.028	-	-	-	-	-	-	-
.001	.003	.001	1.001	.004	.067	.031	.004	.001	.004	.001	.005	.005	.001	.001	.003	.007	.003	.006	.003	.061	.001	.004
-	-	-	-	1.000	-	-	-	-	-	-	-	-	-	-	-	-	-	-	-	.050	.011	-
-	-	-	-	-	1.000	-	-	-	-	-	-	-	-	-	-	-	-	-	-	-	-	-
-	-	-	-	-	-	-	.475	.129	.420	.055	.071	.074	.018	.017	.018	.018	.036	.047	.037	.032	-	.009
-	-	-	-	-	-	-	.785	.223	-	.083	.068	.044	.014	.030	.030	.022	.036	.048	.032	.035	-	-
-	-	-	-	-	-	-	1.000	-	.106	.081	.042	-	.025	.010	.018	.027	.050	.039	.042	-	-	-
-	-	-	-	-	-	-	.034	1.000	-	-	.021	.053	.061	.046	.103	.035	.066	.040	.007	.011	-	-
-	-	-	-	-	-	-	.047	-	1.000	.076	.115	.023	-	-	.013	.035	.046	.045	.027	-	-	.021
-	-	-	-	-	-	-	.018	-	.008	.071	.490	.462	-	-	-	.014	.016	.037	.009	.017	-	.010
-	-	-	-	-	-	-	-	-	-	1.000	-	-	-	-	-	-	-	-	-	-	-	-
-	-	-	-	-	-	-	-	-	-	-	1.000	-	-	-	-	-	.009	.020	-	-	-	-
-	-	-	-	-	-	-	.038	-	.017	-	.051	1.000	-	-	-	-	.030	.026	.060	.019	.037	-	.021
-	-	-	-	-	-	-	-	-	-	-	-	-	.075	.073	.153	.132	.199	.368	-	-	-	-
-	-	-	-	-	-	-	-	-	-	-	-	-	1.000	-	-	-	-	-	-	-	-	-
-	-	-	-	-	-	-	-	-	-	-	-	-	-	1.000	-	-	-	-	-	-	-	-
-	-	-	-	-	-	-	-	-	-	-	-	-	-	-	1.000	-	-	-	-	-	-	-
-	-	-	-	-	-	-	-	-	-	-	-	-	-	-	-	1.000	-	-	-	-	-	-
-	-	-	-	-	-	-	-	-	-	-	-	-	-	-	-	-	1.000	-	-	-	-	-
-	-	-	-	-	-	-	.005	-	-	-	-	.005	-	-	-	-	-	.060	.225	.116	.109	.353
-	-	-	-	-	-	-	-	-	-	-	-	-	-	-	-	-	-	1.000	-	-	-	-
-	-	-	-	-	-	-	-	-	-	-	-	-	-	-	-	-	-	-	1.000	-	-	-
-	-	-	-	-	-	-	-	-	-	-	-	-	-	-	-	-	-	-	-	1.000	-	-
-	-	-	-	-	-	-	-	-	-	-	-	-	-	-	-	-	-	-	-	-	1.000	-
-	-	-	-	-	-	-	-	-	-	-	-	-	-	-	-	-	-	-	-	-	-	1.000
-	-	-	-	-	-	-	-	-	-	-	-	-	-	-	-	-	-	.212	.050	-	.210	.336
-	-	-	-	-	-	-	.059	-	-	-	-	.064	-	-	-	-	-	.028	-	-	-	-
.002	.009	.003	.003	.010	.002	.013	.011	.003	.010	.002	.012	.012	.003	.003	.007	.006	.009	.016	.008	.004	.002	.010

367	369	371 A	371 T&B &TT	371 MVP	372	373	374	379	381 å4	385 å7	CDM 39	V&P	CDF URN	CDO	CNF OOD	CNC S	CNG AS	CNO O	CSH OUS	CSH MDP	CST RAN S	CSO
.026	.009	.040	.029	.034	.022	.008	.003	.003	.016	.014	.021	.022	.021	.017	.090	.037	.010	.050	-	.050	-	.021
.001	-	.038	.014	.001	.015	.007	.003	.005	.013	.021	.048	.040	.034	.025	.146	.063	.012	.059	-	.036	-	.035
-	-	.048	.018	-	.019	.007	.003	.004	.017	.027	.023	.052	.044	.017	.189	.082	.016	.064	-	.047	-	.045
-	-	.077	-	-	-	-	-	.006	-	.043	.037	.076	.061	.022	.304	.131	.025	.102	-	.076	-	.073
-	-	-	.064	-	-	-	.012	-	.058	-	-	.017	.022	.007	-	-	-	-	-	-	-	-
-	-	-	-	-	.201	.074	-	-	-	-	-	-	-	.018	-	-	-	-	-	-	-	-
.002	.001	.007	.001	.003	.001	.005	-	.010	.001	.001	.132	-	-	.049	-	-	-	.040	-	-	-	-
.074	.024	.052	.054	.094	.007	.002	.002	.002	.025	.006	.010	-	.003	.002	-	.006	-	.001	-	-	-	-
-	-	-	-	-	-	-	-	-	-	-	-	-	-	-	-	-	-	-	-	.742	-	-
.030	.010	.046	.033	.039	.025	.009	.003	.003	.018	.016	.024	.026	.024	.013	.103	.042	.012	.057	-	-	-	.023
.050	.018	.078	.057	.064	.045	.016	.005	.006	.030	.026	.037	.047	.041	.024	-	-	-	.014	-	-	-	.033
.005	.001	.007	.003	.007	.002	-	-	-	.004	.003	.007	-	.003	-	.229	.093	.026	.111	-	-	-	.048
.008	.005	.034	.015	.034	.006	.003	.003	.004	.006	.005	.012	-	.004	-	-	.002	.032	.014	-	-	-	-
-	-	-	-	-	-	-	-	-	-	-	-	-	-	-	-1.006	-	-	-	-	-	-	-
-	-	-	-	-	-	-	-	-	-	-	-	-	-	-	-	-	-1.000	-	-	-	-	-
-	-	-	-	-	-	-	-	-.016	-	-	.048	-	-	-	-	.961	-	-	-	-	-	-
-	-	-	-	-	-	-	-	.035	-	-	.022	-	.521	-	-	-	-	-	-	-	-	-
-	-	-	-	-	-	-	-	-	-	-	-	-	.760	-	-	-	-	-	-	-	-	-
-	-	-	-	-	-	-	-	-	-	-	-	-	.087	-	-	-	-	-	-	-	-	-
.008	.002	.007	.003	.007	.007	.002	.001	.001	.004	.004	.006	-	-	-	-	-	-	-	-	-	-	-
.009	.003	.007	.003	.008	.007	.002	.001	.001	.005	.004	.006	-	-	-	-	-	-	.415	-	-	-	-
-	-	.001	.001	.001	-	-	-	-	-	.005	-	-	-	-	-	-	-	.147	-	-	-	.183
-	-	-	-	-	-	-	-	-	-	.017	-	-	-	-	-	-	-	-	-	-	-	-
-	-	-	-	-	-	-	-	-	-	-	-	-	-	-	-	-	-	-	-	-	-	.859
-	-	-	-	-	-	-	-	-	-	-	-	-	-	-	-	-	-1.000	-	-	-	-	-
.011	.003	.037	.017	.039	.009	.001	.001	.001	.006	.005	.008	-	-	-	-	-	-	-	-	-	-	-
-	-	-	-	-	-	-	-	-	-	-	-	-	-	-	-	-	.540	.210	-	-	-	-
.037	-	.054	.025	.057	.004	-	-	-	.021	.011	.064	-	-	-	-	-	.050	-	.013	-	-	-
-	-	.123	.056	.130	-	-	-	-	-	-	-	-	-	-	-	-	-	-	-	-	-	-
.004	.001	.074	.034	.079	.020	.001	-	-	.047	.002	.054	-	-	-	-	-	.291	-	.067	-	-	-
.061	-	.024	.011	.026	-	-	-	-	.019	.018	.088	-	-	-	-	-	.983	-	-	-	-	-
-	-	.019	-	-	-	-	-	-	-	-	-	-	-	-	-	-	-	-	-	-	-	-
.016	.018	.087	.040	.092	.016	.010	.017	.009	.009	.008	.016	-	-	-	-	-	-	-	-	-	-	-
-	-	.131	.060	.139	.005	.107	.029	-	-	-	-	-	-	-	-	-	-	-	-	-	-	-
-	-	.137	.067	.144	.001	.022	.030	-	-	-	-	-	-	-	-	-	-	-	-	-	-	-
-	-	.112	.051	.118	.020	-	.024	-	-	-	-	-	-	-	-	-	-	-	-	-	-	-
.038	.044	.027	.012	.028	.031	-	-	.022	.020	.019	.038	-	-	-	-	-	-	-	-	-	-	-
-	.012	.065	.029	.068	.015	.009	-	.006	-	-	-	-	-	-	-	-	-	-	-	-	-	-
-	-	-	-	-	-	.019	-	.012	-	-	-	-	-	-	-	-	-	-	-	-	-	-
-	.025	.140	.064	.148	.032	-	-	-	-	-	-	-	-	-	-	-	-	-	-	-	-	-
-	-	-	-	-	-	-	-	-	-	-	.024	.027	-	-	-	-	-	-	-	-	-	-
-	-	-	-	-	-	-	-	-	-	-	-	-	-	-	-	-	-	-	-	-	-	-
-	-	-	-	-	-	-	-	-	-	-	-	-	-	-	-	-	-	-	-	-	-	-
-	-	-	-	-	-	-	-	-	-	-	-	-	-	-	-	-	-	-	-	-	-	-
-	-	-	-	-	-	-	-	-	-	-	-	-	-	-	-	-	-	-	-	-	-	-
-	-	-	-	-	-	-	-	-	-	-	.064	.072	-	-	-	-	-	-	-	-	-	-
.284	.084	.015	.006	.013	.005	-	-	-	.012	.006	-	-	.118	-	-	-	-	-	-	-	-	-
-	-	-	-	-	-	-	-	-	-	-	-	.811	-	-	-	-	-	-	-	-	-	-
-	-	.048	-	-	-	-	-	-	-	-	-	-	.484	-	-	-	-	-	-	-	-	-
1.000	-	-	-	-	.017	-	-	-	.041	.020	-	-	-	-	-	-	-	-	-	-	-	-
-	1.000	.149	.068	.158	-	-	-	-	-	-	-	-	-	-	-	-	-	-	-	-	-	-
-	-	.344	.293	.268	.242	.082	.020	.020	-	-	-	-	.253	-	.020	-	-	-	-	-	-	-
-	-	.540	.460	.421	-	-	-	-	-	-	-	-	.398	-	-	-	-	-	-	-	-	-
-	-	1.000	-	-	-	-	-	-	-	-	-	-	-1.000	-	-	-	-	-	-	-	-	-
-	-	-	-1.000	-	-	-	-	-	-	-	-	-	-	-	-	-	-	-	-	-	-	-
-	-	.338	.667	1.000	-	-	-	-	-	-	-	-	-	-	-	.247	-	-	-	-	-	-
-	-	-	-	-1.000	-	-	-	-	-	-	-	-	-	-	-	-	-	-	-	-	-	-
-	-	-	-	-	-1.000	-	-	-	-	-	-	-	-	-	-	-	-	-	-	-	-	-
-	-	-	-	-	-	-1.000	-	-	-	-	-	-	-	-	-	-	-	-	-	-	-	-
-	-	-	-	-	-	-	.520	.480	-	-	-	.150	-	-	-	.058	-	-	-	.060	-	-
-	-	-	-	-	-	-	-1.000	-	-	-	-	.118	-	-	-	-	-	-	-	-	-	-
-	-	-	-	-	-	-	-	-1.000	-	-	-	.185	-	-	-	.120	-	-	-	.124	-	-
.011	.003	.009	.004	.010	.009	.003	.001	.001	.006	.005	1.008	-	-	.386	-	-	-	.313	-	-	-	-

IPD ER	IPD ICR	EMR	ICN R	INV CH	EXE NDO	EXE ND1	EXE ND2	EXE ND3	EXE ND4	EXE ND5 &6	MEN D0	MEN D1A	MEN D2	MEN D3	MEN D4	MEN D5	MEN D10	GFM L	GFO	GSL
.007	.038	.093	.035	.003	.001	.021	.034	-	.005	.008	-.001	-.004	-.016	-.001	-.004	-	-.017	.050	.006	.016
.012	.065	.145	.057	.004	.002	.021	.056	.003	.009	.009	-.003	-.009	-.027	-.004	-.009	-.001	-.009	.065	.006	.014
.015	.017	.180	.008	.004	.001	.002	.068	.001	.011	.011	-.002	-.003	-.033	-.002	-.008	-	-.004	.084	.007	.018
.024	.013	-	.001	.006	.002	.003	.004	.001	.017	.001	-.004	-.005	-.002	-.008	-	-.004	.084	.007	.018	
.024	.013	-	.001	.006	.002	.003	.004	.001	.017	.001	-.004	-.005	-.002	-.003	-.013	-	-.007	.007	.002	.019
-	.029	.565	.025	.001	-	-	.212	-	-	-	-	-	-.083	-	-	-	-	.046	.014	.021
-	-	.216	-	-	-	-	.064	-	-	.108	-	-	-.083	-	-	-	-	.708	.026	-
-	.227	.027	.220	.005	.006	.087	.013	.004	.003	.002	-.007	-.031	-.006	-.010	-.012	-.002	-.024	.002	.002	.003
-	.037	.023	.036	.003	-	.043	.009	-	-	-	-	-.001	-.005	-	-	-	-.038	.009	.004	-
-	-	-	-	-	-	-	-	-	-	-	-	-	-	-	-	-	-.257	-	-	-
-	-	-	-	-	-	-	-	-	-	-	-	-	-	-	-	-	-	-	-	.079
.008	.044	.106	.040	.004	.001	.024	.039	.001	.006	.009	-.002	-.004	-.019	-.001	-.005	-	-.004	.057	.007	.012
.014	.066	.192	.069	.005	.002	.033	.071	.001	.006	.017	-.002	-.007	-.034	-.003	-.007	-	-.006	.102	.011	.008
-	.016	-	.005	.003	-	.012	-	-	.005	-	-.001	-	-	-	-.002	-	-	.002	.003	.016
-	.092	.009	.036	.003	-	.053	-	-	-	-	-	-.005	-	-	-	-	-	.002	.003	.002
-	-	-	-	-	-	-	-	-	-	.114	-	-	-	-	-	-	-	.886	-	-
-	-	-	-	-	-	-	-	-	-	-	.006	-	-	-	-	-	-	-	-	-
-	-	-	-	-	-	-	-	-	-	-	-	-	-	-	-	-	-	-	-	-
-	.078	-	-	-	-	-	-	-	-	-	-	-	-	-	-	-	-	-	-	-
-	-	-	-	.025	-	-	-	-	-	-	-	-	-	-	-	-	-	.015	-	-
-	.459	-	.142	-	-	-	-	-	-	-	-	-.073	-	-	-	-	-	-	-	-
.045	.117	.276	.021	.011	-	-	-	-	-	-	-	-	-	-	-	-	-	.010	-	-
.070	.142	-	-	.013	-	-	-	-	-	-	-	-	-	-	-	-	-	.016	-	-
-	.071	.776	.058	.009	-	-	-	-	-	-	-	-	-	-	-	-	-	-	-	-
-	.055	-	-	-	-	-	-	-	-	-	-	-	-	-	-	-	-	-	-	-
-	-	-	-	-	-	-	-	-	-	-	-	-	-	-	-	-	-	-	-	.092
-	.009	-	.004	.002	-	.045	-	-	.019	-	-	-	-	-	-.007	-	-	.003	.009	.016
-	-	-	-	.005	-	.143	-	-	-	-	-	-	-	-	-	-	-	-	.03?	-
-	-	-	-	-	-	-	-	-	-	-	-	-	-	-	-	-	-	-	-	-
-	-	-	-	-	-	-	-	.088	-	-	-	-	-	-.033	-	-	.013	-	.073	
-	.258	-	.104	-	-	-	-	-	-	-	-	-	-	-	-	-	-	-	-	-
-	-	-	-	-	-	-	-	-	-	-	-	-	-	-	-	-	-	-	-	-
-	-	-	-	-	-	-	-	-	-	-	-	-	-	-	-	-	-	-	-	.022
-	.041	-	.040	.003	-	-	-	-	-	-	-	-	-	-	-	-	-	.003	-	.006
-	-	-	-	.015	-	-	-	-	-	-	-	-	-	-	-	-	-	.015	-	.031
-	.068	-	.066	-	-	-	-	-	-	-	-	-	-	-	-	-	-	-	-	-
-	-	-	-	.024	-	-	-	.032	-	-	-	-	-	-	.046	-	-	.007	-	-
-	.276	-	.217	.006	-	.290	-	-	-	-	-	-	-	-	-	-	-	-	-	-
-	.024	-	.105	.008	-	.030	-	-	-	-	-.006	-	-	-	-	-	-	-	-	-
-	.009	-	.101	.003	-	-	-	-	-	-	-.011	-	-	-	-	-	-	-	-	-
-	.006	-	.104	-	-	-	-	-	-	-	-.014	-	-	-	-	-	-	-	-	-
-	.017	-	.090	.012	-	-	-	-	-	-	-	-	-	-	-	-	-	-	-	-
-	.044	-	.112	.015	-	.071	-	-	-	-	-	-	-	-	-	-	-	-	-	-
-	.135	.049	.273	.004	-	.050	-	-	-	-	-	-	-	-	-	-	-	.011	-	-
-	.239	.106	.540	.008	-	.038	-	-	-	-	-	-	-	-	-	-	-	.010	-	-
-	.505	-	.045	-	-	.070	-	-	-	-	-	-	-	-	-	-	-	.013	-	-
-	.031	.602	.027	.002	-	-	.240	-	-	-	-	-	-.095	-	-	-	-	.029	.014	.028
-	-	.932	-	-	-	-	.268	-	-	-	-	-	-.201	-	-	-	-	-	-	-
-	-	.624	-	-	-	-	.376	-	-	-	-	-	-	-	-	-	-	-	-	-
-	-	.932	-	-	-	-	.268	-	-	-	-	-	-.201	-	-	-	-	-	-	-
-	.055	.698	.039	.008	-	-	.309	-	-	-	-	-	-.154	-	-	-	-	.047	-	-
-	.054	.473	.052	-	-	-	.178	-	-	-	-	-	-.061	-	-	-	-	.053	.039	.026
.031	.005	.149	.003	.012	-	.023	.048	-	.006	-	-	-	-.062	-	-.007	-	-	.159	-	-
-	-	-	-	-	-	-	-	-	-	-	-	-	-	-	-	-	-	-	-	-
.092	.047	-	.024	.026	-	-	-	-	-	-	-	-	-	-	-	-	-	-	-	-
.405	-	-	-	.075	-	-	-	-	.131	-	-	-	-	-	-.141	-	-	-	-	-
-	-	.534	-	-	-	-.185	-	-	-	-	-	-.242	-	-	-	.524	-	-	-	-
-	-	-	-	.018	-	-	.275	-	-	-	-	-	-	-	-	-	-	.066	-	-
-	-	.136	-	-	-	.275	-	-	-	-	-	-	-	-	-	-	-	.061	-	-
-	.020	.145	-	-	-	-	.027	-	-	.070	-	-	-	-	-	-	-	.167	.031	-
-	-	.140	-	-	-	-	.042	-	-	-	-	-	-	-	-	-	-	-	-	-
-	-	.769	-	-	-	-	.231	-	-	-	-	-	-	-	-	-	-	-	-	-
-	-	-	-	-	-	-	-	-	-	.289	-	-	-	-	-	-	-	.583	.127	-
-	-	.434	-	-	-	-	-	-	-	-	-	-	-	-	-	-	-	.319	-	-
-	-	1.000	-	-	-	-	-	-	-	-	-	-	-	-	-	-	-	-	-	-
1.000	-	-	-	-	-	-	-	-	-	-	-	-	-	-	-	-	-	-	-	-
.147	.046	.201	.037	-	-	-	.144	-	.079	-	-	-.058	-	-.051	-	-	-	.107	.044	.035
-	.075	.386	.060	-	-	-	.276	-	-	-	-	-	-.111	-	-	-	-	.139	.056	-
.307	.015	-	.012	-	-	-	-	-	.164	-	-	-	-	-	-.106	-	-	.072	.032	.073
-	-	-	.008	.050	.085	.104	.029	.021	-	.016	-.056	-.127	-.051	-.078	-.091	-.013	-.187	-	.013	.025

solving the model for the period of the change (1977:3) and observing relative changes in each production index. Accordingly, the elasticities shown reflect not only the direct effect of final demands filtering back through the industrial sector to supplying industries, but also (although typically to a much smaller extent) the secondary effects on other final demand categories generated by the spending multipliers of the model.

Table 15.2 presents the relative importance of the various intermediate and final demands in the generated output for each industry. Reading across the row for *JQIND251* (furniture), for example, it can be seen that 76% of its market is represented by consumer expenditures on furniture and appliances. Although the table reveals that there are many industries which sell both to final demands and to other industries in various stages of manufacturing, it is nevertheless possible to break down the list of industries into five rough categories corresponding to stages of manufacturing. The columns of industries in the production block of fig. 15.2 show these categories.

2. Industry Employment

2.1 Introduction

The industry employment equations relate employment to industry output levels using a partial adjustment mechanism.

2.2 The Framework

The equations are derived from a production function which is assumed to be of the form:

$$Q = kL^d e^{f(\text{time})}, \tag{2}$$

where Q is output and L is labor input (in man-hours). *time* is used here as a proxy for the long-run trend in productivity and for a relatively smoothly growing capital stock. For the manufacturing industries, the Federal Reserve Board indexes of production are used for the output term. For nonmanufacturing industries, output is represented by the relevant National Income Accounts category; for example, employment in state and local government *(EGSL)* depends on real spending by state and local government *(GSL72)*.

Such a production function implies a desired employment level corresponding to any given level of output. The adjustment that employers

Table 15.3
Elasticities of Industry Outputs With Respect to Final Demand Expenditures

	CDM / V&P	CDF / URN	CMF / CDO	CMF / OOD	CNC / S	CHG / AS	CNO / O	CSH / HOP	CSH / CSO	IPD / ER	IPD / ICR	IPO / ENR	ICN / R	INV / CH	GFM / L	GFM / GFC	GFM / CSL
JQIND	0.11	0.07	0.02	0.08	0.10	0.04	0.08	0.08	0.09	0.01	0.04	0.21	0.03	0.01	0.14	0.02	0.07
JQINDPF&I	0.08	0.06	0.03	0.07	0.09	0.02	0.05	0.05	0.09	0.01	0.04	0.19	0.04	0.01	0.14	0.02	0.05
JQINDPF	0.09	0.06	0.02	0.07	0.10	0.02	0.05	0.06	0.10	0.01	0.02	0.21	0.01	0.01	0.17	0.02	0.05
JQINDC	0.12	0.08	0.03	0.07	0.15	0.02	0.06	0.09	0.11	0.02	0.02	0.01	0.02	0.02	0.02	0.01	0.05
JQINDEQPBUS	0.06	0.06	0.02	0.09	0.04	0.01	0.04	0.03	0.09	-	0.04	0.62	0.02	-	0.21	0.03	0.??
JQINDEQPD&S	-	-	0.02	-	-	-	-	-	-	-	-	0.20	-0.10	-	1.07	0.03	-0.01
JQINDPI	0.04	0.07	0.06	0.06	0.03	0.01	0.07	0.02	0.06	-	0.13	0.14	0.13	0.01	0.03	0.01	0.05
JQINDMATL	0.17	0.09	0.02	0.10	0.14	0.07	0.09	0.06	0.11	0.01	0.04	0.26	0.07	0.01	0.11	0.03	0.10
JQINDMI	0.06	0.03	0.01	0.05	0.04	0.36	0.16	0.20	0.07	-	0.03	0.07	0.06	-	0.04	0.03	0.09
JQIND49&G	0.03	0.02	0.01	0.06	0.02	0.02	0.03	0.78	0.06	-	0.01	0.04	0.02	-	-0.03	0.01	0.14
JQINDM	0.11	0.07	0.03	0.08	0.11	0.02	0.08	0.02	0.09	0.01	0.04	0.23	0.03	0.01	0.16	0.02	0.07
JQINDMD	0.17	0.10	0.04	0.08	0.04	0.01	0.05	0.03	0.09	0.02	0.05	0.37	0.04	0.01	0.24	0.03	0.08
JQINDMN	0.04	0.04	0.01	0.08	0.21	0.03	0.11	0.02	0.10	-	0.02	0.05	0.02	0.01	0.05	0.02	0.06
JQINDMPP	0.12	0.08	0.02	0.08	0.15	0.04	0.07	0.03	0.09	0.01	0.06	0.18	0.08	0.01	0.07	0.02	0.07
JQIND19&G	-0.02	-0.02	-0.01	-0.06	-0.02	-0.01	-0.03	-0.02	-0.06	-	-0.01	-0.03	-0.02	-	1.44	-0.01	-0.06
JQIND20	-	-	-	0.17	-	-	-	-	-	-	-	-	-	-	-	-	-
JQIND21	0.01	0.03	0.01	0.05	0.03	-	1.04	0.02	0.06	-	0.01	0.01	0.02	-	0.02	0.02	0.08
JQIND22	0.02	0.11	0.01	0.02	0.83	0.01	0.02	0.01	0.03	-	0.04	0.03	0.02	0.02	0.03	0.01	0.03
JQIND23	-0.01	-0.01	-	-	0.99	-	-	-	0.01	-	-	-0.01	-	0.03	0.01	-	0.01
JQIND24	0.03	0.23	0.02	0.05	0.02	-	0.06	0.02	0.06	0.01	0.25	0.01	0.15	0.01	0.02	0.01	0.05
JQIND25	0.01	0.59	0.01	0.05	0.02	-	0.02	0.02	0.07	0.04	0.06	0.32	0.04	0.01	0.01	0.01	0.05
JQIND251	-	0.84	-	0.03	0.01	-	0.01	0.02	0.05	0.06	0.07	0.01	0.01	0.02	0.02	0.01	0.05
JQIND252&4&9	0.03	0.12	0.01	0.08	0.03	0.01	0.04	0.03	0.09	-	0.04	0.87	0.08	0.01	0.01	0.01	0.03
JQIND26	0.07	0.05	0.02	0.10	0.07	0.02	0.21	0.02	0.06	-	0.04	0.16	0.03	-	0.09	0.02	0.08
JQIND27	0.04	0.03	0.01	0.06	0.05	0.01	0.44	0.04	0.06	-	0.02	0.08	0.02	-	0.10	0.04	0.15
JQIND28	0.05	0.06	0.02	0.06	0.15	0.01	0.04	0.02	0.26	0.01	0.03	0.06	0.03	0.01	0.04	0.02	0.08
JQIND281	0.06	0.06	0.02	0.06	0.17	0.03	0.05	0.02	0.09	0.01	0.03	0.07	0.04	0.01	0.06	0.04	0.06
JQIND282	0.10	0.13	0.03	0.10	0.34	0.01	0.07	0.03	0.12	0.01	0.05	0.11	0.07	0.02	0.06	0.02	0.09
JQIND283	-	-	-	0.01	-	-	-	-	0.90	-	-	-	-	-	0.02	-	0.09
JQIND284	0.01	0.01	-	0.02	0.02	-	0.01	0.01	0.02	-	-	-	0.01	-	0.01	0.01	0.03
JQIND285	0.15	0.06	0.02	0.12	0.08	0.02	0.07	0.04	0.13	0.01	0.08	0.12	0.03	0.01	0.10	0.03	0.34
JQIND287	0.02	0.02	0.01	0.10	0.02	0.01	0.02	0.02	0.06	-	0.01	0.02	0.01	-	0.02	0.01	0.06
JQIND29	0.01	0.01	-	0.02	0.03	0.48	0.20	0.03	0.04	-	0.01	0.01	0.01	-	0.04	0.03	0.06
JQIND30	0.15	0.11	0.04	0.09	0.11	0.01	0.08	0.03	0.11	0.01	0.04	0.15	0.07	0.01	0.07	0.02	0.08
JQIND301	0.30	0.04	0.02	0.06	0.05	0.01	0.05	0.02	0.07	-	0.01	0.19	0.04	0.02	0.04	0.01	0.10
JQIND302@6	0.19	0.09	0.04	0.08	0.41	0.01	0.13	0.03	0.10	0.01	0.03	0.16	0.04	0.01	0.12	0.03	0.09
JQIND307	0.08	0.14	0.05	0.11	0.04	0.01	0.08	0.03	0.12	0.02	0.05	0.13	0.10	0.01	0.07	0.02	0.07
JQIND31	-0.03	-0.02	-0.01	-0.05	1.12	-0.01	-0.02	-0.01	-0.04	-	-0.01	-0.05	-0.01	0.03	0.57	-0.01	-0.03
JQIND32	0.03	0.01	-	0.02	-	-	0.01	0.01	0.02	-	0.15	-0.08	0.26	0.01	-	-	0.01
JQIND33	0.27	0.09	0.03	0.10	0.04	0.01	0.05	0.04	0.11	0.01	0.05	0.39	0.13	0.01	0.12	0.02	0.11
JQIND331VR	0.34	0.10	0.02	0.14	0.06	0.02	0.06	0.05	0.15	-	0.04	0.43	0.14	0.01	0.11	0.03	0.15
JQIND331	0.36	0.11	0.02	0.15	0.06	0.02	0.06	0.05	0.15	0.01	0.04	0.41	0.15	0.01	0.10	0.03	0.16
JQIND332	0.30	0.06	0.02	0.11	0.05	0.01	0.05	0.04	0.12	-	0.04	0.47	0.11	0.02	0.15	0.02	0.14
JQIND333VR	0.15	0.07	0.03	0.04	0.02	-	0.03	0.02	0.05	0.01	0.07	0.33	0.10	0.02	0.15	0.02	0.03
JQIND34	0.19	0.07	0.02	0.13	0.05	0.01	0.05	0.04	0.13	-	0.07	0.43	0.05	0.01	0.10	0.03	0.10
JQIND341	0.01	0.01	-	0.17	0.01	-	0.01	0.01	0.02	-	0.01	0.01	0.01	-	0.01	-	0.03
JQIND342@4	0.04	0.04	0.02	0.09	0.04	0.01	0.04	0.03	0.10	-	0.13	0.55	0.11	0.01	0.04	0.02	0.07
JQIND345@9	0.37	0.12	0.02	0.16	0.07	0.02	0.07	0.06	0.17	0.01	0.02	0.39	-0.01	0.01	0.18	0.04	0.14
JQIND35	0.05	0.06	0.01	0.08	0.03	0.01	0.04	0.03	0.08	-	0.04	0.64	0.01	-	0.24	0.02	0.08
JQIND351	0.03	0.03	0.01	0.10	0.04	0.01	0.04	0.03	0.10	-	0.01	0.91	0.02	-	0.01	0.01	0.05
JQINDEQPAF	-	-	-	0.06	-	-	-	-	-	-	-	-	-	-	-	-	-
JQIND353	0.10	0.07	0.03	0.13	0.10	0.02	0.09	0.04	0.15	0.01	0.13	0.71	0.21	0.01	0.12	0.03	0.16
JQIND354	0.04	0.04	0.01	0.12	0.05	0.02	0.05	0.04	0.13	-	0.02	0.97	-0.10	-	0.41	0.01	0.07
JQIND355&6	0.04	0.03	0.01	0.10	0.04	0.01	0.04	0.04	0.11	'	0.04	0.92	-0.18	0.01	0.06	0.01	0.05
JQIND357@9	0.07	0.08	-	0.02	0.01	-	0.01	0.01	0.03	-	0.03	0.45	0.06	-	0.43	0.04	0.08
JQIND36	0.04	0.17	-	0.01	-	-	-	-	0.01	0.05	0.01	0.35	0.01	0.02	0.27	-	-
JQIND361&2	0.03	0.02	0.01	0.07	0.03	0.01	0.03	0.03	0.08	-	0.01	0.57	0.06	-	0.01	0.01	0.04
JQIND363	-0.02	0.79	-0.01	-0.05	-0.02	-0.01	-0.03	0.07	0.08	0.34	0.14	0.02	-0.03	-0.01	-0.04		
JQIND365	0.01	0.43	-0.01	-0.14	-0.05	-0.03	-0.07	-0.05	-0.14	0.30	-0.02	0.05	0.07	-	-0.07	-0.03	-0.15
JQIND366	0.01	0.01	0.01	0.04	0.02	0.01	0.02	0.02	0.05	-	-	0.36	0.01	-	0.55	0.01	0.03
JQIND367	0.01	0.13	-	0.06	-0.02	-0.01	-0.02	-0.02	-0.06	0.09	-	0.29	-	0.04	0.45	-	-0.06
JQIND369	0.37	0.07	0.02	0.17	0.07	0.02	0.08	0.06	0.19	-	0.03	0.75	-0.25	0.01	0.12	0.03	0.15
JQIND37	0.60	0.08	0.05	0.19	0.09	0.02	0.09	0.07	0.21	-	0.05	0.50	-0.06	0.01	0.34	0.08	0.20
JQIND371	0.91	0.11	0.04	0.27	0.13	0.03	0.13	0.10	0.31	-	0.05	0.55	0.08	0.01	0.11	0.06	0.29
JQIND371A	1.42	0.06	0.02	0.14	0.06	-	0.06	0.06	0.18	-	0.02	0.04	0.05	0.01	0.05	0.04	0.21
JQIND371T&B&TT	0.16	0.14	0.05	0.36	0.17	0.06	0.18	0.12	0.38	0.01	0.06	0.98	0.10	0.01	0.16	0.07	0.32
JQIND371MVP	0.75	0.14	0.05	0.36	0.17	0.05	0.18	0.13	0.40	-	0.06	0.86	0.10	0.02	0.16	0.08	0.36
JQIND372	-	-	-	-0.01	-	-	-	-	-0.01	-	-	0.18	-0.49	-	1.19	0.15	-0.04
JQIND373	0.04	0.05	0.24	0.13	0.05	0.02	0.06	0.05	0.14	-	0.02	-0.03	0.03	0.01	-0.11	0.03	0.15
JQIND374	0.07	0.07	0.02	0.20	0.08	0.03	0.09	0.07	0.21	-	0.03	1.56	0.05	-	0.04	0.02	0.12
JQIND379	0.44	0.42	0.14	0.08	0.04	-	0.04	0.04	0.11	-	1.19	0.17	0.03	0.01	0.01	0.02	0.11
JQIND38	0.02	0.02	0.16	0.07	0.03	0.01	0.09	0.03	0.14	0.12	0.03	0.12	0.05	-	0.18	0.06	0.11
JQIND381@4	0.02	0.02	0.12	0.06	0.02	0.01	0.03	0.02	0.07	-	0.04	0.21	0.07	-	0.15	0.07	0.06
JQIND385@7	0.02	0.03	0.21	0.07	0.03	0.01	0.16	0.03	0.22	0.25	0.02	0.03	0.03	-	0.20	0.05	0.17
JQIND39	0.06	0.05	0.42	0.05	0.07	0.01	0.36	0.02	0.09	-	0.02	0.08	0.03	0.01	0.07	0.03	-0.01

make from actual employment to this desired level is assumed to be less than complete in any given quarter. Thus,

$$E = E_{-1} + \lambda(E^* - E_{-1}), \tag{3}$$

where λ is the adjustment coefficient. This technique captures the effect of delay in the recognition of an output change as being permanent. In a rising economy, the effects of increased overtime and the cost and time lag inherent in adding new employees hold back employment. In a time of falling output, the effects of shortened hours and the desire of employers to maintain a stable work force buoy employment, at least temporarily.

2.3 The Empirical Implementation

The estimated form of a typical equation is shown in Table 15.4.

There are several exceptions to this general format, principally in the nonmanufacturing sector. For mining, trade, services, construction, and finance, insurance, and real estate, the introduction of the four-quarter change in before-tax profits is intended to model the effects of changes in the adjustment coefficient at different points in the cycle. Mining and petroleum-refining equations were modified to include a relative price-wage term based on the wholesale price index for fuels and the index of hourly compensation to reflect the direct effect of energy prices on productivity and employment.

Table 15.4
Sample Equation for Industry Employment

Ordinary Least Squares

Quarterly (1960:1 to 1980:3): 83 Observations
Dependent Variable: log(E35)

	Coefficient	Std. Error	t-Stat	Independent Variable
	0.0726372	0.02195	3.310	Constant
1)	0.124237	0.04179	2.973	log(JQIND35)
2)	0.135588	0.01946	6.969	log(JQIND35/JQIND35(-4))
3)	-0.140525	0.06511	-2.158	log(JQ%MHNF)
4)	0.848295	0.04539	18.69	log(E35(-1))

R-Bar squared: 0.9974
Durbin-Watson statistic: 1.3093
Standard error of the regression: 0.008225   Normalized: 0.01273

E35 is employment, nonelectrical machinery industry,
JQIND35 is industrial production, nonelectrical machinery industry,
JQ%MHNF is nonfarm productivity.

Total manufacturing, nondurable manufacturing and durable manufacturing employment are identities, the sums of their components. Department of Defense military manpower is exogenous.

2.4 Simulation Properties

The coefficients of adjustment and the long-run elasticities with respect to output are presented in the table 15.5. The short-run elasticity with respect to output is largely determined by the coefficient of adjustment. The intermediate-run elasticity is determined by the coefficients of employment on production in relation to the adjustment coefficient.

Table 15.5
Parameters in the Employment Equations

Industry	Coefficient of Adjustment	Elasticity with Respect to Output
Wholesale and Retail Trade	0.077	0.804
Services	0.094	0.969
Transportation and Public Utilities	0.158	0.795
State and Local Government	0.061	0.874
Federal Government	0.052	0.262
Finance, Insurance and Real Estate	0.045	0.740
Contract Construction	0.129	0.606
Mining	0.089	0.974
Ordnance, etc.	0.201	0.911
Food and Products	0.088	0.228
Tobacco Manufactures	0.441	0.257
Textile Mill Products	0.419	0.630
Apparel and Products	0.387	0.702
Lumber and Products	0.328	0.889
Furniture and Fixtures	0.443	0.681
Paper and Products	0.142	0.674
Printing and Publishing	0.165	0.593
Chemicals and Products	0.073	0.809
Petroleum and Products	0.537	0.968
Rubber and Miscellaneous Plastics	0.379	0.628
Leather and Products	0.336	0.903
Stone, Clay and Glass	0.294	0.700
Primary Metal Industries	0.571	0.563
Fabricated Metal Products	0.428	0.784
Machinery except Electrical	0.408	0.701
Electrical Machinery	0.196	0.767
Transportation Equipment	0.376	0.904
Instruments	0.380	0.602
Miscellaneous Manufacturing	0.159	0.438

Table 15.6
Typical Industry Investment Equation:
The Automobile Industry

Least Squares with First-Order Autocorrelation Correction

Quarterly (1961:1 to 1980:3): 79 Observations
Dependent Variable: IP&E72$371

	Coefficient	Std. Error	t-Stat	Independ Variable
	-0.571555	0.8594	-0.6651	Constant
1)	0.106739	0.04773	2.236	KGP&E72$371
2)				PDL(LETI371(-4),1,6,FAR)
(-4)	0.109062	0.02903		
(-5)	0.0908853	0.02419		
(-6)	0.0727083	0.01935		
(-7)	0.0545312	0.01451		
(-8)	0.0363541	0.009675		
(-9)	0.0181771	0.004838		
Sum	0.381718	0.1016	3.758	
Avg	1.66667	0.0	NC	
3)				PDL(NFCDEBTSERVICE(-1),2,6, FAR)
(-1)	-0.206031	0.4582		
(-2)	-0.651666	0.2443		
(-3)	-0.905311	0.2309		
(-4)	-0.966967	0.2793		
(-5)	-0.836634	0.2712		
(-6)	-0.514312	0.1803		
Sum	-4.08092	1.056	-3.864	
Avg	2.76440	3.576	0.7730	
	0.518251	0.04848	10.69	RHO

R-Bar squared: 0.9555
Durbin-Watson statistic: 1.5680
Standard error of the regression: 0.1768   Normalized: 0.05248

IP&E72$371 is investment of the automobile industry,
KGP&E72$371 is the capital stock in the automobile industry,
LETI371 is the Jorgenson term for the rental price of capital in this industry,
NFCDEBTSERVICE is the ratio of interest payments to cash flow for nonfinancial corporations,
RHO is the first-order autocorrelation correction coefficient.

3. Industry Investment

3.1 Introduction

Investment by industry is built into the DRI model as a necessary element for calculating capacities and utilization rates and as a check on the economy-wide investment estimates. The equations also serve to process the contained in the important quarterly Department of Commerce survey of business investment plans.

3.2 Framework

The industry investment equations follow the theoretical approach used in the aggregate investment equations, discussed in Chapter 7. For each industry, real investment is estimated by a modified neoclassical capital stock-adjustment equation. The price and output components of the Jorgensonian formulation for the desired capital stock are industry specific; for example, the desired capital stock for the food industry utilizes the wholesale price index for processed foods and feeds and the Federal Reserve Board index of production for processed food. Capital stocks by industry are derived from the previous quarter's capital stock plus real new investment minus depreciation.

The economy's cost of capital is applied uniformly to all industries, however, in the absence of rental price measures for each industry. Output expectations have long- and short-run elements where appropriate. Time lags reflect the production processes of investment projects. For example, utility projects display much longer lags than investment in light industry.

CHAPTER 16

ENERGY

1. Introduction

Energy has become a macro topic. Along with industrial capacity and finance, energy has been the effective supply constraint on the economy in recent years and a decisive factor in determining inflation, growth and employment. The DRI model incorporates an energy sector designed to trace these effects of energy and related supply shocks on the economy.

Fig. 16.1 presents the detailed structure of the energy sector in the DRI model. The exogenous variables are an index of the OPEC marker price for crude oil, major tax rates levied by the various levels of government on gasoline, crude oil and electricity, and the price control schedules on domestic energy sources. In addition, the macro model treats energy supply estimates derived from solutions of DRI's energy models as exogenous, including the composition of electricity generation by source (coal, natural gas and other petroleum), and the domestic production of coal, natural gas and petroleum.

On the cost side, the model traces the prices of imported and domestic oil and gas into the retail prices of final energy products bought by consumers, such as gasoline, electricity, natural gas and heating oil. Prices of the basic energy sources enter the stage-of-processing equations for the various wholesale prices of different industries, and into retail prices.

On the demand side, household heating, transportation and electricity energy demands are derived from consumption functions that include income and relative price terms as well as the household stocks to which energy use is related, such as housing and automobiles adjusted for their efficiency ratings. Other energy demand is derived from more aggregate equations that include price elasticities and activity levels.

On the supply side, energy is one of four factors in the model's aggregate production function, along with capital, labor and the stock of research and development. Energy also affects other supply dimensions. The disaggregated industry investment equations include the energy sectors. The growth rate of the residential construction stock depends upon the rental price of housing, which includes energy among the operating costs. The supply of finance to the economy as a whole is affected by energy, both through the general impact of prices on the financial system and through capital requirements of the energy industries.

Figure 16.1
Energy Sector of the DRI U.S. Macro Model:
Major Linkages

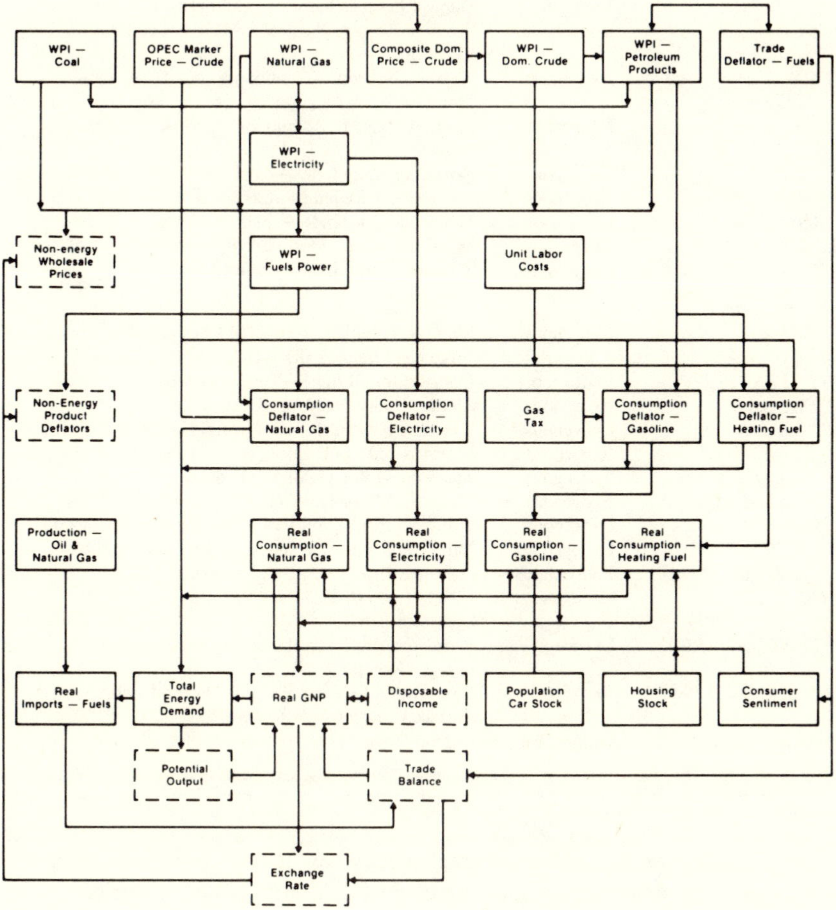

— — — — Primary impact points of energy on rest of model

Table 16.1
Energy Variables

Variable	Endogenous or Exogenous*	Definition
Prices		
JMEND10	Exogenous	Unit Value Index of U.S. Imports—Fuels & Lubricants
PCNFUEL	Endogenous	Implicit Price Deflator—Consumption of Fuel Oil & Coal
PCNGAS	Endogenous	Implicit Price Deflator—Consumption of Gasoline & Oil
PCSHHOPE	Endogenous	Implicit Price Deflator—Consumption of Electricity
PCSHHOPG	Endogenous	Implicit Price Deflator—Consumption of Natural Gas
PCOCP	Endogenous	Average Refiners' Acquisition Price—Crude Oil—Composite
PCOD	Exogenous	Average Refiners' Acquisition Price—Crude Oil—Domestic
PCOF	Exogenous	Average Refiners' Acquisition Price—Crude Oil—Imported
WPI051	Exogenous	Wholesale Price Index—Coal
WPI053	Exogenous	Wholesale Price index—Gas Fuels
WPI054	Exogenous	Wholesale Price Index—Electric Power
WPI0561	Exogenous	Wholesale Price Index—Crude Petroleum
WPI057	Exogenous	Wholesale Price Index—Refined Petroleum Products
Other Variables		
DOM%OIL	Exogenous	Share of Total U.S. Crude Oil Consumption Produced Domestically
DTFUELSALLB	Endogenous	Demand for all Fuels—Total—all Sectors
EUF%COAL	Exogenous	Electric Utility Fuel Use—Coal Share
EUF%NG	Exogenous	Electric Utility Fuel Use—Natural Gas Share
EUF%PET	Exogenous	Electric Utility Fuel Use—Petroleum Share
GASTAXF	Exogenous	Taxes on Motor Gasoline—Federal
GASTAXSL	Exogenous	Taxes on Motor Gasoline—State and Local
JQIND13	Exogenous	Industrial Production Index—Oil and Gas Extraction
JQIND29	Endogenous	Industrial Production Index—Petroleum Products
JQIND49&G	Endogenous	Industrial Production Index—Utilities
MEND1067	Endogenous	U.S. Imports by End-use Categories—Fuels and Lubricants—67$
PET&NG%ENERGY	Exogenous	Petroleum and Natural Gas Share of Domestic Energy Demand
REG%DOMOILPROD	Exogenous	Proportion of Domestic Crude Oil Production Subject to Price Controls
TXGFWF	Exogenous	Federal Government "Windfall Profits" Tax Accruals

*All exogenous variables have simulation rules to approximate their response to domestic inflation.

Energy has various other indirect effects on the economy. Consumer sentiment, one determinant of consumption, contains energy prices as a separate term. The exchange rate in the model is affected by the trade balance, which is, of course, heavily influenced by oil imports. Automobile demand is partly determined by operating costs, of which gasoline price is a component.

The model calculates the aggregate demand for energy in terms of quadrillion Btus (quads). In the case of households, the separate consumption functions are used to calculate energy requirements directly. In the case of industrial, transportation, commercial and other demands, the equations are very simple, relying on activity levels at relative energy prices, leaving it to the DRI energy model to provide the more detailed estimates. Thus, the total energy demand estimates of the macro model are used mainly for simulation exercises and to identify the extent of oil imports.

Oil imports are calculated as a residual. Total energy demand and exogenous domestic energy supplies yield the import requirement. It then becomes a matter of further analysis to assess whether OPEC will, in fact, make the calculated supplies available and at what price. If supplies fall short, policy must choose among allocations, rationing, higher prices, reduced aggregate activity or informal queuing.

2. The Price Block

Determination of primary energy prices, both foreign and domestic, is largely exogenous, with simulation rules (nonstochastic equations) used to capture the impact on energy prices of other prices, regulatory developments, mix changes and structural changes.

Petroleum Prices: Oil prices are primarily determined by appropriate weighting of domestic and imported crude prices. The import price variable is the OPEC price, expressed in dollars per barrel. Through the first quarter of 1979 the data are set at the pretransportation price for Saudi Arabian marker (light) crude. The March 26, 1979 OPEC meeting effectively changed the marker crude price from a ceiling price to a base price. Therefore, after the first quarter of 1979, adjustments are made to reflect the base price plus an average surcharge. The values are designed to capture the price of a crude of similar quality to the Saudi light for consistency with the historical data. Since it is difficult to separate premium differentials from surcharges, the price value is an approximation and not an actual quotation. A simple bridge equation translates the imported crude oil price into the unit value index for imported fuel. This index is used to derive the fuel import bill in the trade sector.

A similar approach is utilized for domestic wellhead crude prices, except that the model accommodates a partial control of domestic crude oil prices. The regulated price of domestic production responds to domestic inflation, since the regulations generally set ceiling prices that are a function of a base price and an inflation markup. The nonregulated portion, on the other hand, moves with the world oil price. With decontrol completed in 1981, this feature of the model is obsolete and will be replaced with an equation to explain the differential between the domestic and foreign refiners' acquisition prices.

Consumer gasoline prices are estimated from input costs, including foreign and domestic crude oil prices and unit labor cost. During the period of violent cost changes, demand or capital cost influences could not be identified from the historical data, though they are likely to reemerge. Table 16.2 shows the equation.

Table 16.2
A Typical Equation: The Retail Price of Gasoline

Ordinary Least Squares

Quarterly (1964:1 to 1980:3): 67 Observations
Dependent Variable: log(PCNGAS—GASTAX/36.130)/(PCNGAS(-1)—GASTAX(-1)/
36.130)

	Coefficient	Std. Error	t-Stat	Independent Variable
	6.39230E-05	0.002563	0.02494	Constant
1)	0.844768	0.04252	19.87	COST@PCNGAS

R-Bar squared: 0.8565
Durbin-Watson statistic: 1.4755
Standard error of the regression: 0.01823   Normalized: 0.7219

PCNGAS is the implicit price deflator, consumption of gasoline and oil,
GASTAX is taxes on motor gasoline, all levels of government,
COST@PCNGAS is the weighted sum of crude petroleum costs and unit labor costs.

Consumer home heating fuel prices are estimated by the same method, with weights for domestic and imported products derived from Department of Energy data.

Coal and Natural Gas Prices: Wholesale coal prices are determined exogenously, with a simulation rule on domestic inflation as measured by a fixed weight deflator. Wholesale wellhead natural gas prices are determined by the same method, with the simulation rule capturing the relation of price ceilings to the inflation rate as set by the Natural Gas Deregulation Act.

Consumer natural gas prices *(PCSHHOPG)* are determined from wholesale gas prices and unit labor costs where *JULCNF* is unit labor costs and *WPI053* is the wholesale price of natural gas fuel:

$$log(PCSHHOPG/PCSHHOPG_{-1}) = -0.000396 +$$
$$0.583log(JULCNF_{-1}/JULCNF_{-2}) + \Sigma^3_{i=1}\alpha_i log(WPI053_{-i}/$$
$$WPI053_{-i-1}) \qquad (1)$$

$\Sigma\alpha_i = 0.378$

R-Bar squared: 0.7545
Durbin-Watson statistic: 1.67
Standard error of the regression: 0.0086

Electricity Prices: Wholesale electricity prices are determined by the costs and relative uses of the three primary input fuels: coal, petroleum and natural gas. The relative weights of the three inputs are exogenous variables derived from the DRI energy model.

Consumer electricity prices are determined by the wholesale price. A dummy variable was used in the estimation to account for the effects of price controls during the Nixon Administration:

$$log(PCSHHOPE/PCSHHOPE_{-1}) = 0.633log(WPI054/$$
$$WPI054_{-1}) + 0.0957log(WPI054_{-1}/WPI054_{-2}) -$$
$$0.00345DMYPRICE \qquad (2)$$

R-Bar squared: 0.7295
Durbin-Watson statistic: 1.63
Standard error of the regression: 0.0077

where *PCSHOPE* is the price deflator for the consumption of electricity, *WPI054* is the wholesale price of electricity and *DMYPRICE* is the price control dummy.

3. The Demand Block

The energy demand block centers on four consumption equations—gasoline, home heating fuel, electricity and natural gas—as well as a total energy demand equation.

Gasoline: Gasoline consumption is estimated on a per-capita basis in log-linear form, using real per-capita disposable income with a four-period linear lag structure; a four-period moving average of the per-capita automobile stock; the average miles per gallon achieved by new model-year cars; and the relative price of gasoline, with a four-period linear lag structure:

$$log(CNGAS72/N) = -1.94 + 0.485log(\Sigma^3_{i=0}\omega_i\, YD72_{-i}/N_{-i}) +$$
$$0.733log((1/4N)\Sigma^4_{i=1}KREGCARS_{-i}) -$$
$$0.0769\ log(AVGMPG) - \Sigma^4_{j=0}\omega_j log(PCNGAS_{-j}/PC_{-j}) \qquad (3)$$

$\omega_i = 0.4,\ 0.3,\ 0.2,\ 0.1$
$\omega_j = 0.104,\ 0.083,\ 0.062,\ 0.042,\ 0.021$

R-Bar squared: 0.9802
Durbin-Watson statistic: 0.47
Standard error of the regression: 0.028

where *CNGAS72* is real consumer expenditure on gasoline and oil, *N* is population, *YD72* is real disposable income, *KREGCARS* is the stock of automobiles, *AVGMPG* is the average mileage per gallon of current year model cars, and *PCNGAS* is the price deflator of gasoline and oil. There is serial correlation in this equation, but the errors are small and correction for serial correlation lowers the elasticities to unacceptable levels. The relevant elasticities are 0.485 for income, 0.733 for the car stock, -0.104 for relative price in the short run and -0.312 for relative price in the long run.

Heating Fuel: Home heating fuel consumption is estimated on a per-housing-unit basis, in log-linear form. The determining variables are real disposable income with a low elasticity (0.209), relative price with a long-run elasticity of -0.336, and consumer sentiment. The small size of this data series relative to the precision with which the data are reported and the effects of weather makes accurate modeling difficult and correlation coefficients low; however, the standard error is small.

$$log(CNFUEL72/KQHUSTS_{-1}) = -3.77 +$$
$$0.209\ log(\Sigma^3_{i=0}\omega_i\, YD72_{-i}) + \Sigma^4_{j=2}(\omega_j log(JATTC_{-j})) -$$
$$\Sigma^4_{k=0}(\omega_k log(PCNFUEL_{-k}/PC_{-k})) \qquad (4)$$

$\omega_i = 0.4,\ 0.3,\ 0.2,\ 0.1$
$\omega_j = 0.101,\ 0.151,\ 0.117$
$\omega_k = 0.112,\ 0.090,\ 0.067,\ 0.045,\ 0.022$

R-Bar squared: 0.7028
Durbin-Watson statistic: 1.22
Standard error of the regression: 0.046

where *CNFUEL72* is real consumer spending on fuel oil and coal, *KQHUSTS* is the stock of housing, *YD72* is real disposable income, *JATTC* is the University of Michigan index of consumer sentiment, *PCNFUEL* is the price deflator for consumer spending in fuel oil and coal, and *PC* is the price deflator for consumer spending.

Electricity: Electricity consumption is modeled as a per-housing-unit function of income, relative price and consumer sentiment, in log-linear form. Transfer income is separated from nontransfer income; the response is more immediate for transfer income. The estimated price elasticity is a modest -0.213 on a given housing stock:

$log(CSHHOPE72/KQHUSTSMII_{-1}) = 5.85 +$
$0.394\ log(\Sigma^3_{i=0}\omega_i(YD_{-i} - VG_{-i}/PC_{-i})) +$
$0.332log(VG_{-1}/PC_{-1}) - \Sigma^4_{j=0}(\omega_j log(PCSHHOPE_{-j}/$
$PC_{-j})) + \Sigma^5_{k=1}(\omega_k log(JATTC_{-k}))$ (5)

$\omega_i = 0.4, 0.3, 0.2, 0.1$
$\omega_j = 0.071, 0.057, 0.043, 0.028, 0.014$
$\omega_k = 0.034, 0.031, 0.027, 0.020, 0.011$

R-Bar squared: 0.9896
Durbin-Watson statistic: 1.40
Standard error of the regression: 0.022

where *CSHHOPE72* is the real consumption expenditure for electricity, *PCSHHOPE72* is its price, *KQHUSTSMH* is the stock of housing including mobile homes, *VG* is personal transfer payments, and *JATTC* is consumer sentiment.

Natural Gas: Natural gas consumption per housing unit is a function of disposable income, relative price and consumer sentiment. The income elasticity is a modest 0.387; the long-run price elasticity is -0.339. The explanatory power of the equation is limited, like the heating fuel equation, by the size and imprecision of the series and the absence of an appropriate weather variable.

$log(CSHHOPG72/KQHUSTS_{-1}) = 4.95 +$
$0.387log(\Sigma^3_{i=0}\omega_i YD72_{-i}) - \Sigma^4_{j=0}\omega_j log(PCSHHOPG_{-j}/PC_{-j}) +$
$\Sigma^4_{k=1}\omega_k log(JATTC_{-k})$ (6)

$\omega_i = 0.4, 0.3, 0.2, 0.1$
$\omega_j = 0.113, 0.090, 0.068, 0.045, 0.023$
$\omega_k = 0.060, 0.054, 0.042, 0.024$

R-Bar squared: 0.6887
Durbin-Watson statistic: 1.30
Standard error of the regression: 0.050

where *CSHHOPG72* is consumer expenditure for natural gas, *KQHUSTS* is the stock of housing, *JATTC* is consumer sentiment and *PCSHHOPG* is its price.

Total Energy Demand and Price Elasticities: Total U.S. energy demand is modeled as a function of consumer energy demands, industrial activity and relative price.

Specifying industrial demand for energy as a function of industrial production in manufacturing, mining and utilities, and defining the relative price term as the ratio of the wholesale price index for fuels and related products and power to the aggregate wholesale price index, the total demand for energy, in quadrillion Btu *(DTFUELSALLB)*, is estimated:

$$log(DTFUELSALLB) = 1.744 + 0.613log(CEN) +$$
$$0.101log(JQINDM) + 0.087log(JQIND49\&G) +$$
$$0.114log(JQINDMI) - \Sigma^5_{i=1}\omega_i log(WPI05_{-i}/WPI_{-i}) \tag{7}$$

$\omega_i = 0.023, 0.019, 0.014, 0.009, 0.005$

R-Bar squared: 0.9974
Durbin-Watson statistic: 1.18
Standard error of the regression: 0.009

where *CEN* is the weighted sum of the energy-related consumer expenditures, *JQINDM* is industrial production of manufacturing, *JQIND49&G* is production of the utility industry, *JQINDMI* is production of the mining industry, *WPI05* is the wholesale price of fuels, related products and power and *WPI* is the wholesale price index.

The price elasticity of energy demand can be calculated from a full model simulation. Such a simulation, conducted on the 1981 edition of the DRI model, and using the period 1981:3-1983:4 as the test period, boosted the relative energy price by 10%. The level of aggregate activity is held constant by an offsetting change in personal taxes. The elasticity is -0.05 after one quarter, -0.28 after four quarters and -0.44 after twelve quarters.

4. The Supply Block

The energy supply block takes domestic crude oil and natural gas production as exogenous, and calculates oil and gas imports as a residual energy supply. An increase in domestic energy demand will be met primarily by the importation of additional foreign oil. An increase in domestic supply will largely displace imports.

Domestic Supply: Production of oil and natural gas is represented by the variable *JQIND13* from the Federal Reserve Board's Industrial Production series. It is a subset of the mining composite, comprising in the base period

(1967) 69.2% of all mining and 4.4% of all industrial production. The variable is exogenous, with a simulation rule which allows for a small (0.05) short-run and moderate (0.44) long-run supply elasticity with domestic wellhead crude oil and natural gas prices.

Import Supply: The model uses the estimates of energy imports of the Bureau of Census, in 1967 dollars, of all imports of fuels and lubricants. Although primarily crude oil and petroleum products, the series includes natural gas, other fuels and lubricants. The figures also include imports for strategic storage. They exclude imports to the Virgin Islands, which appear in the statistical discrepancy to the trade accounts.

5. The Impact of Energy Prices on Economic Performance

Two earlier papers[1] analyzed the impact of energy prices on the performance of the U.S. economy since the OPEC revolution. With the second OPEC shocks complete, it is useful to perform this exercise once more to see how the total energy price increases between 1973 and 1981 changed the pattern of U.S. economic development.

A model simulation has been run in which the world price of oil *(PCOF)* rises at a steady 7-1/4% a year from 1973:1 to 1981:2. Other aspects of the economy are left unchanged, including the fiscal policies and the level of real short-term interest rates (Table 16.3). A comparison to a "tracking" simulation of actual history shows the pertinent effects.

The most dramatic impact of OPEC prices was on the inflation rate. The food price explosion and excessively ambitious demand management policies would have created considerable inflation in any event, but the world energy prices did boost the inflation rate as measured by the GNP deflator for the years 1973-1981 by 1.2%. The CPI was up an extra 1.9%. The core inflation rate rose an extra 1.4%.

High energy prices had numerous other impacts on the economy. Consumption was pushed down directly by the loss of purchasing power which was transferred abroad to energy suppliers. Consumer confidence was damaged by the energy situation leading to additional consumption cuts. The demand for automobiles was set back by the increased operating costs and the demand for housing was hurt by the increased energy outlays required for household operations. Nonresidential fixed investment was reduced by the

[1]Otto Eckstein, "Shock Inflation, Core Inflation, and Energy Disturbances in the DRI Model," *Energy Prices, Inflation, and Economic Activity*, Knut A. Mork, ed. (Boston: Ballinger Publishing Co., 1981), pp. 63-98, and "Energy and Core Inflation," in *Core Inflation* (Englewood Cliffs: Prentice-Hall, Inc., 1981), ch. 5, pp. 35-42.

Table 16.3
Impact of World Oil Prices on the U.S. Economy, 1973-1981:
A Comparison of a "No Energy Trouble" Scenario With Historical Record

	1973	1974	1975	1976	1977	1978	1979	1980	1981
Inflation Rates									
(change in rates)									
Imported Oil	-16.8	-198.1	-4.7	9.3	-0.4	6.6	-40.6	-51.1	-2.6
Fuel and Energy	-6.1	-47.3	-11.0	-1.7	-6.9	0.1	-19.9	-34.3	-14.5
GNP Deflator	-0.1	-1.5	-1.6	0.1	-0.6	-0.7	-1.3	-3.2	-1.9
CPIU	-0.7	-4.0	-1.6	-0.3	-0.8	-0.3	-3.2	-3.8	-2.0
Shock	-0.3	-2.8	-0.9	-0.2	-0.5	-0.1	-1.1	-2.3	-1.1
Core	0.0	-0.7	-1.3	-1.2	-1.2	-1.2	-1.4	-2.2	-3.5
Demand	0.1	0.3	-0.1	0.6	1.1	0.7	0.7	0.2	1.7
Activity Measures									
(percent difference in levels)									
Real GNP	0.5	3.3	5.3	4.5	2.5	1.7	2.0	4.4	5.6
Real Consumption	0.4	3.0	5.6	5.7	4.5	3.8	4.3	6.6	7.9
Real Nonresidential Investment	0.5	5.5	11.5	9.4	6.2	4.4	4.5	9.8	12.3
Real Residential Investment	1.6	12.9	19.5	11.0	2.2	-0.1	0.8	14.6	18.2
Real Government Purchases	0.3	0.9	1.0	1.5	1.3	1.1	1.0	1.3	2.9
Real Net Exports	-1.4	-15.3	-37.5	-64.8	-90.5	-77.1	-61.9	-54.5	-80.5
Industrial Production	0.7	5.2	9.1	7.4	4.1	2.5	3.2	7.7	9.8
Housing Starts	3.0	18.9	23.3	10.8	-0.9	-2.6	-2.2	16.8	20.9
Unit Car Sales	3.3	23.3	29.9	23.2	13.6	10.0	15.6	31.6	34.8
Unemployment	-1.7	-14.1	-19.6	-18.2	-7.5	0.5	2.3	-8.2	-14.4
Supply Measures									
(percent difference in levels)									
Real Potential GNP	0.0	0.1	0.7	1.4	1.9	2.1	2.0	2.2	2.6
Real Net Capital Stock	0.0	0.4	1.5	2.4	3.0	3.2	3.2	3.8	4.7
Labor Force	0.0	0.3	0.8	0.9	0.7	0.3	0.2	0.4	0.6
Productivity	0.4	1.7	1.0	1.3	1.7	1.8	3.1	2.9	3.1

increase in the real cost of capital. While the real federal funds interest rate was held unchanged by the monetary policy assumption, long-term interest rates reflected the worsened inflation, boosting both nominal and real capital costs. Housing activity was damaged considerably by the worsened financial situation, and even the purchases of state and local governments were somewhat reduced. Only real net exports rose, as the United States had to devote increasing resources to paying for its oil on dramatically worsened terms of trade.

Real GNP was substantially lower because of the energy problem. Under the given assumptions for monetary policy, the level of real GNP was lower by 5.3% at the trough of the 1975 recession, and 5.6% lower in 1981. The real growth rate was lowered by 0.6%. The loss of productivity was 3.1% by 1981, a reduction in the productivity growth rate of 0.3%.

The effects on the supply side of the economy were also quite considerable. Relative price adjustments reduced the use of energy in producing aggregate supply, thereby directly reducing the growth of potential output. The reduction of investment had a much larger effect on potential GNP, and even the supply of labor was curtailed slightly by the higher unemployment rate and by the increase in the personal tax burden created by the extra inflation. As a result, potential GNP was lower by 2.6% by 1981, a reduction in the potential growth rate of 0.3%.

AUTHOR INDEX

Adelman, Frank L., 52n
Adelman, Irma, 52n
Anderson, W.H.L., 8, 78n, 131n
Ando, Albert, 3, 3n, 31, 39n, 91, 142n
Arrow, Kenneth J., 4, 141, 220n
Auerbach, Alan, 142

Becker, Gary S., 56
Blinder, Alan S., 141n
Bosworth, Barry, 78n
Brainard, William C., 8, 131n
Brimmer, Andrew F., 129n
Brinner, Roger, 29n, 41n
Brooks, Stephen, 29n
Brown, E. Cary, 142n, 165
Brumberg, Richard, 3, 31, 91
Brunner, Karl, 35

Chazen, Stephen, 27n
Chirinko, Robert S., 140
Choudry, N.K., 174n
Clark, Colin, 2n
Cooper, Frank, 29n

Darling, Paul, 141, 142
DeLeeuw, Frank, 3n, 5, 31, 86, 134n
Denison, Edward F., 56
Domar, Evsey, 56
Dreze, Jacques H., 93n
Duesenberry, James S., 2, 2n, 31, 51, 78n, 91, 92, 97, 186n

Earl, Paul H., 10
Eckstein, Otto, 2, 3n, 5n, 6, 52n, 78n, 86, 151n, 186n, 197n, 200n, 243n
Eisner, Robert, 134n, 140
Evans, Michael K., 3n

Fair, Ray C., 39n, 114n
Feldstein, Martin S., 5n, 86, 142, 147, 186n
Fisher, Franklin M., 4n
Fisher, Irving, 93n
Friedman, Benjamin, 42n
Friedman, Milton, 40, 81, 83, 92, 97

Fromm, Gary, 2, 2n, 3, 4n, 114n, 186n, 197n
Fullerton, Don, 61n

Galper, Harvey, 153n
Goldberger, Arthur S., 2n
Gough, Robert, 53n
Gramlich, Edward M., 3n, 5n, 6, 84n, 151n, 153n
Green, Edward W., 5n
Green, Jerry, 29n
Griliches, Zvi, 56

Haberler, Gottfried, 91
Hall, Robert E., 129n
Halvorsen, Robert F., 6, 151n
Harrod, Roy F., 56
Helliwell, John F., 174n
Hendershott, Patric, 78n
Henderson, James M., 6, 151n
Hicks, John R., 51
Hirsch, Albert A., 2n
Hoffenberg, Marvin, 4, 220n
Houthakker, Hendrik, 174n

Jaffee, Dwight M., 5n, 84n, 114n
Jorgenson, Dale W., 3, 15, 31, 47, 56, 63, 66, 84, 129, 130, 131, 138, 233

Kalchbrenner, John K., 114n
Karaken, John, 142n
Karlin, Samuel, 141
Katowitz, Y., 174n
Kelley, Joseph, 50n, 52n
Kendrick, John W., 56
Keynes, John Maynard, 7, 22, 23, 56, 58, 91
Klein, Lawrence R., 2, 2n, 3n, 4n, 31, 142n
Kruizenga, R.J., 165
Kuh, Edwin L., 2n, 84n, 135n, 186n
Kydland, Finn, 42n

Leamer, Edward E., 174n
Leland, Hayne E., 93n

247

SUBJECT INDEX

249